The Road to Concord

Other Titles in the Series

Grand Forage 1778: The Battleground Around New York City
by Todd W. Braisted

A JOURNAL OF THE AMERICAN REVOLUTION BOOK

THE ROAD *TO* CONCORD

HOW FOUR STOLEN CANNON IGNITED THE REVOLUTIONARY WAR

J. L. BELL

WESTHOLME
Yardley

Westholme Publishing, LLC
904 Edgewood Road
Yardley, Pennsylvania 19067
Visit our Web site at www.westholmepublishing.com

First Printing May 2016
10 9 8 7 6 5 4 3 2 1
ISBN: 978-1-59416-249-7
Also available as an eBook.

Printed in the United States of America.

In memory of Al,
who always believed in me

CONTENTS

List of Maps viii

Introduction: "The Commencement of the War" ix

September 1774 xiii

1. "Ordered Out by the Capt. General" 1
2. "An Extensive Insurrection thro' the Province" 17
3. "Behold, the Guns Were Gone!" 39
4. "Townspeople Took Four Brass Cannon" 56
5. "Not One Lisped a Word" 83
6. "Selling Warlike Stores" 91
7. "Out of Boston to Some Place in the Country" 103
8. "To Act the Traitor" 119
9. "This Town Is Full of Cannon" 134
10. "If You Meet with Any Brass Artillery" 149

Epilogue: "Through All Our History, to the Last" 167
Notes 179
Acknowledgments 223
Index 227

Maps

1. Boston Harbor, 1774 10–11
2. Town of Boston, 1774 47
3. The Road to Concord, April 18–19, 1775 158–159

INTRODUCTION

"The Commencement of the War"

As the sun rose on Lexington, Massachusetts, on April 19, 1775, it warmed the backs of six companies of British light infantry—about 250 soldiers in all—marching swiftly west toward the center of town. Facing them on the town common were about 70 local militiamen. Dozens more men, many armed, milled around a tavern to the right.

The British redcoats moved onto the green space, lining up against the locals. Officers shouted for the militia company to lay down their muskets and disperse. The Lexington men obeyed those demands halfway, dispersing but keeping their weapons. A shot echoed through the village. Some of the British regulars responded by firing at the Lexington men, then more. Some of the locals fired back, though without much effect. By the time the column's commanders restored order, eight militiamen were dead or dying and another ten wounded.

That was, contemporaries and historians agree, the start of the war which led to American independence. But that confrontation was not the first time that the king's soldiers and New England militia units had faced off against each other and fired their guns. The conflict in Massachusetts had grown more and more militarized since the previous September, which was when the bulk of the province had slipped out of the royal government's control. Lexington was simply where that conflict had turned deadly.

The British soldiers did not have business in Lexington. They were not there to search the town, seize the militiamen's muskets, or arrest anyone. They did not stick around. As soon as the British commanders got their regulars back in line, they ordered the column to continue marching west.

Lexington was just one of the towns on the road to Concord, the goal of that march. Those light infantry companies had come so quickly into Lexington because the lieutenant colonel in charge of the mission had ordered them "to march with all expedition to seize the two bridges on different roads beyond Concord" while he followed with more troops. His plan depended on holding those bridges in Concord so search parties could safely cross them and search even farther into the countryside.

Why had Gen. Thomas Gage, commander of the British army in North America and royal governor of Massachusetts, sent his soldiers along that road in April 1775? The usual answer is that Gage knew rebellious provincials had collected military supplies in Concord and wanted to destroy that material. But Gage's superiors in London had ordered him first to arrest the political leaders of the resistance.

Obviously the supplies in Concord seemed important to Gen. Gage, so what had the rebellious government collected there? Most histories speak of gunpowder, musket balls, flour, entrenching tools such as picks and shovels, and the other material that the British soldiers found that afternoon. Listing those items portrays the Massachusetts resistance as an underdog, not really prepared for war. That is how Allen French described the material in *The Siege of Boston*, published in 1911:

> [The Massachusetts] Committee of Supplies . . . gathered together a few hundred spades and pickaxes, some muskets, a thousand wooden mess-bowls, four thousand flints, and a small supply of peas and flour—a pitiful attempt to compete with the vast resources of Great Britain.

Those were actually the low-value supplies that the provincials had not gotten around to moving or hiding by the time the regulars arrived.

Contrast that description with what James Warren of Plymouth, an active member of the Massachusetts Provincial Congress, wrote from Concord to his wife, Mercy, on April 6, less than two weeks before the army raid:

> This Town is full of Cannon, ammunition, stores, etc., and the Army long for them and they want nothing but strength to Induce an attempt on them. The people are ready and determine to defend this Country Inch by Inch.

Warren and his fellow activists did not see themselves as "pitiful," but as determined and well-armed defenders. The provincials were building an army with an artillery force.

Gen. Gage planned the mission to Concord in April 1775 not to look for miscellaneous military supplies but to seek out cannon and the equipment needed to use them. Since the previous fall, the royal authorities and the people of New England had raced to take control of all the artillery in the region. Cannon were the most advanced battlefield weapons of the period, and, unlike muskets, those big guns had no peacetime use. Both sides understood the stakes in that New England "arms race": they were positioning themselves for a war.

Furthermore, Gen. Gage's top objective for the march to Concord was not just any artillery, but four particular brass cannon that had been in the hands of the Boston militia regiment until the end of the previous summer. In the seven months before April 1775, those guns were spirited out of armories under British army guard, smuggled from one safe spot to another, and carted across the countryside past spying eyes. The march to Concord was the second military raid that the general had ordered in hopes of recovering those four guns. Those cannon thus became the trigger that ignited the war for American independence.

The disputes between Britain and its major mainland American colonies were broad and deep-rooted, and there's little doubt that an armed conflict was going to break out somewhere in New England in early 1775. There were other moments when the two forces confronted each other, sometimes violently. If any of those events had proved fatal, the war would have started quite differently and been perceived quite differently, in both America and Europe. Instead, the war started on the road to Concord.

This book tracks how the Massachusetts Patriots and Gen. Gage's forces moved toward war starting in September 1774. It focuses tightly on how the two sides maneuvered to control artillery. For some scholars of this period, that focus may be too narrow. There is a danger that this approach to the sources is like scanning a crowd, spotting familiar faces, and neglecting everyone else. There are certainly other significant stories from that period, some of them even painfully cut from this manuscript. But *The Road to Concord* argues that efforts to seize cannon from the other side, to prepare cannon for use, and to seize cannon back were very significant in how events played out, and the start of the Revolutionary War cannot be recounted without that dimension.

In this book I have tried to quote sources exactly as they first appeared, preserving eighteenth-century punctuation, capitalization, and spelling, as well as eighteenth-century inconsistency about such matters, unless otherwise stated. All dates in this book are New Style. I use the term "Whigs" to refer to those colonial subjects who resisted the new taxes and policies enacted in London in the 1760s and 1770s. In opposition to them were the "friends of the royal government." I shift to "Patriot" and "Loyalist" in late 1774 as the sides harden. Through the start of the war, we must remember, both "Patriots" and "Loyalists" saw themselves as adhering to British constitutional values.

All source citations appear at the back of the book, linked to the relevant quotations or topics by the page number and a key phrase.

September 1774

This calendar of events in and around Boston in September 1774 shows the accelerating arms race between the province's radicals and the British military. By the 17th, all publicly owned cannon in Boston and Charlestown, plus one in Dorchester, had been taken by one side or the other, and in some cases taken back.

1 Army takes two fieldpieces from Cambridge militia.
2 Militiamen march to Cambridge by the thousands.
3 Army mounts four cannon on Neck.
Navy stations warship in Charles.
5 Continental Congress convenes in Philadelphia.
Artillery training in Boston.
6 Suffolk County adopts the Suffolk Resolves.
Crowds close courts in Worcester.
7 Charlestown finishes emptying its battery of cannon.
8 Army and navy find Charlestown battery empty.
9 Army adds twelve cannon to the six now on the Neck.
10 Royal government finishes moving back to Boston from Salem.
11 Army searches Charlestown for cannon from battery.
Braintree citizens raid powder house.
12 Gage asks Suffolk delegates about cannon from Charlestown, sends vague report home.
13 Charlestown moves guns inland.
Great gun moved from Preston's Point in Dorchester.
14 Navy spikes cannon in North Battery.
Boston train's two-pounders taken from old gunhouse.
15 Militia starts fixing North Battery guns.
Army guards Boston train's new gunhouse.
16 Boston train's three-pounders taken from new gunhouse.
17 Army confiscates ordnance from merchant Wells.

18 Army muster prompts alarm over cannon in Boston and Watertown.

20 People take cannon from merchant Timmins; navy recovers these guns.

21 Worcester County convention adopts minute man system.

25 Gage writes to Viscount Barrington that nearly all New England is in arms.

27 Army starts taking ordnance from merchant Scott; people protest with menace.

28 Army finishes taking ordnance from Scott.

Gage cancels General Court.

One

"Ordered Out by the Capt. General"

ABOUT 4:30 IN THE MORNING ON SEPTEMBER 1, 1774, OVER 250 British soldiers were lined up along Boston's Long Wharf. They had started the night in their tents on Boston Common or, as one army captain called it, "a small common on the west side of the town." Each man carried a day's provisions in his knapsack. Led by Lt.-Col. George Maddison from His Majesty's 4th Regiment of Foot, they had quietly marched through the dark streets to the town's largest wharf. Clearly they were on a mission, but those men probably had no idea where they were headed—the regiment had just recently arrived in Boston, and few soldiers would have been allowed to venture off the small peninsula that defined the town.

Long Wharf thrust out into the harbor, pointing to where the sun would appear in another hour. Ordinarily both sides of that wharf would have been lined with merchant ships from London, Bristol, New York, Philadelphia, the Caribbean, and the British Empire's other Atlantic ports. But in March the Parliament in London had passed the Boston Port Bill, closing that harbor to trade from anyplace outside Massachusetts. The only civilian vessels the soldiers could see were schooners and other small ships used for fishing or for ferrying goods from Marblehead, Salem, and other Massachusetts ports that were gaining Boston's usual business. Royal Navy warships towered over them, making sure no captains dared to break the law.

The Boston Port Bill was the Crown's response to how on December 16, 1773, persons unknown had thrown £9,659.6s.4d. worth of the British East India Company's tea into the water beside Griffin's Wharf, a few hundred yards to the south of where the soldiers stood. The destruction of that tea was not spontaneous vandalism but an obviously well planned operation involving scores of men (plus some eager teenagers who had pushed their way into the action). Even worse, many hundreds of Bostonians had watched from the waterfront. The royal authorities were certain that locals had seen through those men's rudimentary disguises or even knew of the plans in advance. They were sure the town's political leaders had helped to organize the tea destruction. And yet not a single eyewitness had come forward with useful information. Parliament had therefore decided to exert force on Boston *collectively*, closing the port to trade with Britain or other colonies until the town paid back the East India Company.

That law hurt Boston's merchants, of course, but it was even harder on waterfront workers. No transatlantic trade meant fewer jobs on the wharves. The shipyards, ropewalks, and sailmakers lost business. Taverns and boardinghouses that catered to mariners lost clientele. Maritime workers' families suffered from lower incomes, and the town's tax revenues fell, meaning less welfare money available for the poor. The government ministers in London had foreseen all that. They believed economic hardship would make Bostonians finally sour on the Whig politicians who had led them into this dead end. Of course, those ministers also expected those politicians to try to spur Bostonians into riots and other violence, as had erupted more than a few times since the Stamp Act of 1765. To clamp down on that possibility, the royal government had sent four army regiments, including the 4th, into the heart of the town.

Now four companies' worth of those soldiers were headed out. Thirteen rowboats manned by sailors from the navy and army transport ships pulled alongside the wharf. The soldiers clambered in, twenty men to each vessel. The oarsmen quietly propelled the boats up around the North End of the peninsula and across the wide mouth of the Charles River. They entered the smaller Mystic River on the north side of Charlestown. Aided by a rising tide, the rowboats traveled upstream to a dock on the farm of Robert Temple, a wealthy farmer inclined to support the royal government. There the soldiers disembarked and lined up again. With them were Joseph Goldthwait, a civilian barrack master who handled some army logistics, and David Phips, royal sheriff of Middlesex County. Following Phips's directions, Lt.-Col. Maddison gave orders to march about a mile along quiet country roads toward Quarry Hill in what is now Somerville.

On top of that hill was a round tower built of stone, about thirty feet tall. It had been built seventy years earlier as a windmill, but in 1747 the Massachusetts government had bought the property. With its remote location, thick walls, and a new wooden roof that could blow sky high to dissipate the force of an explosion, the tower made a fine place to store gunpowder. The province kept its black powder there in wooden kegs, ready to use during militia trainings, celebratory salutes, or times when war with the French or other enemies seemed imminent. Town militia companies and private individuals also stored powder there. The site was thus part of Massachusetts's self-defense infrastructure. And as such, it was a prize in the power struggle between the Crown and the local people.

When the imperial government in London had enacted the Port Bill, it also installed a new royal governor for Massachusetts: Gen. Thomas Gage, commander-in-chief of the British army in North America. Gage was a courteous and cautious man who prided himself on maintaining good relationships with Americans, including his wife Margaret. At age fifty-five, he had lived more than half his adult life in the colonies, mostly in New York City. But he had watched the political unrest in Boston with dismay. After the first public Stamp Act protests, Gage had offered to station troops at

Castle William, on an island in Boston harbor, so they could stifle trouble. In fact, out on that island they would not have been able to stop much—they would have been too far away to respond quickly. After more violence in 1768, the Crown government in London had decided to station troops in the heart of Boston. Gage had visited the town then to check the situation and came away with ideas for tougher government.

Unfortunately for the royal ministers, the regiments that came to Boston in 1768 simply prompted more resentment and more violence until the "Horrid Massacre" of March 1770. Four men and one boy were shot to death, six more injured. That toll might not seem to warrant the label of a massacre, but Boston's population was only 16,000, so nearly everyone in town knew a victim or witness. Gen. Gage, and other royal officials, viewed the soldiers' shots as self-defense against a violent mob. But he had to spend eight months worrying that one of his army captains and eight enlisted men would be convicted of murder and hanged.

With the destruction of the tea at the end of 1773, Boston had regained its place as the British Empire's most oppositional, obstreperous, and downright obnoxious outpost in North America. Gage was a strong believer in royal authority within the British constitution, sending his government superiors recommendations for stricter measures in Massachusetts. He happened to be in London in early 1774 when Parliament considered how to respond to the destruction of the tea. Lord Dartmouth, the secretary of state for North America, and his staff consulted Gage on what military resources it would take to pacify New England. The weakness of the 1768 policy, the general responded, was that the Crown had not been resolute—it had used enough force to rile the people, but not enough to quell them. The Crown must not make that mistake again. When his name came up as a possible governor, Gage personally promised King George III that he would carry out the Boston Port Bill and any other tough measures.

Gage had arrived in Massachusetts as the new royal governor on May 13, and four regiments of British redcoats soon joined him. That meant there was about one soldier for every adult male civilian in Boston. And the general was empowered to bring in more of the troops he commanded in North America. As far as pacifying the town, that level of force worked. Bostonians complained bitterly about the Port Bill and the military occupation. They did what they could to secretly undermine the army, such as sabotaging supplies for new barracks, but there was hardly any open violence against the troops. On June 1, His Majesty's commissioners of customs for North America successfully declared Boston closed to intercolonial trade, a rule that the Royal Navy was on hand to enforce.

Following his instructions from London, Gage announced that the Massachusetts General Court, the province's legislature, would have to move to Salem in June. That change deprived Boston of the prestige and business of being the colony's capital. Royal officials also expected legislators to be more cooperative when they were away from Boston crowds. As the duly appointed royal governor, Gage had authority under the old charter to make that move, and he brought along some companies of soldiers to make sure. The customs commissioners also shifted their operations to that smaller port. When the General Court gathered in the Salem town house on June 7, the Crown's plan to punish Boston by isolation appeared to be working.

Unfortunately for the new governor, the Massachusetts legislature proved as oppositional as ever. On the very first day, a House committee headed by Boston representative and clerk Samuel Adams offered the argument that the provincial charter empowered the governor to move the legislature but did not empower the imperial government to *tell* the governor to do so. That meant the session in Salem was "manifestly inconsistent with the Letter, as well as the Spirit and Intention of the Charter." On June 9 the Council, the upper house of the legislature which was supposed to advise the governor, expressed hope that "your Administration, in the principles and general conduct of it, may be a happy contrast to that of your two immediate Predecessors." Since the king had approved the preceding governors' action, Gage replied, "I consider this Address as an Insult upon His Majesty and the Lords of his Privy Council, and an Affront to myself."

On June 17 the House leaders ordered its chamber's viewing galleries cleared and its door locked to discuss a sensitive proposal: "a Meeting of Committees from the several Colonies on this Continent . . . in the City of *Philadelphia*," or what came to be called a Continental Congress. That gathering was intended to produce a united American protest against the Port Bill, to turn Boston's punishment into a political issue up and down the Atlantic seaboard. As soon as Gage heard about what was going on, he exercised his power to end the assembly. The province secretary read the governor's proclamation to the locked doors of the legislature's chamber. Inside, the House ignored that noise outside and finished electing delegates to go to Philadelphia: Speaker of the House Thomas Cushing, clerk Samuel Adams, and private lawyers Robert Treat Paine and John Adams.

The General Court was therefore no longer in session on August 6 when Gage received official word from Lord Dartmouth that Parliament had passed "An Act for the Better Regulating the Government of the Province of the Massachusetts Bay, in New England." More commonly known as the Massachusetts Government Act, that law changed the colony's constitution in significant ways. Gov. Gage had been aware that this bill was in the works when he left London. Now he moved swiftly to implement one of its major provisions: replacing the chiding Council with men appointed by the ministers in London who would be more inclined to cooperate with his initiatives. Using a legal document called a writ of mandamus, Gage summoned those men to meet with him in Salem. He swore in the first eleven on August 8, thirteen more on August 16. That still left twelve names off London's list, however. One man had died, one had moved to Surinam, one was dithering about whether to take the seat—and nine outright declined.

Some of the gentlemen who declined, and some of those who made it, reported that their neighbors were angry at them for agreeing to be "mandamus Councilors." Gage reported back to London how "a number of people collected on the road near Worcester, with intent to stop" Timothy Ruggles of Rutland from reaching Salem, "but he made his way through them." Daniel Leonard told the governor that in Taunton on August 22 "a written notification . . . was fixed on the Meeting House for the people to assemble" and protest his appointment. Job Williams, once a captain in the French and Indian War, yanked down the paper, tore it into pieces, and then went to warn the new councilor. A crowd massed outside Leonard's house that evening, so he invited Williams to stay overnight. The family went to bed, but "at 11 o'Clock in the evening a Party fixed upon the house with small arms and run off; . . . four bullets and some Swan-shot entered the house at the windows, part in a lower room and part in the chamber above," where Williams was sleeping. This was the first time that members of the Massachusetts resistance had shot a gun at their opponents. On August 29, men outside the house of mandamus Councilor Joshua Loring fired pistols into the air.

More violence seemed to be looming. Councilor Ruggles brought Gage ominous reports from central Massachusetts: "In Worcester they keep no terms, openly threaten resistance by arms, have been purchasing arms, preparing them, casting balls, and providing powder; and threaten to attack any troops who dare to oppose them." Ruggles looked ahead to September 7, when the Worcester County inferior court was scheduled to meet. He was "afraid to take his seat as judge," Gage said; "I apprehend that I shall soon be obliged to march a body of troops into that township, and perhaps into others, as occasion happens, to preserve the peace."

The next phase of resistance came sooner, and closer, than the governor anticipated. The Massachusetts Government Act also forbade towns from having town meetings without the governor's approval, aside from the one needed each spring to elect town officials and representatives. Yet another clause barred towns from sending delegates to a province-wide convention, as they had done in 1768. However, the law did not forbid *county*-wide conventions, for the simple reason that there had never been any before, so Massachusetts politicians decided to have some. On the morning of August 24, Gage learned that at nine o'clock Salem was going to hold an unauthorized town meeting to choose delegates for an Essex County Convention—a clear violation of the new law.

Gage acted quickly to get ahead of the local Whigs. He issued a proclamation forbidding the gathering. Then he turned his attention to the local men he knew were organizing that resistance—the Salem committee of correspondence. Back in 1772, Boston's town meeting had established a standing committee of correspondence and urged other towns to do the same so that they could share news and strategies concerning new Crown policies. Gradually such committees had spread across the province, and then at the colony level as well. The men on those committees did not have responsibilities of local government, like the selectmen, but they became increasingly influential in enforcing boycotts, organizing aid to Boston, and other measures.

The general summoned Salem's committee men to meet him at nine o'clock at the house of William Browne, one of the new Council. There the governor demanded those men disperse the unauthorized town meeting. The committee replied that they, not being selectmen, had no power to do so. Gage replied, "I came to execute the Laws, not to dispute, and I am determined to execute them. If the People do not disperse, the Sheriff will go first; if he is disobeyed, and needs Support, I will support him"—meaning with troops. In a pouring rain, two companies of the 59th Regiment began to march from the Salem Neck toward the town hall. The meeting quickly chose five delegates who had already agreed to serve, including members of the still-detained committee of correspondence, and adjourned.

The next day, Gage was angry enough to ask a Loyalist magistrate to arrest the whole Salem committee for defying the law. Two men paid bail to be released. Merchant captain Richard Derby, Jr., and four others refused to cooperate, remaining in custody. Two sets of rumors spread. In the surrounding county, people speculated that the governor planned to haul those men aboard the Royal Navy ship *Scarborough*, perhaps to ship them out of town. Inside Salem, people heard that the militia companies of nearby towns—perhaps three thousand armed men—were mustering to rescue the committee as soon as night fell. Gage made a tactical decision to let his prisoners go.

At that point, Gen. Gage decided that Salem was just as much of a trouble spot as Boston. And at least in the larger port he could have more troops in a more easily defended position. He therefore moved the government apparatus back to Boston on August 27. That night the governor sent a report on recent events to Lord Dartmouth. He described the rising resistance in the colony but, establishing a pattern that put off troubles without resolving them, did not fully reveal how the locals had gotten the better of him. About the Salem confrontation, Gage said merely, "The people behaved with great decency, and retired immediately" after their town meeting; he made no mention of the next day's arrests, confrontation, and capitulation. To the secretary of war, Viscount Barrington, Gage was just as circumspect about events but more blunt in his recommendations. He told Barrington that the Crown's best strategy would be to arrest Massachusetts's most radical leaders and send them to Britain for trial; New Englanders would resist, but "you wou'd be able to overcome them, no doubt, in a year or two."

With such resistance on his mind, Gage must have paid special attention to a letter that he received around that time from William Brattle, a sixty-eight-year-old general of the Massachusetts militia. Brattle was a big man in the town of Cambridge. He was a model of the mid-1700s country gentlemen, a wealthy farm owner who served in public offices, commanded a militia brigade, and dabbled in both law and medicine. Back in 1765 he had exasperated Gov. Francis Bernard by marching alongside workingmen in a demonstration against the Stamp Act when he was supposed to be in a Council meeting. But in the early 1770s Brattle had switched sides in the political debate, defending the Crown's new measures.

In late August, Brattle wrote to Gen. Gage in the courtly third person:

> Mr. Brattle presents his Duty to Governor Gage. He apprehends it his Duty to acquaint his Excellency from Time to Time with every Thing he hears and knows to be true, and is of Importance in these troublesome Times, which is the Apology Mr. Brattle makes for troubling the General with this Letter. . . .

MAP 1. Boston Harbor, 1774.

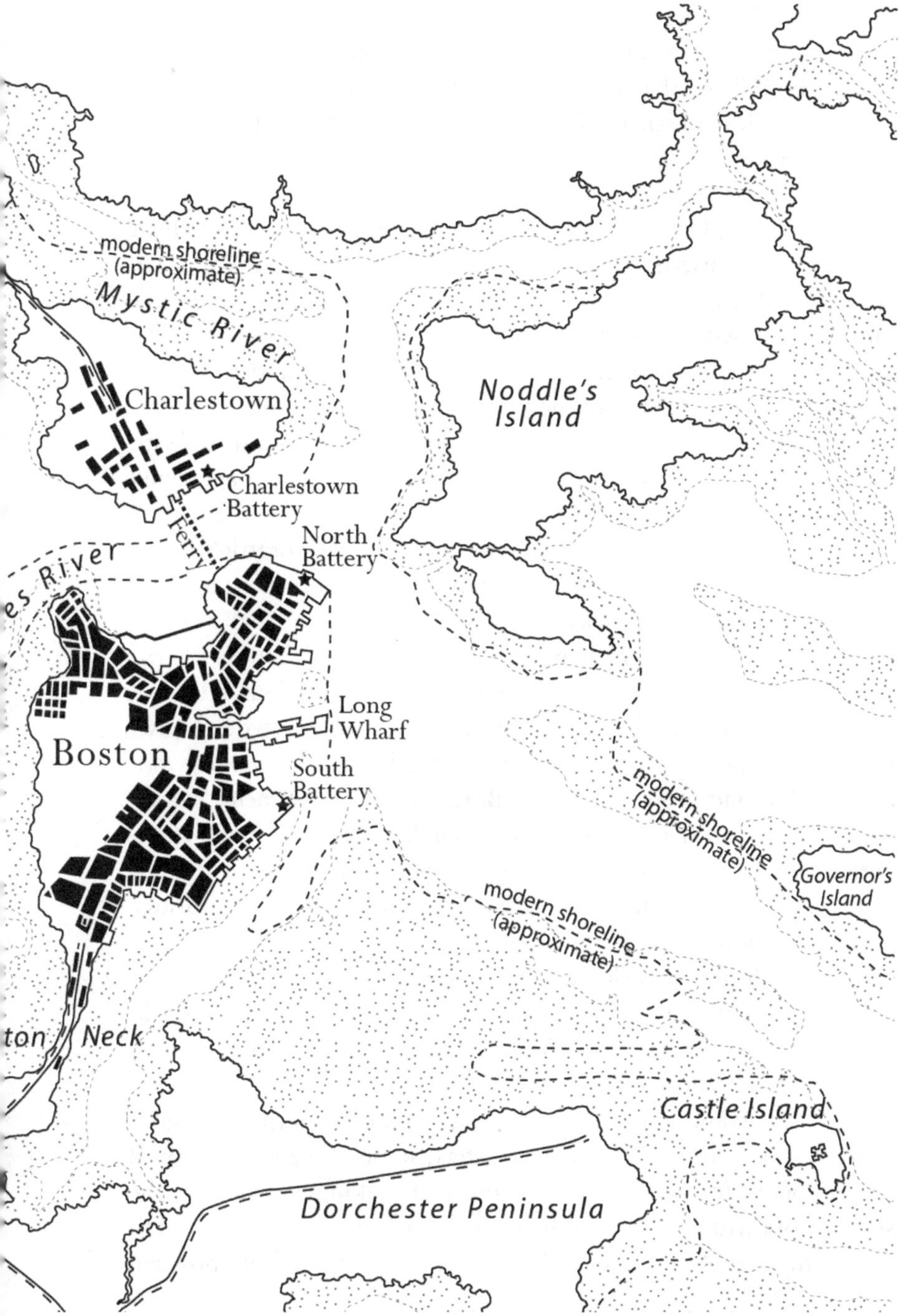
modern shoreline
(approximate)
Mystic River
Charlestown
Charlestown
Battery
Ferry
North
Battery
Noddle's
Island
Long
Wharf
Boston
South
Battery
modern shoreline
(approximate)
Governor's
Island
modern shoreline
(approximate)
Neck
Castle Island
Dorchester Peninsula

> This Morning the Select Men of Medford, came and received their Town Stock of Powder, which was in the Arsenal on Quarry-Hill, so that there is now therein, the King's Powder only, which shall remain there as a sacred Depositum till ordered out by the Capt. General.

As governor, Gage was captain-general, or commander-in-chief, of the Massachusetts militia. Brattle's message for him was clear, despite the fawning and indirect language: the governor could ask for the gunpowder in that stone tower anytime, but it might not be available for much longer. Gage had reportedly chided Byfield Lyde, the Loyalist keeper of the powder house in Boston, about letting people take out "enormous quantities" over that summer. With the thought of the restless Essex County militia fresh, Gage acted soon after his return to Boston.

On the night of August 31, David Phips came to Brattle's house in Cambridge with news that the army would collect that gunpowder the next day. Phips was tasked with helping to carry out the governor's orders in two capacities, as Middlesex County sheriff and as the militia colonel in command of a prestigious troop of horse guards. Brattle handed over the keys to the powder house. Phips also reported that Gen. Gage had asked him to collect two cannon that had been assigned to Brattle's militia regiment. Brattle wrote a note to Thaddeus Mason, the Middlesex County clerk, with instructions to deliver those guns. The sheriff hired a train of eight wagons for the next day, borrowing horses from a Cambridge innkeeper without specifying why.

Sheriff Phips, barrack master Goldthwait, Lt.-Col. Maddison, and the redcoats arrived at the tower on Quarry Hill before dusk. It was the start of another "Very hot dry" day. The men waited until there was enough light for them to see inside the stone building—no one wanted to carry a flaming torch or lantern into a gunpowder storehouse. For additional safety, some of the men removed their boots to forestall the small danger of striking sparks from the stone floors with the nails in their soles. Then the soldiers started to empty the storehouse, removing 260 half-barrels of gunpowder, each weighing fifty pounds, into the waiting wagons. Soon those casks were on their way to "*Temple's* barn" beside the Mystic River.

Maddison detached about twenty men to go to Cambridge with Phips and collect the two small cannon. Those guns were "fieldpieces" mounted on carriages for use on battlefields, as opposed to bigger, heavier artillery designed for sieges, ships, or shore batteries. They may have been stored in a gunhouse or small armory under Thaddeus Mason's control, or perhaps just a barn. Some Cambridge men tried to stop the sheriff and soldiers from taking those two guns. According to a housewright named John Nutting, who lived beside the town common, "the Mob desired and insisted that as an Officer of Militia he should prevent the Ordnance from being removed." Instead, he "readily assisted" Sheriff Phips in the operation.

The soldiers and their civilian helpers rolled the fieldpieces on their carriages out of Cambridge center and past Quarry Hill to the dock at Temple's farm. There the men loaded the barrels of gunpowder and cannon into the waiting rowboats. After the tide turned, sailors rowed those boats back around the Boston Peninsula. The issue of the *Boston News-Letter* printed that morning reported that the military was "now conveying" the powder to Castle William, the army-occupied island in the harbor.

By noon, the operation was over. There had been no injuries or delays, despite the objections from some in Cambridge. The royal government of Massachusetts had removed a large supply of gunpowder to a more secure place and taken control of two weapons that had no use except in warfare. If the people were to resist his attempts to enforce the law, as Gage expected they would, they would have less firepower to work with. As commander of the militia, the governor was well within his authority to move the province's military assets around like that. He probably expected to hear some complaints, but nothing he could not waive off. Indeed, Gage was so confident that morning that he proclaimed that towns should elect representatives for a new session of the Massachusetts General Court, to convene in Salem on October 5.

By the time he sat down to his midday dinner, however, Gage had lost control of the situation. The Boston merchant John Andrews reported in a letter: "The Governor walking up the main street to dine with Brigadier [Robert] Pigot . . . , who improves [i.e., uses] a house just above Liberty tree, by chance or design, in pulling out his handkerchief, dropt a letter" from his pocket. That was the letter that William Brattle had sent him, hinting that he should empty the powder house. Andrews was dubious that Gage had truly lost that paper by accident; he suggested the general had "a view to exculpate himself from being thought to take such a measure of his own head." It is also possible that Patriots stole the letter, or that Gage really did lose it by accident—a very unlucky accident.

By that afternoon, news of Brattle's missive reached Cambridge. People received it as evidence of a "Tratorous plot," in Abigail Adams's words, which naturally produced "Great commotions." Brattle saw that he was in danger. "[N]o sooner did he discover that his treachery had taken air," Adams wrote, "than he fled not only to Boston, but into the camp for Safety." Sheltered by the king's troops on Boston Common, Brattle spent that night and the next day writing a public letter declaring his innocence: "it is affirmed, I advised the Governor to remove the powder: this I positively deny, because it is absolutely false. It never so much as entered into my mind or thought." No one accepted Brattle's excuses or apology, and he never saw his home in Cambridge again.

Unable to find the militia general, the Cambridge protesters shifted their attention to another prominent supporter of the Crown who lived nearby, Jonathan Sewall. Born into a poor branch of an old, established Massachusetts family in 1729, Sewall had set out to build his fortune as a lawyer. In 1766 and 1767 he had deployed his wit in a series of lengthy newspaper essays signed "Philanthrop" which attacked the local Whig movement. Gov. Bernard showed his gratitude by making Sewall the province's attorney general. More recently, Sewall had added the title of Vice-Admiralty Court judge. He had prospered well enough that in 1771 he bought a house in Cambridge about a mile west from Brattle's on the road to Watertown. There he lived with his wife, the former Esther Quincy, and their three children aged four to eight.

Early in the afternoon on September 1, Sewall showed up at his father-in-law's house in Boston saying "he was advised to leave his house, & come to town." Justice of the peace Edmund Quincy was a Whig, but he did not want any harm to come to his daughter's husband, so he invited the attorney general to stay for dinner. Instead, "after writing a Letter, he [Sewall] went out, telling ye people, not to wait, if he did not soon return." No one in his family knew where he was for the next couple of days, though they do not seem to have been particularly surprised by that. Sewall, who appears to have suffered from bipolar disorder, may often have behaved erratically.

That evening, shortly before midnight, about thirty men and boys showed up outside the Sewall home. From her bedroom window, Esther Sewall assured them her husband was not there. Some yelled back that she was "a damned liar." She said "that being a woman she expected civil treatment from them as she had & would treat them," and "if they would go away, they should have anything she could give them out of the house." The crowd refused to be bought off and broke open a door in order to search the building for the attorney general.

At that point the children's tutor, Ward Chipman; two other young men; and an enslaved servant ran downstairs to deliver "an active & vigorous application of the argumentum baculinum"—the argument of the cudgel. This surprise counterattack forced the intruders out of the house. Their friends began to throw rocks and sticks at the back windows. Then Chipman fired a pistol. At the time, the young men inside the house said that shot was an accident, that Chipman had not shot at the crowd but "in the entry near the front window" when most of the mob was at the back. (Much later, Chipman reportedly implied that he had chosen to shoot to protect the Sewalls' home.)

Somehow, instead of inflaming the situation further, the pistol shot brought people to their senses, as if they realized that their ritual political brawling was about to go too far. The young defenders were able to go out and assure the crowd "that the gun went off accidentally, that we were very sorry for it as it was agreed upon since we had got them out of the house not to fire but on the last extremity." Again they asked the men and boys to think of Mrs. Sewall and her young children inside. The crowd, now more subdued, told Chipman and his friends they "had fought like brave fellows" and offered a bargain: "if we would give them something to drink they would not go to Judge Lee's as they intended"—the nearby house of Joseph Lee, another of Gen. Gage's newly sworn mandamus Councilors. That was how the confrontation ended: "after drinking a few glasses of wine" the young men "cordially bid each other Good-Night."

The next day, Justice Quincy chided his daughter in an unhelpful letter from Boston: "Im sorry to understand, that thro. great inadvertency, a Gun or pistol was dischd. from ye. house—ye sole Cause of ye Violence wch. Ensued". The *Boston Gazette* assured the world that this unruly crowd in Cambridge "were mostly boys and negroes, who soon dispersed"—a common way the Whig press tried to absolve the white men of Massachusetts from blame for any unreasonable violence. The Patriots behind that newspaper did not want to continue the confrontation in Cambridge, only to seize the moral high ground.

As for Gen. Gage, he undoubtedly knew about Brattle hiding in Boston, and he might have been hosting Sewall as well—the attorney general became part of his staff in the coming months. But if Cambridge's reaction to his move on the powder house was limited to chasing two more Loyalists out of their homes, that was an acceptable trade-off for securing the powder and guns. The governor had no idea that the news of redcoat activity was spreading west from Cambridge, becoming more wild and incendiary as it traveled.

Two

"An Extensive Insurrection thro' the Province"

While Gen. Gage was arranging to remove the gunpowder from Charlestown, a young Irish merchant named McNeil was traveling from Litchfield, Connecticut, toward Boston, where a relative was baking bread for the king's troops. On August 30, McNeil had watched a large crowd in Springfield pressure the local judges into not holding court sessions under the Massachusetts Government Act. On the night of September 1 he stopped at a tavern in Shrewsbury in central Massachusetts. "[A]bout midnight or perhaps one o'Clock," McNeil later told the Rev. Ezra Stiles of Newport, he woke up to hear "somebody violently rapping up the Landlord, telling the doleful Story that the Powder was taken, six men killed."

The fact that soldiers had emptied the powder house in Charlestown had grown into a report of redcoats and civilians clashing, and then a dire account of a massacre like the one in Boston in 1770. And the rumor continued to grow. A version heard in Hartford, Connecticut, said: "Brattle at Cambridge, a high tory, had petitioned Gage for troops to protect him at his house, which

Gage granted; a mob gathered and demand of Brattle to renounce his toryism or whatever you may term it; but after a short parley the troop fired, kill'd some right out, a large number wounded." By the time the alarm reached Longmeadow, Massachusetts, the story was "that the Ships in ye Harbour—of Boston, & ye Army on ye Land Side were allso fireing upon ye Town so yt. it was like ye Town was Demolishd."

Even in its mild form, the news from Cambridge alarmed the people of Shrewsbury. McNeil described how soon "fifty men were collected at the Tavern" in the middle of the night "equipping themselves & sending off Posts every Way to the neighboring Towns" to share information. They made McNeil repeat his story of how the people in Springfield had closed the courts. As soon as men were "equipt" for a military march, they set off to the east. In the morning McNeil resumed his journey in the same direction, passing one scene of commotion after another:

> all along were armed Men rushing forward some on foot some on horseback, at every house Women & Children making Cartridges, running Bullets, making Wallets, baking Biscuit, crying & bemoaning & at the same time animating their Husbands & Sons to fight for their Liberties, tho' not knowing whether they should ever see them again . . . such Emotions appeared all along the whole Tract of above fourty Miles from Shrewsbury to Boston.

Some of the smaller towns near Boston seemed deserted: "they scarcely left half a dozen Men in a Town, unless old and decrepid, and in one town the Landlord told him that himself was the only Man left." Not until McNeil was "within two miles of Cambridge" did anyone tell him the rumor of men killed by the king's soldiers was false.

The grievous rumor of the British military shelling Boston by land and sea should have been easy to dismiss. Destroying the town would have harmed some of the king's most loyal subjects and left no secure place for the thousands of soldiers to live. But with widespread fear and resentment, and no way to spread corrective news faster than a horse could ride or a ship could sail, both sides of a conflict could easily develop exaggerated ideas of what their rivals had done.

The response that McNeil saw looked disordered, but in fact it was the way the New England militia system was supposed to work. In an emergency, when people perceived their land in danger of invasion, that society could put thousands of armed, trained, and organized men on the march overnight. The system could activate without needing orders from a top authority, such as the royal governor. Instead, each town's companies would gather, and their already-elected officers and community leaders would consult about what to do. New England's militia companies had last mobilized on this scale in 1757 when word came that French and Native Americans fighters had taken Fort William Henry on Lake George. They would do so again in April 1775 and in response to Gen. John Burgoyne's advance from Canada in 1777.

On this September 2, those militia men perceived the threat to their communities coming not from the western frontier but from the royal government. The Massachusetts Government Act had riled the country towns like no other Crown action since the Stamp Act. Unlike the Boston Port Bill, which was directed at one town and could end as soon as someone repaid the cost of the tea, the new law promised *permanent* changes to the whole province. It altered the colony's system of self-government on nearly every level, providing more top-down authority from London and less bottom-up authority from the people. (Or perhaps less "middle-up" authority since New England voters were all white men with a certain amount of property.)

The men of Massachusetts were used to choosing many of their government officials. The colony's new charter of 1692 had established that the government in London would appoint the royal governor, and that he would appoint judges, sheriffs, and some other officials from the top. But there were still plenty of offices for the people to vote on, starting at the lowest level with town selectmen and such positions as overseers of the poor, hog reeves, and sealers of leather. Voters chose their towns' representatives to the General Court. The lower house of that legislature chose the members of the upper house or Council. Thus, even the Council, made up of gentlemen with the highest social standing and wealth in a deferential society, was ultimately a bottom-up institution.

There had long been friction between Massachusetts and the imperial government over various issues. Those distant ministers controlled the British military, choosing where to deploy the ships of the Royal Navy and the regiments of the army. The Treasury Department administered the Customs service, charged with cutting down on smuggling and collecting tariffs to regulate trade. But for the great majority of New Englanders—farming in small towns, attending the town's one church, raising their large families—that top-down authority did not really matter in daily life.

That began to change in the 1760s as the government in London sought more revenue from the North American colonies to run the empire. The Stamp Act of 1765 affected everyone who wanted to file a lawsuit, marry, or read a newspaper. Demonstrations, boycotts, riots, and widespread non-cooperation made sure that law never took effect in Massachusetts. Furthermore, that campaign established a political argument that grew stronger over the following years. First, American colonists agreed that Parliament should not have the power to tax them because they could not elect anyone to Parliament—a position that a printer at *The London Magazine* summarized in 1768 as "No Taxation without Representation." Second, those colonists, especially in New England, came to suspect that power-hungry politicians in London were trying to chip away at their self-government. And indeed, after a seventeenth century riven by civil wars, Parliament would not accept any rivals to its authority within the British Empire.

Massachusetts Whigs viewed every dispute of the next nine years through that lens. For example, in the early 1770s the central government began to grant salaries to governors, judges, and other royal appointees who had previously been paid by the colonial legislatures. One might expect voters to be pleased not to shoulder this expense. However, colonists knew they were already supplying the money for those salaries through Parliament's tax on tea. Furthermore, many American legislatures had used their power to delay paying salaries as a way to signal disapproval of royal appointees; now governors and judges were insulated from such financial pressure. Thus, politically sensitized colonists perceived that budgetary change as yet another way London politicians were strengthening their top-down power.

For most New Englanders, however, new imperial policies had little effect on their daily lives. Those farmers were not directly paying the new tariffs on imports. They saw soldiers when they visited Boston from 1768 to 1770, but their own towns were never under military occupation. The tea boycott of 1773 got some traction outside the ports—in Lexington citizens publicly burned tea three days before the Boston Tea Party—but the issues still seemed remote from rural life. For a decade small-town meetings and legislators expressed solidarity with Boston's political grievances, but the countryside was far less active than the ports.

The Massachusetts Government Act changed that. To start with, it changed how those towns could govern themselves. Under that law, as mentioned in the previous chapter, towns needed permission from the royal governor to hold more than the one meeting each spring when they elected local officials and representatives to the General Court. This clause applied to every town in the province, even if they had not destroyed any tea or mobbed any royal officials' houses. Most communities quickly found a way around the law: instead of formally ending a meeting, citizens simply adjourned to a future date, legally continuing the same meeting. But the law still seemed unjust.

The people of Massachusetts began to resist the Massachusetts Government Act in July 1774, even before its final text arrived from London on August 6. The strongest response arose not in Boston, which was crowded with soldiers, but out west in Berkshire County, where on July 25 committees called for closing the county courts, refusing to conduct normal civil business under the new law. Another set of targets were the gentlemen summoned to join the Council by writ of mandamus. Starting in mid-August, crowds visited those men's houses in the countryside to make clear they should not join this "new-fangled Council." The calls for county conventions and court closings moved from west to east. People worried about how Gov. Gage would eventually respond.

In that political environment, news of the king's troops removing the Middlesex County gunpowder and cannon on the morning of September 1 did not look like a simple redeployment of provincial military resources. It looked like the governor was trying to disarm the militia, perhaps in preparation for harsher action.

The militia was the colony's self-defense system—the people's protection from invaders, emergency police force, training ground for citizen-soldiers in imperial wars, and shield against potential tyrants. Massachusetts law required almost every white male between the ages of sixteen and sixty to gather four times each year to practice military maneuvers. That law exempted various types of men from mandatory trainings, some because they were too high in society (ministers, Harvard graduates, men who had already served as militia officers) and some because they were too low (blacks and Indians, whether enslaved or free). But for the vast majority of Massachusetts men, militia training was as much a part of civic life as elections. Indeed, since one did not have to be twenty-one years old or own a significant amount of property to serve in the militia, it was the main form of civic participation for many young males.

Though militia training was a top-down legal mandate and the governor was the province's commander-in-chief, in practice militia service was more of a bottom-up institution. As royal officials discovered, it was useless to call out the militia against mobs when the same men who made up the militia also made up the mob. During riots in 1747 Gov. William Shirley complained about "the soldiers of the Militia there having refus'd and neglected to obey my Orders given em by their Officers to appear in Arms for quelling the Tumult." Gov. Francis Bernard heard the same warning from his Council in 1765 during the Stamp Act riots: "the Militia, the only force we had, would never act against the Rioters, if they would assemble at all, which was much doubted."

Furthermore, by tradition New England militia companies elected their own captains, lieutenants, ensigns, and sergeants, choosing officers who (in peaceful times) offered the best feasts on training days or (during crises) had the most reassuring military experience. The royal governors accepted those choices, contenting themselves with naming the majors, colonels, and generals at the top. As a result of that tradition, the militia provided a ladder for rising in society. Men from the middling ranks could gain the respect of their neighbors through diligent training and become officers, a step toward being recognized as gentlemen. Once a man was a militia captain or above, he retained his military title for life as a mark of respect. Thus, when the royal governor appeared to be limiting the militia system, he was also limiting the aspirations of men to rise from the bottom (or middle) to the top.

The men of rural Massachusetts adapted that system to organize their opposition to the Crown's new laws in 1774. The crowds in western counties were not simply masses of men, but men in their militia companies—sometimes estimated to be more than a thousand. Councilor Daniel Leonard acknowledged the military nature of the crowd he faced in Taunton: "About five hundred persons assembled, . . . some of them Officers in the Militia, and formed themselves into a Battalion before my House." Most Loyalist appointees did not state that they were facing militia units because that would grant those protesters legitimacy, but many observers spoke of the crowds' discipline.

Those mass turnouts were probably also enabled by the homogeneity of rural New England society. West of the seaside towns, there were practically no non-Congregationalist churches. Eighty-five percent of the Massachusetts population was ethnically English, not even Irish or Scottish. Towns were full of people who were each other's relatives, schoolmates, in-laws, marching comrades, and business partners. Though individuals differed by personality, class, theological nuances, and other factors, that society was basically a monoculture, like fields all planted with the same crop. In the summer of 1774, the idea that Gen. Gage's government was curtailing the people's rights swept across the landscape like a potato blight. For years radical Whigs had issued warnings about corrupt ministers and their appointees oppressing Americans. Now that idea took hold, and the result was thousands of armed men on the march.

The province's leading Patriot newspaper, the *Boston Gazette*, described the militia mobilization that started on September 1 this way:

> the County of Middlesex took the alarm, and on Thursday evening began to collect in large bodies, with their arms, provisions, and ammunition, determining by some means to give a check to a power which so openly threatened their destruction, and in such a clandestine manner robbed them of the means of their defence.

Those "large bodies" headed east with remarkable speed. According to John Andrews, the town of Marlborough heard about the removal of the gunpowder on Thursday night, "yet they were down to Cambridge (which is thirty miles) by eight o'clock Fryday morning, with a troop of horse and another of foot." There were contingents from Cambridge, Charlestown, Concord, Framingham, Sudbury, Waltham, and Watertown, among other towns.

One advance sign of that mass approaching Cambridge was Dr. Joseph Lee riding into town from Concord. At fifty-eight years old, this wealthy physician was immune to the homogeneous thinking of his neighbors. He had a long record of quarrels about church membership, debts, and other small-town issues. Early on the morning of September 2 he arrived at the house of local magistrate Joseph Lee. (The two men with the same name were not related.) Dr. Lee brought the news "that the country was assembling to come down" and would probably demand that Judge Lee resign from the mandamus Council. The judge, who was sixty-three, not a fervent Loyalist, and hoping to live quietly with his neighbors, quickly wrote out a resignation.

Dr. Lee may have taken the same warning to Cambridge's other mandamus Councilor, Samuel Danforth. This man was seventy-seven years old and had served on the governor's Council for thirty-five of those years. He was not known for taking sides. People respected his learning. Among the many sciences he studied was alchemy, also reportedly an interest of Dr. Lee. In 1773 Danforth had written to Benjamin Franklin with the good news that he might discover the philosopher's stone, "curing all Diseases, even old Age itself." Franklin replied from London, "I anticipate the jolly Conversation we and twenty more of our Friends may have 100 Years hence," when they could enjoy "the future glorious State of our America." Danforth was also ready to resign from the Council. In fact, the previous day he had gone into Boston to do that, but Gage had "refus'd to accept of it."

Several men from Cambridge and its eastern neighbor, Charlestown, went to the highest-ranking royal appointee in town, Lt. Gov. Thomas Oliver, and asked him to speak to the oncoming crowds and "make them return peaceably home." It was less than four weeks since Oliver had been sworn in as lieutenant governor, an appointment which probably surprised him as much as everyone else. He was only forty-one years old and had never been active in politics, though he was Brattle's second-in-command in their militia regiment. As an Anglican and heir to wealthy sugar plantations on Antigua, Oliver was a natural Loyalist. The government ministers in London probably thought he belonged to the right family. However he came by his new responsibilities, Oliver took them seriously, and on this morning that meant helping to keep the peace.

Lt. Gov. Oliver lived in a mansion on the road leading from the center of Cambridge west along the Charles River toward Watertown. That was one of the main routes into town, so, he recognized, the throngs "were to pass by my house." Then, "In a very short time, before I could prepare myself to go, they were in sight." Oliver went out and met the men, "enquiring the cause of such an appearance." They spoke of having been "deprived of their Rights and Priviledges." They promised "they were no mob, but sober, orderly people, who would commit no disorders." After some discussion, Oliver thought he had calmed the men down "from the respectful manner in which they expressed their thanks." In fact, they simply proceeded on down the road to Cambridge common and sent word to Councilors Danforth and Lee that they were waiting.

As the crowds approached Cambridge, they had learned that the rumors of soldiers killing people the day before were untrue. According to the *Boston Gazette*, they "left their fire-arms, &c., at some distance behind them." McNeil agreed: "most of the people left their Arms at Watertown, only another Body of 250 had already bro't Arms into Town," so those men left their weapons with some of their group as guards "in a yard at a miles distance." However, the *Gazette* described some men as "armed only with sticks," carrying a threat of violence.

A crowd that Oliver guessed numbered about 1,500 people accumulated on Cambridge common. This was a large swath of grass near the college with elm trees planted along one side for shade. The day was becoming warm and dry. The men grouped "under their regular leaders," or militia officers, and each company chose one or two men to comprise a "committee of the body" and speak to Danforth, Lee, and others on behalf of the whole assembly. The people began to worry that "the troops were on their march to disperse them," which might yet bring about another massacre, so the committee went back to Lt. Gov. Oliver and asked him to "wait on the General to prevent" this. They "promised that no disorders should arise" and in return insisted that the lieutenant governor agree to come back to Cambridge after this errand.

Oliver took on that mission. As he hurried toward the center of Cambridge, he passed a series of estates that almost all belonged to his wife Elizabeth's relatives. These included Judge Lee's old house, remade somewhat clumsily to fit the Georgian style, where the town's two Councilors were preparing to meet with the "committee of the body." Further along came Attorney General Sewall's mansion; Oliver might have seen the broken windowpanes from the night before. Just before the village he passed the home of the suddenly unpopular William Brattle. The families along that road were Loyalist, and their comfortable life in Cambridge was in jeopardy.

By eight o'clock, Andrews heard, the crowd numbered "about three thousand . . . and continually increasing." Oliver hurried on toward Charlestown in order to take the ferry over to Boston. On the road he met a group of men traveling the other way: several of

Boston's leading Patriot politicians. These committee of correspondence members and the lieutenant governor might have eyed each other warily at first. Soon they realized they all wanted the same thing: to see the confrontation in Cambridge end peacefully.

The organizer of the Boston contingent was Dr. Joseph Warren, a thirty-three-year-old doctor, widowed the previous year. About six o'clock that morning he had heard about the damage at Attorney General Sewall's house. While discussing how the Patriot movement should respond, he received a note from the committee of correspondence for Charlestown, who had heard from their counterparts in Cambridge. Those men asked him "to take some step in order to prevent the people from coming to immediate acts of violence, as incredible numbers were in arms, and lined the roads from Sudbury to Cambridge."

Dr. Warren sent for his colleagues in the Boston political leadership. However, he did not tell his messenger about the volatile situation outside of town, no doubt hoping to keep rumors from spreading inside town. His summons therefore carried little sense of urgency. The group that slowly assembled at Warren's house were all gentlemen, but they came from different parts of the Whig movement. There was William Molineux, a hardware merchant who leaned toward a confrontational style of politics that fit his irascible personality. A second merchant, John Bradford, had started as a sea captain; he served on many town committees.

Dr. Thomas Young was a physician who had come to Boston from Albany eight years earlier because he wanted to be in the thick of America's fight for liberty. His ideas on politics, religion, and medicine were all unorthodox, but he was never daunted by criticism. Joseph Greenleaf was a magistrate from Abington, Massachusetts, who had moved into Boston in 1771 to print political tracts and a magazine—a bold step down in eighteenth-century society. Finally, William Cooper was the Boston town clerk, son and brother of leading Congregationalist ministers and thus from New England's traditional elite. Cooper kept notes at town meetings as well as the unofficial meetings about the tea, ensuring the Whigs' interest was always served. Molineux, Greenleaf, Cooper, and Bradford were in their fifties, and Dr. Young was forty-three. The man who had summoned them, Dr. Warren, was the youngest by a decade.

Warren described "waiting some time" for others to arrive. Some prominent Patriot leaders never appeared that morning. James Bowdoin was ill. Dr. Benjamin Church, Jr., may have been out of town with his mistress. But the biggest no-show was the young merchant John Hancock. He had inherited one of Boston's greatest fortunes and finest homes. He was both a town selectman and a representative to the General Court. Six months earlier he had delivered the annual oration to commemorate the Boston Massacre, gaining more visibility and popularity than ever. But there is no evidence of his whereabouts that morning.

At last the six Boston men set off on the ferry. In Charlestown they consulted with that town's political leaders, who urged them onward. Then they met Lt. Gov. Thomas Oliver coming the other way. "He said he was going to the general, to desire him not to march his troops out of Boston," Warren reported; "We thought his precaution good, and proceeded to Cambridge." Dr. Young described what they found on the common: "Judge Danforth was addressing perhaps four thousand people in the open air; and such was the order of that great assembly that not a whisper interrupted the low voice of that feeble old man from being heard by the whole Body."

Samuel Danforth was standing on the courthouse steps, going through what had become a ritual for mandamus Councilors who did not enjoy the protection of the troops in Boston: he was apologizing for having ever accepted the position. The Boston press summed up Danforth's remarks this way:

> having now arrived at a very advanced age, and spent the greater part in the service of the public it was great mortification to him to find a step lately taken by him so disagreeable to his country, in which, he conscientiously had meaned to serve them, but finding their general sense against his holding a seat at the council board on the new establishment, he assured them that he had

resigned said office, and would never henceforth accept or act in any office inconsistent with the charter right of his country.

To reinforce that message, Danforth held up a paper certifying that he had already resigned, "signed with his own hand" and witnessed by Nathaniel Cudworth, a militia officer from Sudbury. Judge Lee made a similar speech, reading out "what I wrote to the Governor." Both men declared that they had been treated with respect, "Sobriety and Decency."

Around this time the committee men from Boston and Charlestown arrived and tried to take charge. They mounted the courthouse steps and addressed the crowd below. Unfortunately, they had not coordinated their message. After praising "their Readiness to serve the Cause of their Country," Cooper told those men they should not resist the loss of the gunpowder and cannon. Gen. Gage had the authority to take them, and anyway the powder was probably useless, old and caked. Molineux echoed that message. (Two days later, William Gamage, who had the duty of "sunning and turning" the powder regularly to keep it fresh, disputed that claim in the newspapers.) Bradford interrupted his colleagues to disagree. Richard Devens from Charlestown disagreed with Bradford. Greenleaf, who had more experience with rural Massachusetts society than any of his colleagues, apparently did not speak.

Finally, one of the Boston men tried to restore order by turning the vast gathering into a formal public meeting. "[A] Vote was called for to see if the body was satisfied" with what Danforth and Lee had said. The Patriot newspapers reported that question "passed in the affirmative, nem. con."—i.e., without a single dissenting voice. Then a Boston man made a motion "to know whether that body would signify their abhorrence of mobs, riots, and the destruction of private property." Once again, the four thousand men were unanimous in so signifying.

The question of what to do about Sheriff Phips was thornier. He had helped to remove the militia gunpowder and cannon. He had also sent out summonses for jury duty and other legal documents as sheriff. Phips complained to the committee that people had spoken of him "hardly" for working under the Massachusetts Government Act. His case required consultation. Not realizing that the assembly had already chosen a committee to speak for them, Cooper suggested that they do that now and those men could join the Boston gentlemen in a nearby tavern for a conference about Phips, perhaps over midday dinner. As for the larger crowd, it could wait on the hot common. Though Cooper's suggestion was impolitic, that appears to be what happened next.

Genteel Whig witnesses emphasized the crowd's stoic calm. Dr. Young praised how they "kept their particular stations for three hours in the scorching sun of the hottest day we have had this summer. Such patient endurance is certainly a principal ingredient in the composition of that character emphatically called a Good Soldier." John Adams's law clerk Edward Hill described the maturity of the crowd: "They were dress'd just as they are at work. Every man appeared as composed as if they were at a funeral. I saw many among them whom I should judge were 60 and 70 years of age." The news of "the vast number of country people" was so striking that the Rev. Manasseh Cutler visited Cambridge to see for himself.

At length the combined committees returned and "reported to the body, that it was their opinion the high sheriff was excuseable, as he had acted in conformity to his order from the commander in chief." Both elite gentlemen and militia officers were sensitive to hierarchy, after all. As for his civil duties, however, Phips had to deliver a written statement that he would rescind the writs "that I have sent out under the new Establishment." Likewise, Thaddeus Mason was not formally chided for giving the army the militia cannon, but he had to apologize for continuing to send out legal papers under the Massachusetts Government Act. Either publicly on the common or from his home, Mason resigned after thirty-eight years as county clerk.

Around this time Lt. Gov. Oliver returned with the reassuring news that he had spoken to Gen. Gage and "no troops were ordered." The committee thanked him and then made one more request. In Oliver's words, "They began with expressing their regard and respect for me, and ended with observing how happy I should make them, if I would quit" the Council. The lieutenant governor replied that this additional demand was "very ungrateful treatment." He noted that resigning would "undoubtedly incur his Majesty's displeasure." He argued that as lieutenant governor he answered to the whole province, not simply the "particular County" represented on the common that day. Finally, Oliver promised "that when all the other Councillors had resigned, if it appeared to be the sense of the Province I should resign, I would submit." The committee considered Oliver's arguments and "Voted them satisfactory." They just had to sell their decision to the whole crowd.

The leaders were "preparing to deliver it to the body, when Mr. commissioner Hallowell, came through the town on his way to Boston." Benjamin Hallowell, Jr., was one of His Majesty's commissioners of customs, responsible for collecting tariffs and stopping smugglers in all the ports of North America. Out of a very unpopular group of officials he was one of the most unpopular. One reason was his short temper; he was hotheaded enough to get into a fistfight with Adm. Samuel Graves during the siege of Boston, and they were on the same side. Another reason was that Hallowell was a Boston native, not a bureaucrat from Britain; he therefore appeared to have betrayed his own community. A good measure of the bad feelings Hallowell engendered is that other customs commissioners happened to pass through Cambridge at the same time, all moving back from Salem to Boston, but only he attracted attention.

Of course, the inland farmers had no reason to recognize that gentleman riding past in a chaise with an enslaved black servant in livery following on horseback. Hallowell later told Gage, "No Insult or Affront was offered me untill I came to . . . where some people from Boston Stood, who called to me, Dam you how doe you like us now, you Tory Son of a Bitch"? In a letter to London he specifically blamed "One Thomas of this town and one of the inflammatory printers" for pointing him out. Isaiah Thomas was the publisher of the *Massachusetts Spy* newspaper. The gentlemen from Boston and Cambridge were trying to tamp down trouble, but Thomas was not.

The printer's yell riled up the crowd. The *Boston Gazette* reported, "The sight of that obnoxious person so inflamed the people that in a few minutes above 160 horsemen were drawn up and proceeding in pursuit of him on the full gallop." The September 8 *Massachusetts Spy* put the number of horsemen at "above an hundred." Again, this was not what the political leaders wanted. Thomas Gardner of Cambridge, a committee of correspondence member and militia captain, "began a parley with one of the foremost [riders] which caused them to halt till he delivered his mind very fully in dissuasion of the pursuit." Devens of Charlestown and Young of Boston agreed with Gardner, saying that anything that "might introduce confusion into the proceedings," such as violence, would spoil the accomplishment of making the councilors resign. Hallowell later heard that the Boston men argued "that the Shedding of one mans blood wou'd answer no good purpose, and at the same time bring on the loss of many thousand lives, for they expected every moment the arrival of the troops from Boston."

The customs commissioner wrote that of all the horsemen "6 or 8 wou'd not be prevailed upon to goe back." The Boston press insisted that only "one gentleman, of a small stature, pushed on." Both Hallowell and the *Massachusetts Spy* said that man's name was Bradshaw. He overtook the commissioner's chaise in Roxbury, about five miles from Boston; rode in front of the horse; and slapped it until it stopped. Hallowell pulled out "a brace of pistols." Bradshaw backed off. Hallowell drove on again. Bradshaw chased him from a distance, shouting, "Stop the Murderer the Tory Murderer he has killed a man."

After another mile, the commissioner's carriage horse began to falter. He mounted the steed that his slave was riding and set off on his own, gripping both pistols. Hallowell reached his house in Jamaica Plain but, deciding it was not safe enough, headed on to Boston. Reportedly his horse collapsed just as he got past the sentries, and he ran into the army camp. Hallowell declared that "not less than one hundred people" were behind him. The Patriot newspapers sniffed that he claimed "he was pursued by some thousands, who would be in town at his heels, and destroy all friends of government." As for Bradshaw, Hallowell accused him of having looted the abandoned chaise of a gold-headed cane, a holster, and three pounds of gunpowder.

Both sides of the conflict were now scared that the other was about to attack. Reportedly Gen. Gage "sent out all day several trusty Soldiers in Sailors Habits to loiter on the rode from Roxbury to Cambridge & return & bring accounts unnoticed." In Cambridge a man arrived on a "very fleet Horse" from the Charlestown ferry to warn about activity in the army camp. Some of the men on the common rushed to retrieve their guns. Others reportedly prepared "to take up the bridge" over the Charles "to prevent their [the army's] bringing the artillery to bear upon 'em." Adopting a military term, the Patriot press reported that "light horsemen were dispatched both ways to gain more certain advice of the true state of the soldiery." Even when those riders returned with news that there were no troops approaching by land or water, the assembly was still aroused. And it was not the same assembly as it had been that morning; more "large companies [were] pouring in" from the west.

The crowd now "resolved to leave no unconstitutional officers, within their reach, in possession of his place." That meant, first and foremost, Lt. Gov. Oliver. He had taken advantage of the tumult when Commissioner Hallowell passed by to slip back to his house. "I chose to get out of the way," he later wrote. "I was just going into my carriage to proceed to Boston, when a vast crowd advanced, and in a short time my house was surrounded by 4000 People, and one 4th part in arms." There was a knock at the door. "I waited in my hall, when 5 persons entered, with a decent appearance, who informed me they were a Committee from the body of the People to demand my Resignation as a Councillor." The assembly had chosen new leaders, and Oliver did not recognize these visitors. As for the quibbling gentlemen from Boston, they were clearly no longer a factor (though they had "provided some refreshment" for the crowd).

The new committee had brought a paper for Oliver to sign. It called the Massachusetts Government Act "a manifest infringement of the charter rights and privileges of this people," and ended with the royal lieutenant governor promising to resign from the Council formed under "the present novel and oppressive plan of government." Oliver reproached his visitors for "ingratitude & false dealings," reminding them that he had reached an agreement with their colleagues earlier in the day. This committee acknowledged that but said "that the People were dissatisfied with the Votes of their Committee in the morning."

Around that time the Irish trader McNeil caught up with the militiamen he had seen march off the night before. He told Ezra Stiles that he found

> the Multitude . . . formed & standing before Lt. Gov. Oliver's House. He judged those drawn up regularly in Lines were about Two Thousand & not three—& that the Bystanders were I think a thousand more. . . . there was no Tumult, but an awful Stillness, Silence thro' the Lines, and among the surrounding Body of People. All was negotiated by the Committee but in the presence of the Body, the Committee communicating by the Officers Information thro' the Lines, so that all knew what was transacting.

The negotiations were not going well. Lt. Gov. Oliver "absolutely refused to sign any paper." The committee asked him to "consider the consequences of refusing the demands of an inraged People." McNeil watched "some Gentlemen & Officers nearest, pressing thro' the Gate into the [lieutenant] Governors Yard." Soon Oliver saw people "pressed up to my windows, which were then open." Men in the background were "calling for vengeance against the Foes of their Liberty." The committee "appeared anxious . . . and, impressed with some humanity, endeavoured to appease the people; but in vain." Oliver heard "the distresses of my Wife and Children" from the next room. He made a wild suggestion to the committee: "I proposed that the People should take me by force." Startled, the men refused to allow that.

Finally, Oliver surrendered—to a point. He added one line to the resignation letter the committee had written for him: "My house at Cambridge being surrounded by about four thousand people, in compliance with their command I sign my name." The committee took the document out to the assembly. McNeil reported it was "immediately handed along the Lines & read publickly at proper Distances till the whole Body of the people were made to hear it," prompting a "a chearful Murmur or general universal Voice of Joy." In contrast, Oliver, who was trying to justify his choices to higher-ups in the royal government, stated that the committee "found great difficulty in getting it accepted." He wrote:

> I had several messages that the people would not accept it with those additions, upon which I walked into the court-yard, and declared that I would do no more, though they should put me to death. I perceived that those persons who formed the first body which came down in the morning, consisted of the landholders of the neighboring towns, used their utmost endeavors to get the paper received with my additions; and I must, in justice to them, observe, that they never invaded my enclosures, but were still not able to protect me from other insults which I received from those who were in arms.

That confrontation ended about an hour before sunset. At five o'clock "came on hard Thunder & Lightning with a great Shower," driving the militia men back to their homes and taverns for the night.

That evening, Gage received a letter from Lt. Gov. Oliver "to beg I wou'd on no Account send any Troops there, or it wou'd prove fatal to him." The general acted with the utmost caution. McNeil visited the army camp that evening, observing "all Hurry, Activity, lively preparation, & . . . Anxiety." Shortly after sunset, the veteran 23rd Regiment "marched without Music, slowly, stilly, to set the Watch on the Neck; and then returned into Camp," seeking to increase the town's security without causing any further alarm outside.

That evening Gage wrote to Gen. Frederick Haldimand, whom he had left in charge at New York: "Affairs in this Province are grown so very bad that I must get all [forces] I can together." He did not think that it would be safe to move additional artillery up to Boston by land; "the Cannon shou'd be sent up to the Vessells." The next day Gage told Lord Dartmouth, the secretary of state: "Tho' I saw Things were bad when I wrote from Salem, I found them much worse the I expected. . . . Tho' the People are not held in high Estimation by the Troops, yet they are numerous, worked up to a Fury."

Lt. Gov. Oliver went into Boston to stay by September 2, bringing his family shortly afterward. William Brattle, Attorney General Sewall, and Customs Commissioner Hallowell were already there under army protection. Then, "a Day or two after Govr. Oliver's House was attacked," came Oliver's brother-in-law and neighbor, John Vassall, and his wife and children. On September 16, Judge Lee secured a letter from the Charlestown committee of correspondence certifying that he was going "to take a Tour through the Country for his Ladys health" and should "be treated by all the Friends of our happy Constitution, with such Civility and Respect, as shall do honour to our common Cause." Soon the mansions along the river road in Cambridge were occupied only by servants.

That ended the crisis in Cambridge, but news of the seizure of the gunpowder, in its exaggerated form, was still working its way through the New England countryside and still putting militia companies on the march. A few days later Dr. Warren wrote:

> The people from Hampshire County crowded the county of Worcester with armed men; and both counties received the accounts of the quiet dispersion of the people of Middlesex with apparent regret, grudging them the glory of having done something important for their country without their assistance.

Dr. Young added:

> The western Post tells that on Friday afternoon and Saturday morning the people from the [Connecticut] River had reached

> Worcester Shrewsbury when they were met by expresses telling them the business was over, and it was merrily said that had not Worcester men been absent themselves the town would not have held the volunteers.

People guessed that at least "twenty thousand" militiamen had been active at one point or another, vastly outnumbering Gage's forces in Boston.

Israel Putnam received word of the Royal Artillery shelling Boston in Pomfret, Connecticut, around 11:00 A.M. on Saturday, or about eighteen hours after the confrontation had ended. He sent off letters to rouse that colony's militia. Handbills printed with Putnam's alert arrived in New Haven on Sunday afternoon. By Monday, September 5, word of the trouble reached Gen. Frederick Haldimand in New York. On Tuesday the Continental Congress in Philadelphia received their first "Intimation of the Bombardment of Boston," John Adams wrote; "a confused account, but an alarming one indeed." There were similar, less documented chains of communication to the west and northwest as the corrective good news followed behind.

The dire reports disrupted Sunday services in many New England towns. In Milford, Connecticut, thirteen-year-old Joseph Plumb Martin felt the alarm keenly:

> In the afternoon, one Sabbath day, while the people were assembled at meeting, word was brought that the British (regulars, as the good people then called them) were advancing from Boston, spreading death and desolation in their route in every direction. . . . I went out of the house in the dusk of the evening, when I heard the sound of a carriage on the road, in the direction of Boston; I thought they were coming as sure as a gun; I shall be dead or a captive before to-morrow morning; however, I went to bed late in the evening, dreamed of "fire and sword," I suppose; waked in the morning, found myself alive, and the house standing where it did the evening before.

Young Joseph's house was the same that morning, but the world around Boston had changed profoundly. The militia mobilization that historians later dubbed the "Powder Alarm" had reshaped the political situation in Massachusetts. First, it was clear that Gen. Gage's authority now stopped at the gate of Boston. Where he had soldiers—inside the town and at Castle William—the governor could still exercise power. Everywhere else in the colony was effectively free from royal control. Patriots grew more confident about their military might. The response to the powder seizure, wrote the Rev. Ezra Stiles, "shews that New England are ready to fight for their Liberties." Dr. Warren declared: "Had the troops marched only five miles out of Boston, I doubt whether a man would have been saved of their whole number."

Second, the people of rural Massachusetts were now more militant than the people of Boston. Dr. Young stated, "That treacherous, sneaking and cowardly action, of seizing our Province powder set all the Country in a flame. Every one now feels the matter coming home to him. . . . By all our advices from the westward the Body of the people are for resuming their old Charter, and organizing a government immediately." Echoing a message Oliver had brought into Boston, Gage warned Lord Dartmouth that the opposition was "not a Boston Rabble but the Freeholders and Farmers of the Country"—the great and respectable majority of the population. Col. Hugh Earl Percy laid out the situation for his father on September 12: "In short, this country is now in as open a state of rebellion as Scotland was in the year '45."

Three

"Behold, the Guns Were Gone!"

INSIDE BOSTON, GEN. GAGE RECOGNIZED THAT HIS ARMY WAS vulnerable to attack. Even as the confrontation on Cambridge Common went on, rumors swirled inside Boston about the size of that threat. The merchant John Andrews recorded this report about the rural militia leaders:

> their determination is to collect about forty or fifty thousand by night (which they are sure of accomplishing) when they intend to fling in about fifteen thousand by the way of the Neck, and as many more over the ferry: when once they got possession, to come in like locusts and rid the town of every soldier.

Nearly all the numbers in Andrews's letters tend to be double the likely figures, but even a force of twenty thousand would have dwarfed the troops that Gage had. (It would also have been more men than Gen. George Washington ever commanded during the siege of Boston.)

The British commander therefore strengthened the town's land defenses. By the end of the day, Andrews wrote, "the Guard upon the Neck is doubled," and "the whole battalions have had new flints, &ca., delivered out to them." The general stopped all withdrawals from the powder house on Boston Common, even individuals' private property. On September 3, Boston smith Thomas Newell wrote in his diary, "Four large field-pieces were dragged from the common by the soldiery and placed at the only entrance to this town by land" on the Boston Neck. Soon the army added more artillery there and began to build a stronger gatehouse that extended all the way across the narrow stretch of dry land. Gen. Gage wrote to his subordinates in Quebec and New York, summoning more regiments to Boston. On September 22, Abigail Adams would look around the town and send her husband John a letter from what she tartly called "Boston Garison."

The Royal Navy moved to guard the town's flanks. On September 2, H.M.S. *Lively*, a "frigate of 20 guns, came to her moorings in the ferry way" in the Charles River between the North End and Charlestown. Adm. Samuel Graves ordered that the ferry boats be anchored under his guns for eight hours each night so they would not be available for any amphibious invasion. Andrews wrote, "They have haul'd the Men of War close in upon the town at all quarters," each of those ships bristling with artillery. The British military thus had Boston and its nearest neighbors within cannon range.

No Massachusetts citizens could miss the significance of those actions: the taxes Parliament collected from them were now paying to threaten them with cannon fire. Rural towns responded by moving their military supplies out of reach of the governor and his supporters and discussing stronger action. Even before nightfall on September 1, Brookline held a special town meeting "to Examine into the state of Said Town as to There Milatary preparations for War, in case of a Suden attack from our Enemies." At a meeting on September 5, the men of Watertown voted to have "the Selectmen Secure the town Stock of ammunition."

The men of Braintree took action on September 11, nominally a day of rest, as Abigail Adams reported to her husband:

> In consequence of the powders being taken from Charlstown, a general alarm spread thro many Towns and was caught pretty soon here. The report took here a fryday, and a Sunday a Soldier was seen lurking about the common. Supposed to be a Spy, but most likely a Deserter. However inteligence of it was communicated to the other parishes, and about 8 o clock a Sunday Evening there pass by here about 200 Men, preceeded by a horse cart, and marched down to the powder house from whence they took the powder and carried [it] into the other parish and there secreeted it. I opened the window upon there return. They pass'd without any Noise, not a word among them till they came against this house, when some of them perceiveing me, askd me if I wanted any powder. I replied not since it was in so good hands. The reason they gave for taking it, was that we had so many Tories here they dare not trust us with it.

Six days later one of Adams's former law clerks, William Tudor, told him that in Boston, "Guns are so scarce here now that there is not a complete firelock to be purchased."

Boston harbor was ringed with artillery emplacements to protect the port from naval invaders. Some of those sites were large, such as the well-fortified Castle William. Others were as small as one or two guns on a harbor island or at the mouth of a small river. The artillery in those places tended to be very large, rather old, and mounted on carriages not built to travel more than a few feet. It had been decades since they were fired for anything other than drills or celebrations. Nevertheless, they were cannon.

Across the Charles River from Boston to the north, Charlestown maintained a small battery stocked with powder and ordnance to guard the town's wharves and the entrance to the river. In 1770 the British military engineer Capt. John Montresor had deemed that battery "irreparable," and he found only five cannon inside—eighteen-pounders, meaning they could fire balls weighing eighteen pounds. He may have helped to install more guns at that time as part of a general upgrade of coastal defenses.

In the first week of September 1774, Charlestown Patriots began to cart away the cannonballs and other shot from that battery.

Word of what was happening in Charlestown made its way across the river to Boston. The merchant Andrews wrote that "A Scotch Captain, who is building a ship at Charlestown, . . . came over and inform'd the Governor of it." This is plausible since people with homes and families in Britain were naturally more loyal to the imperial center, but New Englanders were also becoming even more suspicious than usual of recent immigrants, especially from Scotland, and Andrews may have blamed a convenient scapegoat. On September 7, Gen. Gage sent an army officer to the old fort to see what was going on, and his presence tipped off the Charlestown locals to the governor's interest. British troops arrived that night to dismantle the battery. It was empty.

As Andrews explained, "The inhabitants, suspecting what would take place, provided a number of [ox] teams, such as carry ship timbers, and slung all the guns belonging to the battery, and carried up country, together with the reposit of shot." In 1845 town historian Richard Frothingham reported that the ordnance had been hidden on Schoolhouse Hill under what he delicately termed "stable dirt." Frothingham could identify only three likely participants: Timothy Thompson, William Calder, and William Lane. Even sophisticated Bostonians had to acknowledge the resourcefulness of their Charlestown neighbors: "So much for the honor of *Pig Village!*" Andrews marveled. The provincials now had at least five big iron cannon under their control, and the only reassurance Gage could give himself was that those battery guns were too big to maneuver around usefully.

The army responded by adding twelve more cannon to the fortifications at the Boston Neck gate, making eighteen in all. They also set up a search for the missing guns. During Sunday services, Andrews complained, British officers were in Charlestown "traversing the streets and by-ways, and tampering with the children, to get out of them where the cannon were hid." The next day, locals feared that the army had learned that crucial information. On September 13 Andrews wrote, "Am just inform'd that the officers prevailed on a negro at Charlestown to inform 'em where the cannon were lodg'd; which being known there, they [the inhabitants] mustered about three thousand, and with teems carried 'em about ten or a dozen miles further up" into the countryside.

Again, the army may or may not have actually obtained information from a black man in Charlestown. The blame cast on that supposed informant, as on the "Scotch captain," might simply have reflected white New Englanders' fear of outsiders, as well as a slave-owning society's fear of an uprising by the enslaved people. Later that month, Abigail Adams wrote from Boston about whispers of "a conspiracy of the Negroes." There does not appear to be evidence to support those rumors beyond the safe assumption that African-Americans in Massachusetts, like other people, were seeking to improve their lives. Blacks in rural New England, unlike the enslaved in other parts of Revolutionary America, generally perceived their best chance of liberty as coming from serving the Patriot cause rather than sabotaging it.

In the meantime, on September 12 Gage received a protest from a committee representing the Suffolk County Convention—another county convention getting around the Massachusetts Government Act. At that time Suffolk County still included the towns outside Boston southwest all the way to the Rhode Island border, including those just on the other side of the Neck such as Roxbury, Dorchester, and Brookline. The country delegates asked why their own empire's army was pointing cannon at them. Gage assured those visitors that he deployed his artillery to protect citizens. Then he added his own accusatory question: "What is the reason that the cannon were remov'd from Charlestown?"

The Massachusetts radicals offered no answer, but they now knew that losing control of the province's cannon annoyed the general. That evening Samuel Pierce of Dorchester recorded in his diary, "The greate gun was Removed from Preston's Point" in his town at the mouth of the Neponset River.

British officials tracked those developments, and even more dire news from the countryside. On September 12, the governor reported to the secretary of state that "The Country People are exercising in Arms in this Province, Connecticut, and Rhode Island, and getting Magazines of Arms and Ammunition in the Country, and such

Artillery, as they can procure good and bad." Hugh Earl Percy, Gage's second-in-command during the summer, wrote to his father: "A few days ago, they mustered about 7000 men at Worcester, to which place they have conveyed about 20 pieces of cannon." The next day, Customs Commissioner Henry Hulton told a friend, "The people for their part are all arming, melting their lead into bullets, and draging Cannon into the Country."

Within the town of Boston, two large artillery batteries usually staffed by militia companies overlooked the main harbor. In 1770 Capt. Montresor had counted twenty-two artillery pieces between them. When the royal troops arrived with the new governor in the spring, they had occupied the South Battery to store their supplies, but the North was still in the hands of a militia company led by Nathaniel Barber, an active Whig. Bostonians started to whisper about following the example of their Charlestown neighbors. Andrews mentioned the "intentions of a number of ye. inhabitants, who have had it some time in contemplation to remove [the North Battery guns] . . . least they might be made use of to fortifie the Neck."

Instead, the Royal Navy acted first. Its commanders were no doubt very aware that those batteries' cannon pointed out at their ships. Early in the night of September 14, two warships approached the North Battery, "ready for an engagement." Sailors approached from the water, got inside, and spiked all the guns, blocking up their touchholes with small metal rods so they were unable to fire. Andrews chuckled that when two navy officers returned to inspect the work a resentful townswoman had managed to lock them inside the battery. A "Ridiculous Maneuvre," sniffed merchant John Rowe.

The *Boston Post-Boy* reported the cannon were "cleared again the next Day without much Difficulty." Whig activist Joseph Palmer assured Robert Treat Paine that "they have been drill'd" and made usable again. Since workers could often reclaim spiked cannon with a good drill, spiking was a quick way to disable an enemy gun during battle rather than a long-term solution. British naval commanders presumably knew that, so this action was probably designed to remove the North Battery as a threat just long enough for another operation.

Even as Bostonians congratulated themselves on restoring the North Battery, the *Post-Boy* added that "the Cannon in the Batteries back of Governor's Island were removed by the General's Order."

The competition for artillery then moved away from the harbor. Cannon in batteries were important to keep out of the enemy's hands, but tended to be old and heavy. For battle, a provincial army would need field-pieces: smaller cannon, light enough to mount on carriages and move with teams of horses or men. The best were "brass" (what today we would call bronze), not iron, and thus more durable for their weight. The Royal Artillery had brought several such weapons. Boston possessed only four, belonging to the town's militia artillery company, or "train." The train's fieldpieces were probably in use on September 5, when Thomas Newell wrote "Artillery training" in his diary.

The Boston train was founded in 1762 by David Mason and Adino Paddock, who had probably met as apprentices in the 1740s. Paddock, born in England in 1728, trained to be a coachmaker. Mason, a Boston native two years older, was apprenticed to a decorative painter named John Gore, whose business included painting coaches.

In November 1755, during the run-up to the French and Indian War, Mason succeeded to the command of the artillery at Fort William Henry on the southern end of Lake George in New York. He told his daughter there were "6 pieces of cannon" in the fort—not enough to hold off a siege by the French and Native alliance in early August 1757. The European commanders negotiated a surrender that let the British regulars, colonial troops, and civilians in the fort withdraw unarmed to Fort Edward on the Hudson River. Some Native soldiers seeking captives, scalps, and other trophies broke that agreement, attacking the British captives on August 10.

Mason was among the people taken prisoner by Natives allied with the French. He told his daughter Susan that his captors carried him upriver, stripping off most of his garments as prizes. Mason still had his "small clothes," and in one pocket was "a tobacco stopper" with a "burning glass," or magnifying lens, attached to one end. When a teenager he took to be a chief's son wanted to smoke a pipe, Mason showed him how to light the tobacco with sunlight. The "supernatural power" of the lens frightened the Indians so much, he believed, that they were all too happy to hand him over to a passing Frenchman. In fact, the French commanders were working hard to retrieve all the British prisoners they could. Mason then described an arduous journey to Albany, clothed mainly in the kind Frenchman's coat, fearful of being recaptured, and starving except for "a piece of ginseng" that he luckily had in his pocket.

Back in Boston, Mason turned down further commissions in the army because his wife wanted to keep him home and safe. That took some effort. Mason was reportedly in charge of the powder supply in the South Battery during the great fire of March 20, 1760. According to his daughter:

> The fire was fast approaching the building and there was a considerable quantity of powder in the house [at the battery] that was thought might be removed before the fire could reach it. He accordingly went to his house for the key, which was some distance from the fire. When my mother learnt his intention it threw her into great distress in apprehension of the danger he was going to expose himself, and after he had used many arguments to quiet her mind and had made his way out of the house, she followed him to the door entreating him not to venture upon so dangerous a step, and in the midst of her pleadings the [powder] house blew up.

Mason used his experience as an artillery officer during the war to co-found the artillery company of the Boston militia a couple of years later. He took the rank of captain, and his younger friend Paddock was lieutenant. The train made its first "very fine Appearance" on June 11, 1762. For the next celebration of the king's birthday, on June 6, 1763, "the new Artillery Company, with

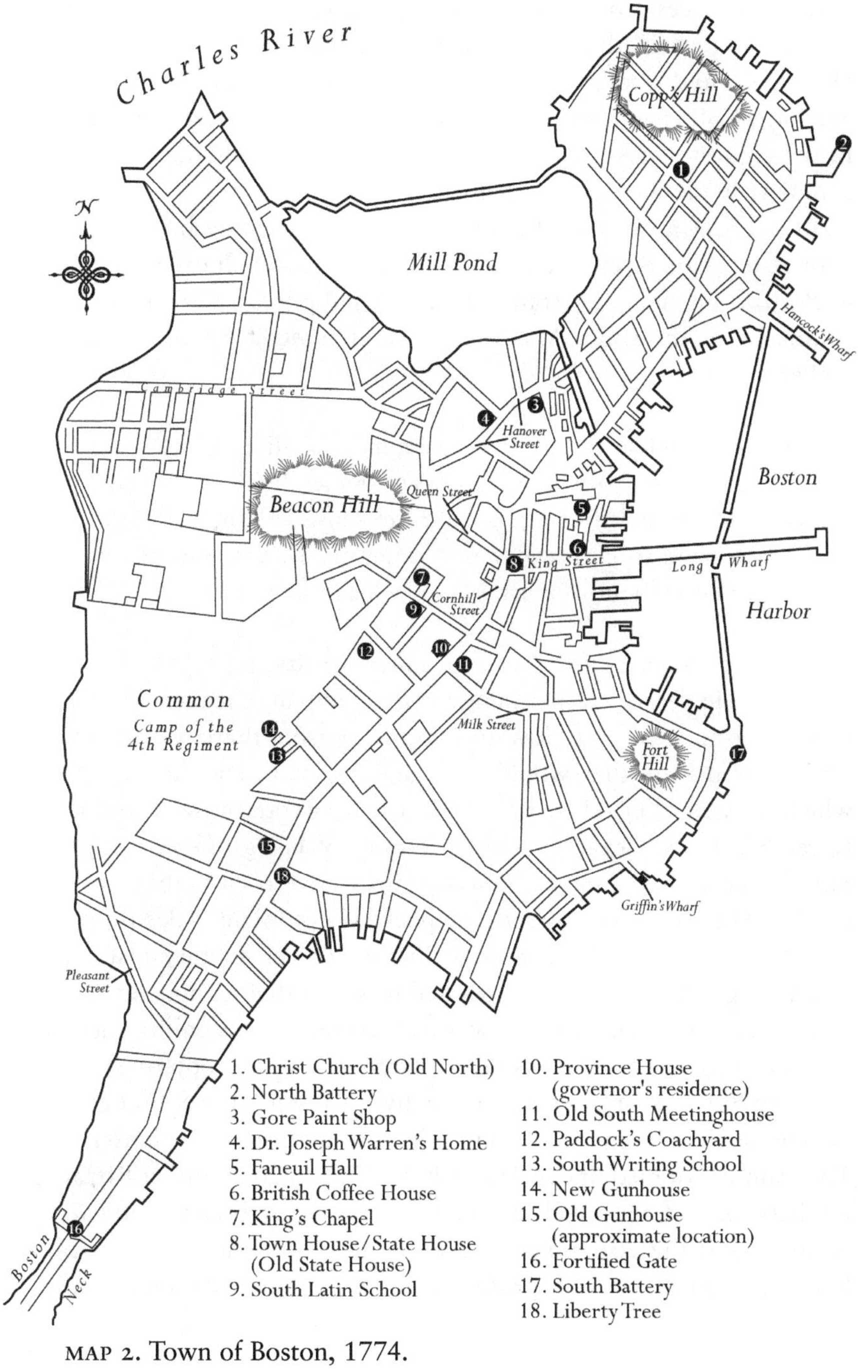

MAP 2. Town of Boston, 1774.

two Field Pieces, commanded by Capt. David Mason" played a prominent part in the festivities. Placing their guns near Faneuil Hall, they fired a salute after each toast that Gov. Francis Bernard and other officeholders offered to the king and other important British figures. Those cannon were probably small and old, but the company made the most of them.

In 1765, Mason moved his family and his painting business to Gloucester—for economic reasons following a smallpox epidemic in Boston, his daughter stated. Paddock happily succeeded to the command of the train. Mason's daughter understood the coachmaker this way:

> He was an ambitious, aspiring young man, qualities which may be seen made no part of my father's character. Be this as it may, his friend persuaded him, as it was an expensive affair, to give up the command to him who was a young man and could better attend to it without so much injury to his business.

Another member of the train, Thomas Crafts, Jr., told a different story. He described the change in the company's leadership this way: "Mason was . . . so low and mean a person, thare was not an Officer or private that would train under him In consequence of which he was oblige'd to retire." When he wrote those words in December 1775, Crafts was bitter about not being offered a high rank in the Continental army, so he might have been unduly critical. Or Mason's personal style or pocketbook might indeed have kept him from presenting himself in the genteel military fashion that younger men in the train wanted to see in their commander.

As a coachmaker, Paddock was used to serving a wealthy clientele. Starting in 1760 he built a large workyard opposite the Granary Burying Ground and was active in town service, firefighting companies, Freemasonry, and other avenues of social climbing. The train blossomed under Paddock. In 1766, a company of Royal Artillery bound for Quebec wintered in Boston because of bad weather, and the coachmaker took advantage of the situation to have his men trained by professionals. Gov. Bernard's unilateral decision to allow the regular army to use Castle William in that winter became a political issue, but nobody objected to the lessons those professionals offered. Soon the Boston train enjoyed respect from both royalists and Whigs. Having a field artillery company made the Boston regiment stand out within the Massachusetts militia.

In 1766 the Massachusetts General Court voted to buy four new fieldpieces for the Boston train. Two seem to have been purchased in America. They were small brass guns, apparently two-pounders. In February 1768, Boston newspapers proudly announced two more cannon newly arrived from England:

> In the Brigantine Abigail, Capt. Stevens from London, came two beautiful Brass Field Pieces, 3 pounders, with the Province Arms thereon, for the Use of the Train of Artillery of the Regiment of this Town. They were cast from two old Pieces which were purchased some time since by the General Court of this Province.

The shiny new three-pounders were soon mounted on carriages designed by William Burbeck, keeper of ordnance at Castle William.

The train was storing its older pair of cannon in a gunhouse that Henry Burbeck, a young member of the train (and son of the Castle keeper), recalled as being "under a large Elm tree near the corner of Essex and Tremont," then called Frog Lane and Common Street. That spring, Paddock convinced the town of Boston to build a new gunhouse for its new three-pounders "upon the Towns Land near the Common" just south of West Street. This building was made of brick, 24 feet wide and either 42 or 52 feet long, its slate roof over 15 feet high at the apex.

The train showed off its new weapons and new maneuvers at a celebration of the king's birthday on June 4, 1768:

> His Excellency the governour's troop of guards, under the command of Colonel [David] Phipps, the regiment of the militia of this town, commanded by Colonel [Joseph] Jackson, with the

> train of artillery under Capt. Paddock, mustered in King-street, where the troop and regiment fired three vollies, and the train several discharges of their new field pieces, after which the troop and regiment marched off: Then the train performed the exercise of a mock fight, during which their soldier-like behaviour, their management of the artillery, and the good order observed, gave general satisfaction to a numerous crowd of spectators.

For such exercises, the *Post-Boy* clarified, "The Artillery Company divided into two Parties," each side probably equipped with a matched pair of cannon.

Within a few years Paddock was promoted to major. The *Boston News-Letter* devoted considerable space to the train's elaborate display at the militia training on September 14, 1772:

> The Company of Artillery under Major Paddock, having first been exercised as usual, performed another Mock Battle, as follows, A Detachment of the Company under Capt. [Jabez] Hatch and Lieut. [George] Trott drew off with two Cannon and a Mortar, and marched to Fox-Hill, so called, the Bottom of the Common, and encamp'd with French Colours flying: Upon which Major Paddock, with Lieutenants [Thomas] Crafts and [Edward] Tuckerman, and the Remainder of the Company march'd and took Post on a Hill opposite; from thence began to cannonade and bombard with artificial Bombs, which was answered from those in the Encampment: At this Station it was supposed no advantage could be had, the Major therefore marched off by the Right between the Powder-House and a Ridge of Hills, and form'd on the Right of the Ridge, which brought him on the Left of Fox-Hill, where he again began the Engagement, after firing a few Shot, he ordered Lt. Craft with one Cannon and a Party with Firelocks to pass a Defile in Front, at the same Time Capt. Hatch sent Lt. Trott to a Redoubt below his Post to oppose him, which Lt. Craft forced and obliged Lt. Trott to give way and run up to the Encampment. As soon as the Assailants mounted the Breastwork, a Parley was beat by Capt.

> Hatch and a Flag sent out offering to surrender on Conditions of being allowed all the Honors of War, which being refused, a brisk Firing began again from the Encampment. Whereupon the Remainder of the Company were ordered to join Lt. Craft who ascended the Hill briskly and forced the Encampment with charged Bayonets, flaming Hand-Grenades flying all the Time amidst the contending Parties: On which Capt. Hatch with his Party retired precipitantly down the opposite side of the Hill, the French Colours were struck and the Encampment represented to be set on Fire. Both Parties joined and marched with their Cannon in regular Order to their Parade, and after going through several Firings, retired.
>
> The whole was executed in a Manner that did Honour to the Officers and Privates.
>
> His Excellency the Governor [Thomas Hutchinson], was on the Common to see the Performance of the Regiment and Artillery Company; as were also a great Number of Gentlemen and Ladies, and People of all Ranks, who were highly pleased with the present Spirit for Military Art.

Spectacular war games and gleaming brass guns were not the company's only distinctions. They also had a fine set of "Fifes and Drums" which could play alongside the upper-class Company of Cadets' musicians. And in April 1773, "Major Paddock apply'd to the Selectmen for Liberty to make a Scuttle through the Roof of the Gun House in order to have a Platform to exhibit Fire works." The train was so popular, and its members' expertise with explosives so trusted, that "Liberty was accordingly granted." The enthusiastic audiences for such displays show how much the militia train meant to the town of Boston. Four small fieldpieces would have little weight in a war, but to Bostonians their artillery company proved that they participated in their own defense and did not have to depend on the royal military.

The train carried even more symbolic value for its members. The company "was composed principally, if not altogether, of the mechanics of Boston," recalled Gov. William Eustis. In contrast,

Gen. Henry Burbeck later explained, "The Cadet Company was formed by the *Aristocracy* and called the 'Governor's Guard' and no Mechanic was admitted as a member." The train was thus an avenue for ambitious young craftsmen to distinguish themselves in militia service, to become more than ordinary mechanics. Artillery officers were recognized for their scientific skills, using mathematics to aim their mortar shots and surveying skills to lay out fortifications. An artillery command was a step from the working class of mechanics into gentility.

By founding the train and making themselves officers, Mason and Paddock got a jump start in society. Mason had become a lieutenant at Fort William Henry, but now he was a captain. Paddock gained officer's rank without seeing combat. In the early 1770s another set of young men, including future artillery commander Henry Knox, took a similar step upward by forming Boston's first grenadier company, also "formed of Mechanics and other professions." Perhaps because their genteel standing was so new and fragile, Continental army artillery officers seem to have been especially touchy about relative military ranks and protocols.

Training probably also gave artillerists a feeling of unity and group cohesion unusual even by the standard of colonial New England. While infantry soldiers were taught to march and shoot in a body, each man still maintained, carried, loaded, aimed, and fired his own weapon. In a militia company, each man usually *owned* his weapon as well. A cannon had to be worked by several men together, all well trained as gunners and matrosses—the approximate equivalents of corporals and privates in the infantry. The Royal Artillery standard was to assign thirteen men to each fieldpiece, though in emergencies that number could dip as low as three. Top squads could fire three or more times in a minute. But if those men did not coordinate their movements—if, for instance, the commanding officer did not firmly place his thumb over the touchhole before a gun was swabbed out—they could easily blow up their guns and maim or kill each other. The Royal Artillery listed sixteen different accidents that could be caused by "the Man that Sponges," "the Man who serves the Vent," "the Man who puts the

Cartridge into the Gun," and "the Man who Fires the Gun." Gun crews had to grow close to each other and work in tandem.

Gov. Thomas Hutchinson praised Paddock's train to the General Court in January 1773 and urged legislators to fund similar companies in other counties and to buy "twelve brass field-pieces," enough to field an entire Massachusetts artillery regiment. (That build-up also provided several more militia commands for the royal governor to dole out, building up favors.) The following October an artillery company for the militia regiment in the part of Suffolk County outside Boston "made their first public appearance, under Capt. Lemuel Robinson" of Dorchester. By 1775 the second and third regiment of the Suffolk County militia regiments also had trains. Another artillery company was founded in Middlesex County—it trained with the two cannon that the British army removed from Cambridge on September 1, 1774.

In the early 1770s, Hutchinson promoted Paddock to major. As a native of England and a manufacturer dependent on elite patronage, the coachmaker was a natural Loyalist. During the non-importation movement of 1769, the *Boston News-Letter* had praised "elegant COACH in the modern Taste" from his shop for being "as compleat and as good as any one ever imported," but he was never involved in Whig politics. In 1774 Paddock publicly declared his loyalty to the Crown by protesting the Boston committee of correspondence's Solemn League and Covenant and signing the Farewell Address to Gov. Hutchinson.

Most of the men in the train, like most of the men in Boston, did not share Paddock's loyalty. In fact, Lt. George Trott and Lt. Thomas Crafts were members of the "Loyall Nine," the club of young men who organized the anti-Stamp Act protests of 1765. Members of the artillery company objected when their commander cooperated with Gen. Gage in stationing sentinels outside the gunhouses, or small armories, where they stored their four small brass guns. Back in August, the Company of Cadets had dissolved to protest the governor's decision to remove John Hancock as their elected captain. Likewise, the train "ceased meeting" in early September when their gunhouses were put under British guard. The militiamen just refused to show up, and there was no way for Paddock to enforce his authority.

In later years, these men expressed their complaints in the language of property rights and self-government, tying the dispute within the train to the larger political conflict. But losing control of those four shiny fieldpieces to the governor probably also had a deep personal meaning for them. Without the guns they had trained on and cared for, those young mechanics may well have seen themselves losing their identity as artillerists, the army cutting off their opportunities and aspirations. Characteristically, the members of the train responded by acting in small, unified squads.

The company's older gunhouse backed onto the estate of Francis Johonnot, a distiller and Anglican Loyalist. There was a large garden between Johonnot's home on Sheaffe Street and the militia building—large enough to muffle sounds of workmen. The half-moon set at about ten o'clock on Wednesday, September 14, the night when Royal Navy sailors were spiking the North Battery's guns. Burbeck remembered it as a "dark stormy night." Boston's skies provided little light until dawn, around quarter to six. Andrews reported what had happened in the darkness:

> Ever since ye. cannon were taken away from Charlestown, the General has order'd a double guard to ye. new and old gun houses, where ye. brass field pieces belonging to our militia are lodg'd: notwithstanding which, the vigilance and temerity of our people has entirely disconcerted him, for We'n'sday evening, or rather night, they took these from the Old house (by opening the side of the house) and carried away through Frank Johonnot's Garden.

The next day, the Patriot activist Joseph Palmer sent news from Boston to Continental Congress delegate Robert Treat Paine, highlighting the military preparations outside town:

> Our People in the Country are busy making Carriages for Cannon &c. &c., so that preparations for war are carrying on

> as if the last reason of States was soon to be tried. May God preserve Our rights without that severe trial; but if it must be, let us shew ourselves men. The Country people, as 'tis said, have turn'd Paddock's Field p——s into Dung, & have carried them into their Fields; what Crop they will produce is only written in the prophecies.

Palmer managed both to convey that the Paddock company's two small guns had been smuggled away under manure, like the cannon in Charlestown, and to spin that image into a metaphor for the growing crisis.

Having lost the train's two-pounders, Gen. Gage ordered his officers to put an even stronger guard on the town's newer gunhouse. That site already seemed quite secure. It was, in Thomas Newell's words, "near, very near the common"—across Common Street from its front door were the tents of the 4th Regiment. That put hundreds of soldiers within earshot of the sentries. That front door was also locked, with Paddock holding the key. There was a side entrance, but that double door was latched from the inside. Even to reach that side entrance required getting into a "yard inclosed with a high fence" that the gunhouse shared with the South Writing School. The school was rarely empty in daylight hours: Master Samuel Holbrook held sessions on six days of the week and welcomed paying students in his off-hours. And the front door of the school faced West Street, where anyone coming out would have been visible from the Common.

Even that situation did not seem secure enough, however. Gen. Gage or his artillery commander, Col. Samuel Cleaveland, apparently met with Paddock to discuss moving his unit's three-pounders into the British camp, just as Lt.-Col. Maddison had moved the Middlesex County militia's cannon to the Castle at the start of the month. "At the fixed hour" on September 16, Andrews related, "the officer on guard . . . went with a number of Mattrosses to execute his orders, but behold, the guns were gone! He swore the *Devil* must have help'd to get 'em away."

Four

"Townspeople Took Four Brass Cannon"

Most Bostonians were baffled by how the cannon disappeared from the gunhouse beside the Common. John Andrews, normally a gossip sponge, had to admit, "Its amazing to me how our people manag'd to carry off the guns, as they weigh near seven hundred weight apiece; more especially that they should do it, and not alarm the centinels. Am told their business was not executed above 10 or 15 minutes before the officer came." Andrews overstated the weight of those missing guns. Though some cannon designed to throw three-pound balls weighed over 600 pounds, the Boston train had ordered smaller brass guns of a sort designed to be lifted by four determined men. And apparently, they had been.

So how did Patriots remove those two yard-long, three-hundred-pound cannon without any redcoats spotting them? In 1823 the Boston writer William Tudor, Jr., offered an answer in *The Life of James Otis, of Massachusetts*. Tudor's source was a man who claimed to have helped sneak the second pair of fieldpieces out of the gunhouse. His name was Samuel Gore. In 1823 he was seventy-two years old, head of his family's decorative painting firm and part-owner of a company that manufactured window glass. Tudor presented little evidence to corroborate what Gore told him—no confederates, witnesses, or documents. Gore apparently did not even tell him the date of the theft.

Samuel Gore might have had reasons to embellish his Revolutionary past. His father had been a Loyalist, leaving Boston with the British army in March 1776 and sailing to England. That family history became a political issue when Gore's younger brother ran for governor in 1809. The Massachusetts legislature had even ordered Samuel Gore himself arrested in April 1776 since he had stayed in Boston through the siege. During the rest of the War for Independence, he had served in the military for only twenty-one days, marching with the Massachusetts militia in a brief assault on British-occupied Newport in 1777. Gore might have wished for a more heroic history.

Once Tudor put the story into print in 1823, however, no one complained that Gore was taking credit for someone else's action. When Gore died eight years later, his *Columbian Centinel* obituary not only retold the story but made it seem more important by ignoring all the other artillery pieces moving around:

> Mr. G. was one of the very small number of mechanics, who obtained, secured, and sent out of the town of Boston, when it was in the hands of British power, at the commencement of the Revolution, the only two pieces of cannon then in the town.

In 1848 the last known survivor of Paddock's militia train, retired U.S. general Henry Burbeck, confirmed the story for an inquiring historian: "my impression was and is that Samuel Gore (brother to Govr. Gore) and his associates were the persons" who secured the three-pounders.

Unfortunately, aside from Tudor's account, Samuel Gore left no remarks of the cannon theft. No letters or journals by him survive from this period. He did not participate in formal politics before the war and published no newspaper essays, as far as we can tell. Therefore, the only way to understand why Gore risked his freedom, perhaps even his life, to secure two small brass cannon is to reconstruct his life up until 1774.

Samuel Gore was born on January 26, 1751, to decorative painter John Gore and his wife Frances. Sammy, as his family called him, was his parents' sixth child, though two older brothers had died in infancy. Eventually Sammy would have seven younger sisters, five of them surviving to adulthood, and one little brother. His siblings ranged from seven years older to eleven years younger.

The single surviving picture of Samuel Gore shows him as a little boy posed with three older siblings. It is one of John Singleton Copley's earliest works, painted around 1755. Since John Gore imported paint, he probably wished to encourage the young artist's ambitions. At the center of the painting stands John Gore, Jr., born in 1745 and thus the family's first-born male. Sisters Frances (Fanny), born in 1744, and Elizabeth, born in 1749, are seated at the left, letting John be the tallest figure in the composition. Sammy is at the right, still wearing the petticoat of a four-year-old.

The simple existence of this portrait reveals the Gore family's social ambitions. Sammy's parents had not been born into the genteel class who normally hung portraits of their children. His mother, born Frances Pinkney, was a shopkeeper's daughter. His father, John Gore, Sr., was the son of a carpenter, grandson of a yeoman farmer in Roxbury. Their ancestors had arrived in the great migration of Puritan settlers in the 1630s, exactly like hundreds of other Massachusetts families.

John Gore had learned the trade of "japanning," named for the technique of coating furniture or ornaments with black enamel in a supposedly Japanese style. As a specialty, he painted coats of arms, which wealthy customers wanted on carriages, wall hangings, hatchments (diamond-shaped panels displayed on houses in mourning), and other ornaments. The family kept a notebook on the heraldry of ninety-nine New England families as they existed in the early 1700s. Gore's shop sign was also heraldic: "The Painter's Arms," symbol of London's painters guild. For decades it hung outside the family shop on Queen Street, near the center of Boston. Newspaper advertisements invited readers to seek out that shop for "Coach & Carpet Painting done in the best and cheapest Manner."

In his early twenties Gore took on the fatherless teenager David Mason as an apprentice and started growing his business.

As an ornamental painter specializing in heraldry, Gore was at the highest social level among Boston's "mechanics," or craftsmen, alongside silversmiths, carriage-makers, upholsterers, fancy tailors, milliners, bookbinders, portrait painters, and a few other professions. All these men (and, in a few cases, women) produced luxury goods. They still worked with their hands, like the less prestigious shoemakers, blacksmiths, tanners, coopers, and so forth. But makers of luxury goods had the elite as their customers, and they charged high prices. They could thus more easily develop the connections, manners, and wealth necessary to rise in society themselves.

Over time Gore expanded his painting service to sell paints and the colors needed to make them, as well as brushes and other supplies, most ordered from London. His stock ranged from genteel retail items ("Watercolours ready prepared in shells," "The best of London Crown Glass for Pictures") to industrial quantities ("for House and Ship Painting, Whiting by the Hogshead, and Rozin by the Barrell"). He thus qualified as a low-level merchant, an economic step upward. Eventually he had customers as far away as Philadelphia.

Along with building his wealth, John Gore took other steps toward gentility. He joined Boston's militia regiment and rose to command a company in 1763. For the rest of his life he was addressed publicly as "Captain Gore." As for the religious side of life, in this period families bought their meeting-house pews, a specialized sort of real estate. Capt. Gore chose a pew in the fashionable Brattle Street Meeting, presided over by the Rev. Dr. Samuel Cooper.

Capt. Gore also made himself available for town offices. Eventually, in 1767, he was elected Overseer of the Poor for Boston's seventh ward. With the eleven other Overseers, he shared responsibility for supervising the town's almshouse, workhouse, and bridewell (for unmarried expectant mothers); for committing poor people to those institutions or doling out public assistance;

and for indenturing children who were born out of wedlock or whose parents could not feed them. The Overseers of the Poor were among the town's most respected officials, ranking just below representatives to the General Court and selectmen. By that year the title "Esquire" was appearing after Capt. Gore's name, a sign that his peers had accepted him as a gentleman.

Boston's tax list for 1771 records Capt. Gore as the owner of a house, a separate shop (most craftsmen lived over their shops), one "servant for life" or slave, a horse, and a cow. His other taxable assets included over £802 worth of merchandise plus £575 loaned out to others, a considerable estate. In 1782 Capt. Gore told the British government that before the war "his business brought him in five hundred pounds sterling [per] year, which gave a genteel support to his family." By then he owned four houses, three on Queen Street and one on Hilliard's Alley.

Being "a genteel support to his family" meant giving his children the best opportunities. John and Frances Gore's first step, in common with most parents in New England, was ensuring their children learned to read. Widespread literacy was a legacy of the Puritan emphasis on studying Scripture. Some little boys and girls in Boston were taught at home, but most families sent their children to private "reading schools" run by women in the neighborhood. The favorite reading text was a grim little book called *The New-England Primer*; most editions featured a woodcut of a Protestant martyr being burned to death in front of his children.

As Capt. Gore rose in society, he had his three sons educated for business or professional careers, not simply trained in crafts. The eldest went first to the town writing school a few doors up Queen Street, his name appearing on that school's roll for 1753. In 1756, around the time he was having his portrait painted, it appears that John, Jr., transferred into the South Latin School, one of the town's two free grammar schools. This was an unusual move; he was then eleven years old while most entrants were seven. Presumably he had shown intelligence and diligence at his lessons, and his parents wanted him to try the college-prep curriculum.

In 1758 Sammy Gore turned seven, out of petticoats and old enough to go to a town school as well. For him, his parents made grammar school the first choice. On a designated morning in July, he lined up with other seven-year-olds at Master John Lovell's house on School Street. The South Latin School teacher asked each boy to read "a few verses of the Bible." If a boy read well enough, and appeared mature enough in other ways, he was admitted.

Sammy passed the test and entered the South Latin School a few days later. His class numbered thirty-one boys, a bit larger than usual. The schoolhouse was a ten-year-old brick building on School Street. It had a single classroom, crowded that year with 117 boys in seven classes. Overseeing these scholars were only two teachers: Master Lovell and his assistant or "usher." Each class had its own bench, or "form." At first the new boys sat in the order in which they arrived at Master Lovell's house; Sammy was eighth, between Thomas Hooper and Aaron Brown. As lessons went on, however, the boys had to switch seats according to how well they performed. Most scholars did not complete the Latin School course, in effect falling off the end of the bench. The class entering in 1758 was typical: of thirty-one scholars, only seven finished the course at South Latin. In the great majority of those boys who stepped off the college track were John and Sammy Gore.

Some boys dropped out of Latin School because of economic or health reasons, but neither of those reasons appears to apply to Sammy Gore. Probably he and most other Latin School dropouts left because of a mismatch between the school's curriculum and their priorities. Boston's grammar schools were entirely geared toward sending boys to Harvard, teaching no practical skills. If a boy did not do well at learning Latin or became more interested in business or a craft, he had no reason to stay.

Some boys leaving grammar school before the final year went to work; John Gore, Jr., may have become a clerk for a dry-goods merchant, learning the business of buying and selling cloth. Others switched to one of the town's writing schools, trading their Latin textbooks for quill pens, rulers, and blank copybooks. Given that pattern of transfers, it seems reasonable that at some point around 1760 Sammy Gore moved to the Queen Street Writing School to finish his education.

The main subject at Boston's three writing schools was just what their name stated: writing. That did not mean composing essays but practicing the handwritings that businessmen used. For beginners the schoolmaster would write a sentence at the top of a sheet of paper in his exquisite "round hand," and the boys would try to copy it below. As scholars improved, they copied longer, more ornate pieces. Writing school masters also wrote out arithmetic problems, which the boys not only had to solve with little instruction but to copy in their best round hand. For Sammy Gore, such lessons would be useful in the career chosen for him: the business of decorative painting.

Sammy went to work for his father full-time around the age of fourteen, learning the skills of a japanner and specialized importer. His apprenticeship was thus probably more comfortable than most. He may well have worked alongside his first cousin George Searle, also born in 1751; Searle later became a heraldic painter in Newburyport. Later John Johnston, born in 1753 to another family of painters in Boston, joined the Gore shop as an apprentice. As for the family's hopes to send a son to Harvard, they had one more chance: little Christopher (Kit) Gore entered the South Latin School in 1765.

For Sammy, who turned fourteen that year, his occupational training coincided with Boston's political resistance to new Crown policies. In the summer of 1765 all of Britain's American colonies were roiled by news of the Stamp Act, but protests were confined to legislative sessions and newspaper pages until August 14. On that morning, Bostonians found an effigy of the Massachusetts stamp-tax collector hanging from a large elm in the South End. Gangs of men made a game of "stamping" every load of goods passing by the tree to dramatize how the Stamp Act could affect all citizens.

The Gore family had a close connection to that political protest through the husband of eldest daughter Frances. Thomas Crafts, Jr., had been born in 1740 and married Fanny Gore in 1763. Like her father, he was a carpenter's son who trained as a japanner. He may even have trained with Capt. Gore; it was common for a promising apprentice to marry the boss's daughter. Crafts was "a man of immense stature" with a "fiery-visaged" complexion and a booming voice. He was one of the few vegetarians of the period, living "entirely on vegetable products and milk." And Crafts was among the secret organizers of the Stamp Act protests of 1765.

This group called itself the "Loyall Nine." Besides Crafts the japanner, they included two merchants, two braziers (makers of brass implements), a printer, a rum distiller, and a jeweler. Only one member, young merchant John Avery, Jr., was a Harvard graduate. All were small businessmen, some from the ranks of mechanics. Though they had ties to Boston's Whig leadership—they could enjoy "a very Genteel Supper" with Samuel Adams—they were not high above the working men who made up the crowds.

In December, one Loyall Nine member wrote to his father-in-law about how the group secretly organized an anti-Stamp demonstration: "The whole affair [was] transacted by the Loyall Nine, . . . getting the advertisements Printed, which were all done after 12 oClock Monday Night, the Advertisements Pasted up to the amount of a hundred was all done from 9 to 3. oClock." This man closed by saying, "I must desire you'd keep this a profound Secret and not to Let any Person see these Papers." Secrecy was vital because the anti-Stamp protests in August had led to violence after nightfall, with mobs trashing the homes of stamp agent and province Secretary Andrew Oliver, Lieutenant Governor Thomas Hutchinson, and other officials. Not only was such violence illegal, but it frightened wealthy Whigs and besmirched the Stamp Act resistance.

As a result, after August 1765 both the Loyall Nine and Boston's Whig politicians worked to keep political protests under control. On September 11 they put a plaque on the great elm where the effigies hung, naming it "The Tree of Liberty" and establishing it as a political gathering-place. They tamed Boston's traditional celebration of the Fifth of November—locally called "Pope Night" and climaxing with a brawl between North End and South End gangs. In 1765, all the young men of the town marched together, united against the Stamp Tax, with William Brattle, general of the

Massachusetts militia, beside their leader. When the anniversary of the Stamp Act repeal rolled around in March 1768, someone else hung effigies of two customs officials on Liberty Tree; Crafts and two comrades quickly cut them down before things got out of their control.

The Loyall Nine had issued their first public announcements over the mysterious initials "M.Y.," but they soon adopted the label "Sons of Liberty." In some American towns, such as Albany, men created formal organizations under that name. In Boston, however, the Sons of Liberty seems never to have been an organized group with a defined membership. Rather, the Loyall Nine and other political groups used the term to call for resistance whenever they saw the need. Any man who worked against the Crown's new taxes could see himself as a Son of Liberty—and any man who did not was, by implication, rejecting his birthright as a free British subject.

Formal politics was reserved for propertied white men over age twenty-one, but public demonstrations let boys like Sammy Gore be Sons of Liberty, too. As early as the first anti-Stamp protest in 1765, there were "two or three hundred little boys with a Flagg marching in Procession." Friends of the royal government complained about how Whig politicians recruited children into their protests. One royal official later complained, "According to common Custom, when a Riot was to be brought on, the Factioneers would employ Boys & Negroes to assemble & make Bonfires in the Streets." On some occasions adults encouraged or watched over the youths; even a clergyman was said to have exclaimed, "see how those Boys fight for us."

Boys could take political actions on their own as well. On September 24, 1766, a North End merchant named Daniel Malcom refused to let customs officials search his cellar for smuggled liquor. The customs men had a writ but could not find magistrates willing to enforce it. Men gathered outside Malcom's house, silent but intimidating. Then the schools let out, and "the Boys came running along and they got together enquiring what the Matter was." Soon more than twenty boys were milling around Bennet Street, making up half the crowd. At sunset, the customs officers' writ expired.

Town leaders probably hoped the affair would fade away, but some of the boys decided they knew who had told the customs office about Malcom's liquor: a North End neighbor named Ebenezer Richardson, who a few years earlier had been unmasked as a confidential "informer" for royal appointees. These boys announced "that they knew where he lived and they they'd goe and give him three Cheers for the great Prize he'd got"—sarcastically shaming him.

The eyewitness accounts of this event collected by authorities show another side of boys' political activity: they could be convenient scapegoats when something went wrong. One man reported hearing that if the customs officials tried to storm Malcom's house someone would ring the bells in Old North Church to summon a mob. That rumor threatened to put Boston in a bad light, and in a second deposition three weeks later the same man blamed "the Scholars . . . from the Latin School" for spreading it. Similarly, back in 1765 newspapers had said the worst of the August riots had started with "Boys and Children" making a bonfire on King Street. A friend of the royal government bitterly criticized the Whigs' response to violence: "their usual sayings . . . repeated again, that it was done by Boys & Negroes, or by Nobody."

Boys started to take on legal responsibilities at age sixteen when they served in the province militia. When Sammy Gore reached that age in 1767, he probably joined the Boston artillery train like many men in his circle. Capt. Gore's former apprentice David Mason had cofounded that unit, and its commander was a close family friend, Adino Paddock. Third in command was Sammy's brother-in-law, Thomas Crafts. Eventually Capt. Gore's apprentice John Johnston served in the train as well. For a young crafts apprentice like Gore, serving in the artillery train had appeal beyond discharging his militia obligation among friends, beyond even making a very loud BOOM. The artillery was a prestigious branch of the military. In the political atmosphere of 1767, furthermore, the artillery train's discipline and skills carried a political message: we colonists can defend ourselves, so there is no need for a large army in America or for higher taxes to pay for that army.

The ministry in London disagreed. That year Chancellor of the Exchequer Charles Townshend instituted new taxes on all tea, lead, painter's colors, and glass shipped into the American colonies. A new Customs Commission, headquartered in Boston, would oversee the collection of those duties. The Townshend duties presented a particular problem for Capt. John Gore. His main business was importing painter's colors, hard to obtain locally. How could he avoid importing them and paying the taxes?

In 1768 John Gore, Jr., set up a business "opposite Liberty-Tree" selling a long list of clothes and imported garments. He followed his father into town government in March 1768, winning a beginner's-level office as a Clerk of the Market. That same month, he wed Sarah Foster, niece of the Rev. Dr. Henry Caner, rector at King's Chapel. Marrying into a clerical family confirmed that young Gore was from the genteel class. Notably, Caner was an Anglican and true Tory, championing stronger royal authority in New England and thus at odds with at least some of his niece's new in-laws. A year later, John and Sarah Gore had their first child, whom they had baptized at the West Meetinghouse in a newly developing part of town.

In October 1768, four regiments of the British army arrived in Boston to protect the Customs Commissioners. Whigs were philosophically opposed to such a "standing army." Even for apolitical Bostonians, the troops were a daily bother—taking over public buildings as barracks, patrolling the streets, competing for women and odd jobs and breathing room. Boston's political temper quickly rose back to a boil.

Boston's merchants were already trying to overturn the Townshend duties with "non-importation"—a boycott (though that term was not coined yet) of goods from Britain. In 1768 their agreement barred luxuries only, but for 1769 they extended it to cover all but essential items. The merchants of New York joined in, followed slowly by those in Philadelphia and other ports. The boycotters hoped that non-importation would spur English merchants into lobbying Parliament to repeal the Townshend duties. American politicians foresaw other benefits as well. In the absence of British goods, they said, local manufactures would grow, helping the colonial economy.

Thus, the campaign for non-importation involved both discouraging people from buying imported goods and encouraging them to make and buy domestic products. Newspapers, pamphlets, town meetings, and provincial laws supported local production. In May 1768 the *Boston Gazette* reported that William Dawes, Jr., had married Mehitable May while "dress'd wholly in the Manufactures of this Country, wherein he did Honor to himself, and merits the respect of his Province." The marriage of a leather-tanner and a young woman from Roxbury was very unlikely to have appeared in a newspaper if the printers had not been making a political point.

The Gore family participated in the non-importation campaign. In 1768 Capt. Gore still marketed his stock as "Just imported from London," but in December 1769 he assured customers that all his goods were either "the Produce & Manufacture of North-America" or "imported before the Agreement of the Merchants for Non-importation took Place." In 1768 John, Jr., offered "a general Assortment of English and India GOODS"; by June 1769 he was advertising "North-American Manufactures" and offering to trade his imported inventory for "All sorts of Mens and Womens Ware manufactured in New England."

Through 1769, Boston's merchants and politicians worked together to maintain non-importation. On the fourth anniversary of the first Stamp Act protest, they gathered for a celebratory dinner. John Adams reported: "We had two Tables laid in the open Field by the Barn, with between 300 and 400 Plates, and an Arning of Sail Cloth overhead." He praised such festivals because they "tinge the Minds of the People, they impregnate them with the sentiments of Liberty." In fact, "the People" were not on the guest list. To keep Boston's working class from intruding, these Sons of Liberty met not at Liberty Tree in the South End but at Lemuel Robinson's Liberty Tree tavern in Dorchester, a carriage-ride away.

Capt. Gore was among the diners in Dorchester, along with all the other Overseers of the Poor, all the selectmen, all the Boston representatives to the General Court, and all the public-school teachers but Master Lovell. Thomas Crafts and most of the Loyall Nine attended, as did John Gore, Jr. For entertainment, Nathaniel Balch, a handsome hatter with the soul of a stand-up comic, offered imitations of "the Lawyers Head, and the Hunting of a Bitch fox." The company sang patriotic anthems by John Dickinson, a guest of honor from Philadelphia, and local Whig Dr. Benjamin Church. At the end of the afternoon, John Hancock led the way back to Boston in his chariot (which the Gores had repainted in 1765). A patriotic young printer recorded: "300 Coaches & Chaises . . . passed through the Main Street, round the Town-house, and then home."

One week after this festival of unity, however, a customs official began to leak records showing that some of those merchants—indeed, even some who served on the committee to promote the boycott—had imported goods. These documents appeared in the *Boston Chronicle*, a newspaper founded in 1767 by two Scottish immigrants who were willing to buck the town establishment. In its September 4–7 issue, the *Chronicle* revealed that in April the *Thomas* had brought in eighteen casks of "Painters Colours" and one case of "Painters Colours, brushes and leaf Gold," all marked for "J.G."

Such disclosures did more than embarrass men like Capt. Gore. They threatened the whole program of non-importation. For the boycott to succeed, *all* the merchants in Boston had to stick to the program. Otherwise, those few importers who did ship in British goods—still generally better and cheaper than the local equivalents—would reap extra profits. Furthermore, if other American merchants decided Bostonians were not serious about non-importation, they would start buying from Britain as well. Therefore, the merchants loudly insisted that all the goods listed in the *Chronicle* had been mislabeled, or consigned to the army, or shipped before agents in London had gotten orders to send nothing, or put aside under lock and key, or . . .

Tempers rose. On October 27, a group of merchants confronted the *Chronicle* publishers on King Street. No one was hurt, but with men firing pistols and swinging shovels, someone could have been killed. That night, Boston politics reached an even higher level of personal violence with its first tar-and-feathering, of a sailor from Newport who had worked for the customs service.

Boston's non-importation agreement was due to run out at the end of 1769. Most merchants, including the Gores, were ready to extend it. A few declared that they wanted to start selling what had already arrived from Britain and shipping in new goods. Whig activists took the decision out of the merchants' hands by convening "a Meeting of the Merchants & Traders, at *Faneuil*-Hall," on January 23. Instead of a private meeting of the merchants, this was a public event for all businessmen. The meeting voted that the handful of shopkeepers already selling imported goods were "obstinate and inveterate Enemies of their Country, and Subverters of the Rights and Liberties of this Continent."

This added pressure did not change the importers' minds. It may even have hardened their determination. One of these shopkeepers, Theophilus Lillie, had already penned a protest in the *Boston Chronicle* for January 11–15:

> I cannot help saying, although I never entered far into the mysteries of Government, having applied myself to my shop and my business, that it always seemed strange to me that People who contend so much for civil and religious Liberty, should be so ready to deprive others of their natural Liberty;—that men who are guarding against being subject to Laws which they never gave their consent in person or by their representative, should at the same time make Laws, and in the most effectual manner excute them upon me and others, to which Laws I am sure I never gave my consent either in person or by my representative.

While Boston's Whigs clamored for the colonists' collective liberty to set their own laws, Lillie pled his case for individual liberty from unjust majority rule.

As the Whigs increased the pressure on importers, the *Chronicle* continued printing customs documents. In late January 1770, it revealed that Capt. Gore had paid the Townshend duties on those goods from the *Thomas*, and on "4 barrels Painters colours" that had arrived on the *Abigail* before that. He was only one of several merchants who had brought in goods, and not that many of them. Still, the Gore family may have felt a need to show their commitment to the non-importation cause.

In the third week of February, the Gores—more probably, Frances Gore and her daughters and perhaps daughters-in-law—hosted a spinning bee at their house on Queen Street. More common in rural towns than in Boston, spinning bees brought together several women with their wheels to turn flax or wool into thread. This was a social occasion that also showed the women's support of American manufacturing: the cloth woven from their thread could advance the local economy by a few square feet. Usually the events also had a moral message, with the women gathering at a minister's home and leaving their spun yarn to benefit the poor. Of ten spinning bees in and around Boston in 1766-70, the Gores' was one of only two not in a minister's home.

The *Boston Gazette* put a strong political spin on the Gores' spinning bee:

> One Day last Week a Number of Patriot Ladies met at the House of John Gore, Esq; of this Town, when their Industry at the Spinning Wheel was at least equal to any Instance recorded in our Paper. It is principally owing to the indefatigable Pains of Mr. William Mollineux; and it will be said to his lasting Honor, that the laudable Practice of Spinning is almost universally in Vogue among the Female Children of this Town; whereby they are not only useful to the Community, but the poorer Sort are able in some Measure to assist their Parents in getting a Livelihood—The Use of the Spinning-Wheel is now encouraged, and the pernicious Practice of Tea-drinking equally discountenanced, by all the Ladies of this Town, excepting those whose Husbands are Tories and Friends to the American Revenue-Acts; and a few Ladies who are Tories themselves.

In the same month, some Boston boys were promoting non-importation in a more aggressive way. On Thursdays the town schools closed early, after only a couple of hours of lessons, so the boys could attend the religious "Thursday Lecture" (though a 1770s schoolboy could not recall any classmate taking advantage of that opportunity). Starting on February 8, some boys used their free Thursdays to march in front of one of the shops selling imported goods, "insulting Every body who went in, or out of the Shop, by Hissing and pelting them with Dirt." A witness described how the boys set up a "board . . . with a Hand painted on it, pointing to Mr. [William] Jacksons Shop and below, the word Importer, in Large Letters." Later they erected "a large Wooden Head carved and painted," like the effigies Bostonians had seen on Pope Nights or hanging off Liberty Tree. The boys also made "a Board faced with paper, on which was painted the figures of four of the importers." Sammy Gore or his workmates may have been involved—somebody had to paint those signs.

It is not clear how much adult activists organized the boys, but they were on hand to support them. When Jackson tried to remove the sign in front of his shop, he "was Repulsed by a Number of Idle people, who were standing by, with Clubs and Sticks in their Hands. . . . During this Exhibition a Number of considerable Merchants Stood at a Little distance, and seemed highly pleased with what was going on." The *Chronicle* announced satirically that "a Company of young Tragedians" was in town to stage *The Witches*—both alluding to the Salem witch hunt and tweaking Boston's prohibition against theater.

On Thursday, February 22, the importing shopkeepers discovered their windows "besmeared . . . with tar & feathers." That morning the boys shifted their attention to the shop of Theophilus Lillie, the shopkeeper who had written the newspaper protest about personal liberty. They set up their "Pageantry" on Union Street in front of his door. Along came Ebenezer Richardson, the customs service employee already notorious for "informing." He tried to persuade two men from the country to knock down the carved head with their wagons, but the drivers refused and brought up an old scandal in his past. Richardson stomped off to his nearby home, shouting, "Perjury! Perjury!" at some Whigs watching the affair.

As the *Boston Evening-Post* reported, "The Boys on hearing the words began to gather round, and call him an informer." Richardson and his wife shooed them away. The boys said, "they would not, Kings high Way"—claiming their right to be on the street. Richardson flourished a stick. The boys ran around "with the squeeling and noise they usually make on such occasion." The young mob, now numbering at least "60 or 70 Boys," no longer cared about Lillie's shop. They started pelting Richardson's house with "Limon Peels" and hit his wife with an egg. Someone inside the house tossed out a brickbat, striking a sailor. He threw it back through a window.

A low-level customs employee named George Wilmot came to the house and offered help. According to one of Richardson's daughters, "Wilmot asked [my father] if he had any Gun." Both men armed themselves with muskets. Richardson came out his front door and shouted, "as sure as there was a G[od] in heaven, he'd blow a Lane thro 'em." He "snapped" his gun—firing it with powder but no ball, like a blank shot. The boys scattered and came back again, no longer tossing "light rubbish of one kind or another" but throwing stones through windows.

Whether he had been part of the demonstration all along or was drawn by the noise, Sammy Gore was now at the front of the crowd. Richardson reappeared with his musket at an upper window. The boys continued to throw rocks. Richardson fired again. This time he had loaded his musket with buckshot pellets, "about the bigness of large peas." Eleven pieces flew into the chest of Christopher Seider, a servant boy around eleven-years-old "stooping to take up a Stone." More sliced through the baggy pants of a sailor named Robert Patterson. A few pieces pierced the right hand and thigh of Sammy Gore.

Infuriated at seeing little Christopher fall, men joined the attack and soon dragged Richardson and Wilmot off to the magistrates. Printers of Thursday newspapers scrambled to include the late-breaking story. In a neighboring house, Dr. Joseph Warren, Dr. Thomas Young, and other surgeons were examining the wounded boys. Christopher Seider's chest, peppered with shot, was filling with blood. Although the surgeons could drain that blood—eighteenth-century surgeons were eager to drain blood—they could not repair the damage. His parents, poor German immigrants, were called from their little home at the far end of the Common. Clergymen came to pray with the family. Christopher died around 9 o'clock that night.

As for Sammy Gore, Richardson's shot had wounded him "thro' both thighs and two fingers of his right hand." Dr. Warren extracted two pieces of metal from his leg and bandaged his hand. The radical *Boston Gazette* suggested "his Life was endanger'd," and other newspapers agreed only that "in all probability he will lose the use of the right fore finger, by the wound received there; much important to a youth of his dexterity in drawing and painting." Like the fictional Johnny Tremain, Sammy had been trained in a lucrative craft and now, due to a sudden injury, faced the prospect of losing his livelihood before he had even come of age. As it turned out, Samuel Gore would enjoy a long and healthy career. In the 1830s a Boston barber recalled that he would show off his scarred fingers and "tell the story with some relish." But in 1770, at age nineteen, Sammy had gained a personal reason to resent people who worked for the Crown.

The Gores never filed an assault case against Richardson; they most likely figured that since the man would be convicted of murder, or at least manslaughter, there was no value in suing him for damages. Meanwhile, the Whigs made the most of young Christopher Seider's death. On Monday, February 26, they organized one of the largest funerals the town had ever seen for "this little hero and first martyr to the noble cause."

Passions were driven even higher after weekend brawls between soldiers and ropemakers. On the night of Monday, March 5, a handful of barber's apprentices ran around the center of town reporting how the sentry at the customs office on King Street had clonked one of them on the head. Locals thus heard about another Crown lackey attacking another boy. An angry crowd gathered. The sentry sent for reinforcements, which simply made the crowd madder. By the end of the evening eleven more townspeople had been shot, five fatally.

No Gores reported being at what the Whigs quickly dubbed "the Horrid Massacre," but their house was only blocks away. They undoubtedly heard the ringing bells, the shouting, the seven shots followed by shocked silence. Some of Sammy's Latin School classmates had been in the crowd, Henry Knox up front warning the army captain not to let his men fire. Patterson the sailor was shot in the arm. Edward Payne, a merchant wounded in his own doorway, later became Christopher Gore's father-in-law. Thomas Crafts was one of the two coroners Boston elected that month, so he oversaw inquiries into the deaths.

To the Whigs, the Boston Massacre proved that a standing army in a crowded town would produce oppression. On the day after the shootings, Samuel Adams and the Boston citizenry, peacefully but angrily assembled outside the Town House, pressured the governor and military commander into moving both army regiments to Castle William, the offshore fortress. Customs officials followed them or found reasons to be out of town. Theophilus Lillie chose to move far away to the small town of Oxford.

On April 20, after delays over lawyers and witnesses, Ebenezer Richardson and George Wilmot were brought to trial on the charge of murdering Christopher Seider. Robert Treat Paine and Samuel Quincy served as prosecutors while Josiah Quincy, Jr., a well-born young attorney, represented Richardson. Everyone agreed that Richardson had killed the boy, but had he acted in self-defense? The courtroom was packed as witnesses described the fighting. Sammy Gore was not called to testify, nor any other boy. After the attorneys' arguments, the judges announced that Wilmot, who had never fired his gun, should be found innocent. As for Richardson, "they were convinced that the jury could find him guilty of nothing more than manslaughter." One went further and "charged the death of the Boy upon the promoters of the Effigies and the Exhibitions." A spectator yelled, "Damn that Judge, if I was nigh him, I would give it to him!"

The jury men, confined without food and drink, deliberated from eleven at night to nine the next morning before delivering their judgment: Wilmot was innocent, Richardson guilty of murder.

The crowd cheered until one Whig shouted, "for Shame, for shame Gentlemen!" The judges had to accept this verdict but put off imposing the only legal penalty, death by hanging. Over the following months, session after session of the court passed without sentencing. Many Bostonians suspected that a cabal of royal officials was determined to save Richardson from punishment.

Gradually, Boston quieted down. The imperial government repealed the Townshend duties on all goods except tea. The army regiments remained out of town. The *Boston Chronicle* stopped publishing after its founder's London creditors asked John Hancock to sue him for unpaid bills. In 1770 Lt. Gov. Thomas Hutchinson became the new royal governor, the first native Bostonian to hold that position in decades. Though he hoarded political appointments and consistently supported royal authority, most people perceived him as a personally upright man. Diehard activists like Samuel Adams, Dr. Thomas Young, and Dr. Joseph Warren still complained about many actions of the Crown government, such as the salaries for judges, and they tried new organizing tactics, such as the committees of correspondence, but nothing roused the populace as the presence of soldiers had.

The Gore family had their own good news to celebrate. In August 1770, John, Jr., and Sarah Gore had their second child, a healthy boy also named John. The next summer, youngest son Christopher started his last year at the North Latin School, on his way to fulfill his parents' hopes and enter Harvard. The family seemed to be passing on a prosperous gentility to the next generation. But on September 3, 1771, the Gores suffered a sad surprise, described by printer John Boyle:

> This Morning (Tuesday) Mr. John Gore, Junr. intending an Excursion in the Country with his Friends arose vigorous and cheerful: being casually detained longer than he expected, his friends Set out without him, with the expectation that he would soon overtake them, but alas! *his bounds were determined that he could not pass* He was seized with an Apoplectic Fit at ten o'Clock, and expired at four in the Afternoon.

Capt. Gore and the Rev. Dr. Caner were suddenly responsible for a young widow and her baby boy. And Sammy was now his parents' oldest son.

Samuel Gore turned twenty-one on January 26, 1772. Though his father still occasionally called him Sammy, he was legally a man and a partner in the family firm. The April 9, 1772, *Boston News-Letter* presented a large advertisement for "John Gore and Son," selling paints, varnishes, gums, brushes, "the best London Linseed Oil," and "Pencils of all sorts." At the bottom of the notice was a poignant list of goods still for sale from "the Estate of John Gore, jun., deceased."

Sam Gore could not have been pleased by the news of March 10, 1772, that the imperial government in London had pardoned Ebenezer Richardson. Royal officials in Massachusetts, believing the customs man's conviction for murder was unjust, had lobbied for that pardon for almost two years. But they carefully timed its official delivery for a morning when Boston's Whig leaders were engrossed in a town meeting, giving Richardson time to get out of town before a mob formed. The man who shot Sam Gore in the hand and leg was thus free and, in the eyes of the local radicals, unpunished.

At that time, Gov. Hutchinson was trying to split the Whigs by winning over their richest member, John Hancock. This young merchant opposed royal policies as a Boston selectman and representative, but he usually preferred to wait until popular opinion became clear instead of trying to push it along. Like other wealthy young men, Hancock was doing his militia service in the prestigious Company of Cadets, traditionally the governor's honor guard. In April 1772 the Cadets unanimously elected him to command them. Sensing an opportunity, Hutchinson ratified the choice. Hancock threw himself into writing a drill manual and designing new uniforms, devoting less time to politics.

That calm did not last. In the spring of 1773 Benjamin Franklin, then acting as lobbyist for the Massachusetts House in London, sent speaker Thomas Cushing copies of letters that Gov. Hutchinson and other royal officials had written to a contact in

London a few years before. Those candid discussions not only criticized the Massachusetts Whigs but in some cases suggested serious changes to the province's constitution. Cushing, Adams, and Hancock maneuvered to have the letters published as proof of a conspiracy against their rights as citizens of the British Empire.

At a banquet on May 26, 1773, Hancock and the Company of Cadets were serving as Gov. Hutchinson's honor guard when the Customs commissioners arrived. Not only were those officials unpopular as collectors of the tariffs, but Commissioner Charles Paxton had written some of the controversial letters. A crowd booed the royal appointees. Two cadets, upholsterer Moses Grant and bookseller James Foster Condy, "quit the ranks" to show their displeasure. Grant was already politically active, meeting with the North End Caucus to organize votes at town meetings. Hancock, upset to see cadets behaving rudely in his fine new uniforms, marched the unit away.

Rather than going home, however, Grant and Condy returned to the banquet site and "When the commissioners came out, they joined the mob in pelting them with mud." Commissioner Benjamin Hallowell chased Grant off with his sword. At a meeting of the cadets a few days later, Hancock criticized Condy and Grant's "unmilitary conduct." After a vote "they were expelled from the corps." The two ex-cadets had to find less prestigious militia companies. Since Grant would serve as an artillerist during the war, he probably joined Sam Gore in the train.

Given that charged atmosphere in Boston, this was the wrong time for Parliament to rewrite the rules for shipping tea to America in an obvious attempt to prop up the debt-ridden, politically connected East India Company. On top of that, the new Tea Act made it easier to collect the tea tax, which American Whigs still opposed, and Gov. Hutchinson's sons gained a share in the tea-importing monopoly. (Hutchinson himself had a £1,000 annual investment in their business.) In late November, the ship *Dartmouth* arrived in Boston harbor, carrying East India Company tea. The Whigs insisted that the crew must not land that cargo and allow the tax to be collected. They called public meetings on the issue—not town meetings, but meetings of "the Body of the People" for anyone from Boston or nearby towns who felt an interest. These gatherings overflowed Faneuil Hall and filled Old South Meeting-House, the largest space in town.

The "Body of the People" called for volunteers to patrol Griffin's Wharf near where the ship lay at anchor and prevent it from being unloaded secretly. The first patrol on November 29 included three members of the Loyall Nine, silversmith Paul Revere, and former Cadets Moses Grant and Foster Condy—all fervent and reliable Whigs. Admiral John Montagu described the armed guards as "like Sentinels in a garrison." For over two weeks, day and night, those men made sure that no tea came ashore. According to a veteran of Paddock's artillery named Ebenezer Stevens, that company was asked to take some shifts on the wharf. "Paddock, whose sympathies were with the Royal authorities, refused his consent, but at a company meeting the charge was accepted and undertaken by them, First Lieut. Jabez Hatch taking the command."

Two more tea ships arrived, but the *Dartmouth* remained the crucial one. Customs rules would not allow it to remain unloaded in the harbor past December 16. Yet other regulations meant the ships could not return to sea with their cargos; if captains tried to sail away without the proper paperwork, they would face the guns of the Royal Navy and Castle William, now manned by the army. The only official who could provide the special permission for the ships to leave was Gov. Hutchinson. If the *Dartmouth* was still in the harbor on December 17, customs officials could seize its cargo, declare it taxed, and let the tea work its way onto the market.

On Thursday, December 16, a contingent from Paddock's artillery company was on guard duty at Griffin's Wharf. Up to five thousand people, including other members of the train, jammed the Old South Meeting-House and the streets outside. At close to six o'clock the owner of the *Dartmouth* returned to the gathering from the governor's country home. Hutchinson had again refused to let him sail away with the tea. Samuel Adams announced that "they had now done all they could for the Salvation of their Country"—mere protests would not be enough. The news spread through the crowd and outside. Some people had already prepared for that contingency. While Adams, Dr. Thomas Young, and other gentlemen continued the meeting inside the Old South, men were making their way to Griffin's Wharf. They passed the meetinghouse, "some imitating the Powaws of Indians and others the Whistle of a Boatswain."

With night falling, the militia artillerists patrolling the dock saw those men coming—"about seventy or eighty," said Stevens, who joined that group from the Old South meeting. Many wore no disguises while "Some of them stopped at a paint shop on the way and daubed their faces with paint." Shoemaker George R. T. Hewes hastily blackened his face with soot. Those rudimentary masks, the "Powaws," and the need to speak about the men without acknowledging who they were became the basis of later claims that they were all heavily disguised as "Mohawks." The artillerists waiting on the docks surely recognized fellow members of the train, as well as other friends and acquaintances. One of the crowd leaders was Lendell Pitts—a classmate of Samuel Gore at the South Latin School and a Cadet who had voted not to expel Moses Grant. There was no confrontation between the patrollers and the new arrivals. Stevens said simply, "At the head of the wharf we met the detachment of our company on guard, who joined us." Working together, the men quickly boarded the three ships and systematically emptied all 342 chests of tea into the harbor.

In 1773 plans for this operation were secret; sixty years later, Americans revered it under the name of the "Boston Tea Party," and hundreds of people claimed they or their ancestors had participated. Many traditions about the event are therefore difficult to verify. Nonetheless, it seems close to certain that Samuel Gore was involved. When he died in 1831, the *Columbian Centinel* stated that Gore was "one of the number (and, so far as we know, has left but three survivors) who on the 16th Dec. 1773, proceeded to the tea ships . . . and destroyed their cargoes." Four years later, Benjamin Bussey Thacher published the earliest list of men who were at the Boston Tea Party. His source, "an aged Bostonian," listed Samuel Gore next to Moses Grant.

The response of the imperial government in London, sending in Gen. Thomas Gage as royal governor and once again stationing army regiments in town, forced Boston's merchants and professionals to declare their allegiances. Traditionally, prominent men signed an address to each outgoing governor thanking him for his services and another to each new governor welcoming him. Whigs insisted that Hutchinson and Gage deserved neither thanks nor welcome. Since the governor was the embodiment of the royal power, however, to show disrespect for a man in that post came close to showing disrespect for His Majesty.

John Gore chose to sign the Addresses to Hutchinson and Gage, as did his friend Adino Paddock. They also then signed a protest against the Boston committee of correspondence's Solemn League and Covenant, the strictest non-importation agreement yet. Though Capt. Gore had agreed to earlier boycotts, advertised domestic goods, hosted a spinning bee, and dined with the Sons of Liberty, he would no longer defy royal authority. He later told the British government, "He always lived in great order & peace with his Countrymen untill these unhappy times, when he could not joine them in taking arms against his King & Country to whom he had often taken Oaths of Allegiance as an Officer of the Militia."

Capt. Gore may have valued the social and economic growth he had achieved under the royal government too much to break with it. Pro-Crown friends like Paddock and Caner might have swayed him. He might never have been that enthusiastic a Whig, just as he never seems to have been that enthusiastic a Loyalist. Whatever his thinking, in the summer of 1774 Capt. John Gore made clear to his neighbors which side he was on. Their response was equally clear. On September 8, his firefighting society voted to expel him "for signing the Address to the late Governor Hutchinson." The following March, he would lose his post as an Overseer of the Poor.

If John and Samuel Gore discussed their political differences, they left no record of it. The only family letters from this period are from Capt. Gore to the firm's London agents, and they betray no turmoil. The captain's son-in-law Thomas Crafts was clearly on the side of defiance. He led Boston's committee to collect donations from other towns for families impoverished by the port closure.

The contributions started arriving in July 1774: 258 sheep from Windham, Connecticut; £40 from the Union Fire Club in Salem; 130 more sheep from Brooklin, Connecticut; . . . Crafts kept busy distributing this aid and sending letters of thanks.

On March 10, 1774, Samuel Gore married Mary (Polly) Pierce, daughter of a deacon in the Brattle Street Meeting. The previous December, her sister Sarah had married the upholsterer Moses Grant. Both men were luxury-craftsmen early in their careers, their upbringing verging on genteel but not securely so. Both had participated in actions against customs officials and suffered for it—Gore by being shot, Grant by losing his place in the Cadets. Together they had helped to destroy the tea, bringing on the latest confrontation with the London government.

On September 5, Sam Gore, his brothers-in-law Moses Grant and Thomas Crafts, his fellow apprentice John Johnston, and the rest of the Boston train mustered for "Artillery training." It had been four days since Gen. Gage's soldiers had taken the province's gunpowder and the Cambridge cannon. It had been two days since the army had mounted its own cannon on Boston Neck, pointing out at the country, and the navy had stationed a warship in the Charles River. The militiamen no doubt discussed what would happen with their company's weapons. Either at this muster or soon afterward the train's commander, Adino Paddock, "was heard to express his intention of surrendering these guns to the British army."

Lower-ranking members of the train objected to that plan. As Whigs, they linked their training and equipment to the people's resolve to defend themselves against foreign enemies and, implicitly, a government that imposed unwanted taxes and shielded employees from punishment for their criminal behavior. Keeping the guns would also be a blow for property rights—the local legislature had paid for those cannon, not the army. As author William Tudor described the decision he heard about from Sam Gore, "a few individuals resolved to secure for the country a property which belonged to it, and which, in the present emergency, had an importance very disproportionate to its intrinsic value."

Late on the stormy night of September 14, someone—probably members of the train—broke into the train's older armory and took away its pair of two-pounders. The next day, Gen. Gage doubled the sentries in front of the new gunhouse beside the Common. That being Thursday, all Bostonians knew the South Writing School was empty after mid-morning. Members of the train probably took the opportunity to scout for holes in the army's security.

Gore, Grant, and two more men—Gore later remembered only their last names, Balch and Gridley—"concerted their plan." The biggest obstacles to overcome were the sentries outside the gunhouse and the 4th Regiment across the street. Yet those obstacles actually canceled each other out for a few minutes each day. During roll call, the British drummers beat assembly, soldiers hustled into line, sergeants shouted orders and counted noses. Because of all that noise a short distance in front of them, the sentries could not hear what was happening behind the tall fence around the gunhouse yard. Thus, "The moment for the execution of the project was that of the roll call, when the sentinel who was stationed at one door of the building, would be less likely to hear their operations."

Early on the morning of Friday, September 16, before the boys showed up for their handwriting lessons, Gore, Grant, Balch, and Gridley "passed through the school house" into the yard behind it. Hidden by the fence, they quietly approached the side doors of the gunhouse. The latch across those doors had a weak point: "a small crevice, through which they raised the bar that secured them." The sounds of the King's Own drums probably penetrated the little building as the men entered. The militia artillerists hoisted the brass guns off their carriages and carried them in their arms back out into the fenced yard. From there, they had only one place to go: back into the South Writing School.

Five

"Not One Lisped a Word"

THE SOUTH WRITING SCHOOL, LIKE BOSTON'S OTHER SCHOOL-houses, contained only one room and minimal furniture. There were seven or eight "forms," or benches, for the boys to sit on, with ink-stained wooden desks in front of them. At the front of the room was the schoolmaster's desk, perhaps covered with a collection of toys he had confiscated. Another desk was provided for the usher, or assistant teacher. Near the master's desk was a stove and a chest full of firewood. Boxes held paper, ink, and bushels of long feathers; Boston's writing teachers bought quills by the thousands. The master probably had a stack of books such as George Bickham's *Universal Penman* to draw on for writing exercises.

The master at the South Writing School was Samuel Holbrook, then forty-five-years-old. He had started teaching in that schoolhouse five years earlier, following the long career of his older brother Abiah. When Gore and his mates lugged those two cannon into the South Writing School, Master Holbrook's morning lessons had not started yet. Otherwise, they would have had to pick their way through about two hundred boys aged seven to thirteen. And that autumn the schoolmaster did not even have a full-grown usher to help him keep order, sharpen quills, and move the lessons along. He had only Andrew Cunningham, a fourteen-year-old assistant who had been a star student in the same school until March.

Master Holbrook was part of the militiamen's plot to secure their cannon from the royal army. His assistant Andrew, son of a major in the Boston militia regiment, was probably in on the secret as well. Certainly, after seven years at the South Writing School, the teen-ager would have known the best place in the building to hide two yard-long cannon. Gore and his comrades lifted the lid of the "large box under the master's desk, in which wood was kept" for the stoves and deposited the two fieldpieces inside. Then the men casually left through the front door, empty-handed.

According to what Gore later told the author William Tudor, Jr., he and his confederates acted just in time: "Immediately after the roll call, a lieutenant and sergeant came into the gun house to look at the cannon, previously to removing them." Seeing the empty carriages, the sergeant swore, "By G—, they're gone! I'll be d——d if these fellows won't steal the teeth out of your head, while you're keeping guard." The lieutenant examined the gate in the high fence onto the street and "observed, that they could not have passed that way, because a cobweb across the opening was not broken." Between the sentry and the spider's web, he deduced, the only way the guns could have left the yard was through the school.

Gore stated that "They went next into the school house, which they examined all over, except the [firewood] box, on which the master placed his foot, which was lame; and the officer, with true courtesy, on that account excused him from rising." By this time, the school day was starting. "Some boys were present, but not one lisped a word."

Loitering nearby as an "*innocent* spectator," Gore suggested to the army officer that the cannon may have been hidden on the other side of West Street—in the garden of Stephen Greenleaf, the royal sheriff. "On this, the sergeant took him by the collar, gave him a push, and said 'it was very likely that he was one of the d——d rebels who helped to get them off, and that he had better make himself scarce!'" That was, Gore later stated, too close a guess for comfort, and he took the opportunity to leave.

Gore's description of speaking so saucily to the soldiers makes his whole story seem almost too good. It offers clever twists, a narrow escape, and pleasing stereotypical characters: the wily Yankees, the exasperated but scrupulously polite British officer, the ill-tempered British sergeant. Yet some of those suspicious details match the account that John Andrews put into a letter on the same day. Furthermore, contemporary evidence shows that Gore's tongue could be too sharp for his own good. During the Battle of Bunker Hill in June 1775, as British soldiers marched by his house either to or from the bloody field, Sam Gore was heard "calling over to his sister to come and see a funeral pass." For this joke he was "taken up and confined some time." So that saucy suggestion about where to find the missing cannon may be something Gore later wished he had said, but he may truly have been foolhardy enough to say it.

According to William Tudor, the train's two cannon lay inside the firewood box inside the South Writing School for about two weeks. At least some of the 200-odd boys attending that school no doubt spotted the glint of brass beneath their firewood. Yet none of those scholars alerted the royal authorities. Master Holbrook used his off-hours from eleven to noon and from five to sunset to teach genteel handwriting to girls from wealthy families. None of them gave away the secret, either. Most Boston children were growing up in families that resented the Crown's increasingly heavy-handed policies. Even in the South Latin School, which had a disproportionate number of boys from Loyalist families, most of the student body supported the Patriots. But it appears that the scholars of the South Writing School must have been almost *unanimous* in wishing to thwart Gen. Gage.

That unity of feeling might have reflected the class origins and ambitions of writing-school students. Boston's free public schools provided unusually good educational opportunities for the time, but the system was still riven by economic class. To begin with, only about half of all white boys aged seven to thirteen were in any of the town schools in 1765. The rest were already working, either in their parents' workshops or as apprentices or servants in other households. (The system was also segregated by sex and race, of course. The town schools did not officially make room for girls until 1789. There is no evidence that any of the approximately 5% of Boston boys classified as black or Indian went to town schools before the Revolution.)

Within Boston's education system, furthermore, there was a clear class distinction between the town's two Latin or grammar schools and its three writing schools. The North and South Latin schools prepared boys for college and subsequent careers as lawyers, doctors, ministers, or top-level merchants. The North, South, and Queen Street writing schools prepared boys for apprenticeships in counting-houses or shops through lessons in handwriting and practical arithmetic. (Neither sort of town school taught English literature or composition, history, geography or navigation, or any of the sciences.) The grammar schools served fewer boys—193 in 1770, compared to 749 at the writing schools. Nevertheless, the Latin masters were paid more. Thus, for every pound that Boston paid in that year to educate each writing scholar, it spent £2.14s. on a Latin scholar. With schoolteachers' salaries set in the open town meetings, it was obvious which form of education the society valued more.

As discussed in the last chapter, many boys who entered the South Latin School dropped out before finishing. Of the four hundred boys Master John Lovell admitted from 1750 to 1764, fewer than a third (130) graduated. Many ended up at one of the nearby writing schools. They were not going on to college and thus less likely to enter the highest rank of gentlemen. Harrison Gray Otis was at the South Latin School in the early 1770s, and he described his schoolmates trying to lord over the boys at Master James Carter's nearby writing school by chanting:

> Carter's boys shut up in a pen
> They can't get out but now and then;
> And when they get out they dance about
> For fear of Latin School gentlemen.

The Latin scholars drove home the developing class distinction by contrasting themselves as "gentlemen" to the writing school "boys."

The situation of the boys in the South Writing School thus paralleled that of the young mechanics of the militia train. They were strivers seizing opportunity to rise above the bulk of their peers, but their advancement was fragile and they were still shut out from the top social institutions. That affinity might help to explain why the boys in Master Holbrook's school were so ready to keep the militiamen's secret. Of course, even with the schoolboy solidarity, the two brass cannon could not stay inside the South Writing School's firewood chest indefinitely. With winter approaching, more and more people would be opening that box, and a single comment might reveal the guns to Gen. Gage's government.

In late September, just as the South Writing School boys were keeping a secret, so was the Boston press. None of the town's newspapers mentioned the disappearance of the train's four cannon. They simply left those guns out of their regular report on which cannon would be fired to commemorate the king's coronation on September 22. But perhaps the Loyalist *Boston News-Letter* was making a point about missing artillery pieces when it added to its account of the day: "*In New York Paper we find the following Paragraph*, A letter in Town intimates, that there are ninety pieces of Cannon now lying at the Town of Worcester; they all belong to the Province of Massachusetts-Bay." Worcester had indeed become a hotbed of resistance to the Crown, but this was another greatly exaggerated rumor.

The men of the train knew they needed another hidingplace. In addition to his brother-in-law Moses Grant, Samuel Gore remembered his companions in moving the train's three-pounders into the school as "Balch, Gridley, Whiston, and two or three more." The first was probably Joseph Balch, thirty-five-year-old brother of the hatter who told jokes at the Sons of Liberty banquet in 1769. Joseph Balch served as the second-in-command of Rhode Island's artillery regiment in 1775 before returning to Massachusetts as an officer in its home-based artillery regiment during the Revolutionary War.

Richard Gridley and Obadiah Whiston were blacksmiths. Gridley owned a smithy on Orange Street in the southern corner of Boston, where the peninsula narrowed down into the Neck. Whiston was a young man from Dorchester who worked at Gridley's forge, first perhaps as an apprentice, in 1769 as a twenty-one-year-old journeyman, and in the early 1770s as a partner. In the spring of 1774 the two smiths were busy installing Boston's first street lamps, ordered specially from Britain. (Other people working on this big project included John Gore, Thomas Crafts, Thomas Newell, Richard Boynton, and William Dawes.) One of Gridley and Whiston's apprentices later described them as "Baptists by profession," which was unusual but had no political implications.

Gridley and Whiston had a record in standing up to the British military in the boldest way. On October 24, 1769, the Whig organizer Robert Pierpoint served a warrant on Ens. John Ness, then commanding the guard on the Boston Neck, for letting his men steal firewood. This was the sort of everyday friction between the army and civilians that Whigs treated as a constitutional issue. The young army officer refused to report to a local justice of the peace as the warrant required until his shift was over. An angry crowd gathered to enforce their town's civil authority over the military.

As Ness marched his troops home, they passed Richard Gridley's forge on Orange Street. A soldier accidentally fired his musket, striking the building and enraging the men who worked inside. In the ensign's words, "Obadiah Whiston a Black Smith came up to the right of the Guard, and Struck a Soldier in the face, and made him Bleed, the same Obadiah Whiston was coming up a Second time, but was prevented by the Serjeant." Another redcoat was hit by a brick. Capt. Ponsonby Molesworth arrived and ordered the soldiers to bayonet the next man who tried to attack them. That kept the crowd back, and the troops staggered on to their barracks. By the time they arrived there, Whiston had gone to a magistrate to swear out a warrant against the sergeant for assault.

As Whiston's employer, Gridley took a keen interest in the ensuing legal cases. Which meant he went to the magistrates' inquiry, pointed out Capt. Molesworth, and shouted, "Here is the fellow who threatened to run me through the body. If there is law in Boston, I'll be revenged." At the court of general sessions, Gridley bellowed, "The Army is a parcel of blackguard rascals!"

The following March 5, Obadiah Whiston heard church bells ring in the center of Boston. He testified that he went out, "Met an Engine [for fighting fires] and help'd drag it along but soon heard the Soldiers were fighting the Inhabitants." Running ahead to see what was happening, and perhaps to get in a few punches, Whiston met Edward Garrick, "a barber's boy, who told me he had been struck by the soldiers." At the Main Guard he watched Capt. Thomas Preston and seven soldiers turn out to protect the sentry who had struck Garrick. In describing the night to sympathetic magistrates, Whiston claimed, "I saw one gun go off," but as a witness at Preston's trial for murder he testified he had only *heard* what came to be called the Boston Massacre.

In March 1774 Whiston bought land around the corner from Richard Gridley's shop on the north side of newly developed Pleasant Street. He was by then married with two sons. He probably hoped to set up his own smithy, to fulfill the typical journeyman's ambition of running his own shop instead of working for someone else. On August 21, John Andrews wrote about a confrontation between an armed blacksmith and two army officers:

> This evening two officers of the 38th were very severely drub'd for going into a house in Pleasant street and ill-using two women, whose husbands happen'd to be at home; whereby one of the officers got a contusion on his head from a stroke of a pistol, apply'd by a son of Vulcan; who followed him, took away his sword and broke it, while the other was feeling the effects of an injur'd husband's rage.

If this smith was not Whiston himself, he must have been aware of that affront to a neighbor.

In sum, Obadiah Whiston seems to have been exactly the sort of man who would be up for hiding two stolen cannon from the king's army. Around the start of October 1774, some of the men who had taken the train's three-pounders returned to the South Writing School with a large trunk and a wheelbarrow, perhaps under the cover of delivering firewood, and trundled them away. According to William Tudor, the men carried the three-pounders to "Whiston's blacksmith's shop at the South-end" and stashed them under a pile of coal.

Those two cannon might be safe from the king's army there, but they were not helping the Patriot cause. The blacksmith Gridley had an older namesake cousin living in Stoughton: Col. Richard Gridley, the province's most respected artillerist. For his service in the 1745 capture of Fort Louisburg and in the French and Indian War, the colonel had been granted a half-pay pension from the Crown and other boons. The Boston Patriots probably considered that if only they could get their weapons out of town to the colonel, he would know how to make the most of them.

Six

"Selling Warlike Stores"

By late September 1774, Boston's batteries and gunhouses had been picked clean. All the artillery pieces that the town's militia companies had manned were either under the control of the king's army or concealed in the Patriot underground.

However, there were still cannon in private hands. A few hardware merchants owned ordnance they had stocked up on during the last war against the French. Some trading merchants also kept heavy guns to arm their ships in case of war. One such businessman was the hatter Thomas Handasyd Peck. He later admitted to the governor, "their is two Iron guns in my store. I think about four Pounders. . . . Those guns have no carrages and have Laid Ever Since Last War." But at this delicate time, when turning over such guns to either side had clear political implications and dangers, Peck chose to keep quiet.

Immediately after losing the train's brass fieldpieces, the royal military became more aggressive about taking control of whatever cannon they could locate. On September 16, John Andrews reported, an army officer went to the merchant Arnold Welles and demanded "seven or eight iron ordnance" that "lay along side his Distil house, at a wharf near the South fish market." Welles was a solid Whig, though not a particularly active one, and he forbade the officer to take those guns "at his peril." The royal authorities could not accept that, Andrews wrote:

> The Military, apprehensive that a delay of their expedition 'till midnight would bilk 'em of their prize, went with a large parade in the evening to take 'em away. Mr. Wells being out, his wife (whom you know has a very voluble tongue) went out and rallied 'em so, that the officer was necessitated to give her a receipt to be answerable for their forth coming, before she would suffer him to take them.

Susannah Welles was a daughter of a merchant from Bristol, but her ties to England did not mean she was quiet about protecting her husband's interests.

The Royal Artillery did not need Welles's seven or eight iron guns. By the end of July the contingent from New York had moved in four mounted twelve-pounders, twelve mounted six-pounders, and four mounted howitzers. By August 21, Col. Percy counted "22 pieces of cannon & 3 cos. of artillery" under his command. Most of those artillery pieces were newer and made of brass, and thus less likely to break than guns left over from the last war. But the army did not want Welles's cannon to end up in the hands of the rebels outside of Boston.

At this point in the conflict, each side saw itself as acting only in its own defense while the opposing side unnecessarily escalated tensions. Both Gen. Gage's royal government and the Patriot committees wanted to keep weapons out of the hands of the other party, which they saw as a step to maintaining peace. But it was all too easy for people on each side to perceive their opponents as preparing for war. A passage from William Tudor's September 17 letter to John Adams captures this dangerous paradox. On the one hand, the young lawyer wrote about the governor with suspicion:

> General Gage professes to act only on the defensive. I wish we may not soon find something else is design'd besides the bare Protection of his Troops. Should he commence one Act of Hostility, such is the Spirit that prevails universally, a civil War would inevitably be the Consequence.

But Tudor reported happily on the province's own military preparations: "The Countrymen almost every where turn out and exercise three Times a Week. There is said to be fifty Cannon in the upper Part of the County of Middlesex completely fitted for Service."

Tudor did not admit that those activities might give Gage good reason to worry. The rumor of fifty mounted cannon in just one part of Middlesex County was another wild exaggeration, but it reflected what Bostonians on both sides of the political divide thought might be going on in the militant countryside.

At the same time, the people in towns right outside of Boston were worried about the army. On Sunday, September 18, John Andrews wrote, the 38th Regiment turned out for inspection with their knapsacks a day earlier than usual because they were assigned to help build fortifications.

> [That] manoeuvre rais'd a suspicion in some people's minds (who were more *credulous* than *wise*) that they were going to Watertown after the cannon: which, by being often *told*, came to be *believ'd*, and the committee here sent to inform their brethren of Charlestown, which broke up their morning service and induc'd them to proceed to Cambridge, and from thence to Watertown, alarming all as they went, to be prepar'd and ready to act upon the defensive, if attack'd.

The Patriots' organizing committees already expected the royal military to go after all the cannon that they were moving around, whether they were from harbor batteries, merchants' stores, or the train's gunhouses.

On September 19, Boston Patriots tried to smuggle out another set of old guns. With redcoat soldiers guarding the Neck and the

Royal Navy patrolling the ferry path at the mouth of the Charles, there were no easy routes out of town. Andrews described the attempt this way: "Last evening six or seven iron cannon were taken by some of the towns people from near Jno. Timmins' store, and put into a *mudscow*, or *Portsmouth pleasure boat*, with a view to carry up Cambridge river by way of the Mill Pond." The lawyer Benjamin Kent said "six good pieces of large cannon" were floated "in a gondola through the mill pond." Timmins was a Loyalist; it is possible those cannon were his property and Patriots stole them, but alternatively that "near Jno. Timmins' store," which meant in the area around Faneuil Hall, was a way of hiding their real owner.

The plan seems to have been to move those iron cannon into boats at night, row them across the pond to the dam that defined that body of water, and at high tide shift the vessel or the guns over the dam into the Charles above where the naval warship lay. Unfortunately, Andrews related, the tide did not lift the vessel high enough in the Mill Pond, so the boatsmen "were oblig'd to leave them there."

In the morning, the royal authorities spotted the boat with its heavy cargo. Andrews completed the story by saying that "the Admiral . . . sent a boat about 11 o'clock this forenoon and towed 'em along side his ship." Adm. Samuel Graves himself described the find in a report to his superiors:

> The people have lately attempted to remove several pieces of cannon by night and have actually carried off some from Charlestown and Boston, which they report are intended to fortify a camp in the country; and two or three days ago the boats of the *Preston* and *Lively* seized a flat with six good guns, 6-pounders, which were carrying up Charles River, I suppose for the above loyal purpose.

The Patriots must have been dismayed to lose "six good guns." Of course, other smuggling trips might have been more successful and left no mark on the historic record.

The arms race inside Boston threatened to turn violent on September 27, after merchant Joseph Scott sold a large stock of ordnance to the army. Craftsman Thomas Newell wrote that Scott's action had "given his countrymen great uneasiness," which was an understatement. Another observer reported:

> The Select Men and the Committee of Correspondence, sent for Mr. Scot, and told him he deserved immediate *Death*, for selling warlike Stores to the *Enemy*; and a Number of People instantly assembled to put this Sentence in Execution, but Mr. Scot was so fortunate as to make his Escape: his House however suffered very much before the People separated, at the Desire of the Select Men.

Andrews wrote that "ten cart-loads" of shot were taken away before townspeople leaned on the men driving those wagons and "forbid the carriers not to transport any more upon their peril."

The next morning at nine, "a company of the train" from the Boston militia regiment came to Scott's store to demand the rest of his artillery supplies. Members of the Boston committee of correspondence arrived to back them up. It seems likely that Thomas Crafts, lieutenant in the train and stalwart on the committee, led these visits. Now under pressure from both sides, Scott tried to bar anyone from touching his inventory. But Col. Samuel Cleaveland of the Royal Artillery came personally to complete the bargain, saying "he had it in orders from the General to take the remainder; and have them they must, at all events." Scott locked his cellar door, but an officer set a guard over it and went to the camp for more hands. Andrews wrote:

> When about noon, they came down with about 100 men and 8 or 10 officers, with a number of *fatigue men* with hand barrows, with about thirty tackled in one of their field carriages with a box fix'd on, when proceeded up the court and brought away about fifty or sixty cohorns. After which, they return'd with a carpenter, broke open the cellar door, and were constantly employ'd in carrying shot, &ca., till nearly sunset, which they reposited in the South battery. . . .

At that point, the only military material Scott had left was "two carriage guns," but the army simply made "two trips more." A deal was a deal.

Scott's Patriot neighbors were unforgiving. On the night of September 28, someone smeared his front door with the contents of the town's outhouses. "[N]ot content with disfiguring the outside of his shop," Andrews wrote, the vandals using "a ladder open'd his chamber window and emptied several buckets full into it." A man visiting Boston from the country called to Scott from across the street that "if he would come across the gutter, he would be the death of him, and think in so doing, he should do God service." The next day, Dr. Joseph Warren wrote that Scott "keeps incog."

In describing this episode to Samuel Adams, Warren wrote that the military authorities no longer respected private property: "They keep a constant search for every thing which will be serviceable in battle, and whenever they espy any instruments which may serve or disserve them, whether they are the property of individuals or of the publick is immaterial, they are seized and carried into the Camp or on board the Ships of war."

On the other hand, Col. Cleaveland kept insisting that the army had bought the ordnance fairly: in fact, he said, "Scott had repeatedly solicited them to take 'em."

Gen. Gage's frustration with the populace boiled over that night in a meeting with Dr. Warren. The doctor asked the general about the fortifications on the Neck, and "What is the Meaning that the General buys military Stores?" Gage reportedly replied:

> as the Country People were all armed, and collecting Cannon and Military Stores from all Quarters, which . . . could indicate nothing but their Intention of attacking his Majesty's Forces in that Town. . . . That it is notorious that many Cannon have been conveyed, notwithstanding the Works, from thence; and Arms are carried out openly, by every Man that goes out of Boston, without molestation.

The general went on to complain about how town leaders were encouraging people to block the building of barracks, and how townspeople were insulting soldiers, all the while complaining that they feared being attacked. The *New-York Gazette* reported on that meeting through "authentic Intelligence from Boston," but Boston's own newspapers published nothing about this encounter. The exchange, portraying the Patriots as bellicose and the royal government as ineffectual, fit neither side's preferred narrative of responding to events with stalwart rationality.

The confrontation outside Scott's store revealed fissures between Boston's official leaders and the citizenry. Some men had started to attack Scott's house in daylight, but the selectmen—though they had just told the merchant he deserved "immediate death"—ordered those men to stop. Publisher Joseph Greenleaf described the conflict to his brother-in-law, Robert Treat Paine: "It was difficult to still the clamors of the people on this accot. who would have destroyed him in the evening, had it not been for the Selectmen & our committee. . . . The spirits of the people both in town & country are so high that we are in danger of a rupture." Dr. Warren told Samuel Adams much the same: "it is as much our grave, serious people can effect to keep people from action at some particular times." Andrews perceived another division, between townspeople and visitors from the countryside: "The countrymen that happen'd to be in town, seem'd to be more enrag'd than the townspeople, whose passions were full high enough likewise."

There was also a split within the king's military. The Royal Navy was more aggressive about seizing weapons than the army, perhaps because its commanders were used to behaving imperiously once they were afloat. On September 29, Samuel Phillips of Andover was transporting a dozen muskets on the ferry to Charlestown. H.M.S. *Lively*, "lying in the river" at that spot, "dispatched a boat & seized" the guns. This is a rare example of the Crown forces seizing firelocks rather than artillery before the war. Anything on water seemed to be fair game for the navy. Phillips "waited on Captain [Thomas] Bishop to obtain a release of" his property, urged on by fellow Patriots who wanted to test the law, but he did not get the guns back.

In contrast to his naval colleagues, Gen. Gage was wary about seizing private property. His reluctance to use his own authority to take weapons from private hands lasted even through March 18, 1775, when Lt. Frederick Mackenzie recorded one incident:

> A Country man was Stopped at the Lines, going out of town with 19,000 ball Cartridges, which were taken from him. When liberated, he had the insolence to go to Head quarters to demand the redelivery of them. When asked who they were for, he said they were for his own use.

According to Andrews, that ammunition was "pack'd in candle boxes, consisting of 13,500 besides 4 boxes balls." The wagon driver "struggled hard before he would deliver 'em, and received two or three bad wounds"—all of which sounds suspicious.

The man who went to Gen. Gage demanding his ammunition back was Patriot activist Robert Pierpoint—the same man who had gotten into a dispute over soldiers taking firewood in 1769. The governor refused to return Pierpoint's property, but took pains to say that the ammunition had been impounded by "two Custom house Officers," not by the army or the provincial government. The Customs service could justify seizing ammunition on the ground that by that time the London government had banned imports of gunpowder and other military supplies into the colonies. Pierpoint reportedly had the last word, saying those bullets "were the last parcel of a large quantity which he had carried out at different times"—a warning to Gage that the rural militia was already well armed.

William Molineux, the hot-tempered hardware merchant and leading Patriot, apparently shipped some artillery out of town in October. According to a July 1776 petition to the Massachusetts General Court from another hardware dealer, Joseph Webb, he sold Molineux "four double-fortified nine pounders, and four four-pounders," which were "sent into the Country, and were in actual service in 1775." In renewing his petition the next year, Webb raised his count of the cannon by one. The first legislative committee chosen to evaluate Webb's petition included a man who was part of the network that handled the Provincial Congress's artillery. The disposition of Webb's petition is unclear, but the legislature trusted him enough to promote him to high ranks in the Boston militia regiment in 1778 and 1780. As for Molineux, he still had "2 Swivel Guns" and "4 Cohorns" or mortars in his shop on October 22 when he unexpectedly died. If he had meant those weapons for the Patriots, they never made it out of town.

It is possible that John Hancock also shipped some artillery out of Boston. In 1779 the Massachusetts legislature "passed a resolve for paying the Hon. John Hancock, Esq; eighteen hundred pounds, in full for eight four-pound cannon, taken at the beginning of the contest for the public use." Unfortunately, this reference is so vague that it is impossible to say when Hancock supplied those weapons and whether they were ever in Boston. They might, for instance, have been on ships he owned sailing out of Marblehead.

Another leading Boston merchant was caught up in the arms race without even being in town: Thomas Cushing, then in Philadelphia as one of Massachusetts's delegates to the Continental Congress. In mid-October, the town was galvanized by yet more news about cannon: a ship was bringing twelve new fieldpieces from England. Gen. Gage asked Adm. Graves to watch for the ship *Thomas*, "to look out for and stop said Vessel before She gets into Marblehead, and to take the said Field Pieces out of her and secure them for his Majesty's Service." The Massachusetts House had voted to buy these in 1773 through Cushing, who was both the Speaker of the House and the province's commissary-general. But that usually reliable Whig had not passed along all the funds. The manufacturer was therefore sending the guns to Sir William Pepperrell, a Loyalist Council member whom he trusted for full payment.

From Braintree, Col. Josiah Quincy wrote to his son, "The Reputation of our Friend Mr. C——g is greatly, and I fear deservedly suffering, on Account of his applying the money he received out of the Treasury, to be remitted for the brass Cannon, to the Discharge of his private Obligations." Fortunately for Cushing, the man who was to supply those cannon decided "that without Lord North's permission they could not be shipped." Since the guns never left Britain, the provincial commissary was never responsible for having them sent right into the royal authorities' hands. Still, in April 1775 a Loyalist could make a piercing allusion to this incident by calling Cushing "A dealer in cannon and other warlike stores."

As September came to a close, Gov. Gage tried to convey the scope of the difficulties he was facing. He sent his bluntest report yet to the secretary of war, Viscount Barrington:

> Affairs here are worse that even in the Time of the Stamp-Act, I don't mean in Boston, for throughout the Country. The New England Provinces, except part of New Hampshire, are I may say in Arms, and the Question is now not whether you shall quell Disturbances in Boston, but whether those Provinces shall be conquered, and I find it is the General Resolution of all the Continent to support the Massachusett's Bay in their Opposition to the late Acts. From Appearances no People are more determined for a Civil War, the whole Country from hence to New York armed, training and providing Military Stores.

All that activity was taking place in a month when most of Massachusetts had no effective government above the level of town meetings. The governor had started September with a quick seizure of gunpowder and cannon and an announcement to convene a new General Court session on October 5. But one week before that date, Gage had to issue a new proclamation acknowledging the new reality: given the "many tumults and disorders" of the past month, the "extraordinary resolves" of the county conventions, and the "disordered and unhappy state of the province," the governor deemed it "highly inexpedient that a great and general court should be convened" in October after all. He held out hope that "a session at some more distant day will best tend to promote his majesty's service and the good of the province." He excused any gentleman already elected to that legislative session from attending.

Massachusetts's Patriot politicians had anticipated the possibility that Gage would rescind his original proclamation. The county conventions had already called for towns to elect delegates to a provincial congress in case the General Court never met. Many town meetings had chosen two sets of representatives or instructed their legislators to attend whichever gathering turned out to take place. Such a province-wide gathering of town representatives without the governor's approval was expressly forbidden by the Massachusetts Government Act. This assembly went beyond skirting that law with county conventions and town meetings adjourned to future dates, or trying to hinder its implementation by closing courts and intimidating Councilors. Depending on how one viewed the situation, the Provincial Congress was either an illegal shadow legislature or the rebuilding of a legitimate Massachusetts government from the bottom up.

Under Massachusetts's official charter, most towns were invited to send two representatives to each General Court. Very small towns, with fewer than 120 voters, could send only one and did not have to send any. In many places, especially those farthest from Boston, the inhabitants might have trouble convincing a gentleman to leave his farm, or balk at paying that gentleman's expenses. Most towns therefore sent a single representative. If a town of moderate size sent no one at all, it was supposed to pay a fine, but that penalty was never levied. As a result, only about two-thirds of the towns participated in a typical General Court before the Revolutionary turmoil.

In contrast, over 180 Massachusetts towns were represented at the first meeting of the Provincial Congress in Salem on October 7, 1774, with only 21 towns listing as having sent no delegate. There was no cap on the number of men who might represent a town in the Provincial Congress, so several towns sent three or more delegates. All told, there were 293 men at the first congress, about twice the legislature's usual number. In other words, even though towns had been legally obligated to represent themselves in the General Court, many chose not to. Even though towns had no legal obligation to this new Provincial Congress, many more chose to participate, in defiance of the law, the general, and Parliament. The Provincial Congress was thus a more representative, broader-based body than the preceding legislatures.

The Massachusetts Patriots thus had an organization with the political legitimacy to become a government. Elected representatives could take over the task of organizing a military force from unknown men working at night—if those genteel leaders were ready to take the risks. But many were reluctant. Reconvening in Concord on October 11 and Cambridge on October 17, the Provincial Congress instead engaged in a high-level epistolary exchange with the royal governor about who was doing more to undermine Massachusetts's charter.

When the congress started to discuss stronger measures, delegates thought that was so potentially treasonous that they voted to debate in private. The Patriot politicians wanted to be sure people did not perceive them as rushing to war. They still held out hope that British voters would force a change in Parliament, bringing more sympathetic ministers to power. And if the Crown continued to use force, Massachusetts needed the support of the other North American colonies to resist.

Finally, on October 20, while also discussing a public thanksgiving and a total end to drinking tea, the Provincial Congress named a committee to "consider what is necessary to be now done for the defence and safety of the province."

Seven

"Out of Boston to Some Place in the Country"

While the Provincial Congress considered how to preserve the safety of the colony, several Massachusetts towns were already arming themselves with cannon. Since this required expending money, that was quite a major step.

One of the first to start gathering military supplies was Wrentham, on the Rhode Island border. Selectmen there had checked the local powder house on August 29 after scheduling a town meeting in defiance of the Massachusetts Government Act and asking people to "appear under arms" in case anyone tried to interfere. But their stock of gunpowder was far short of what they expected. Starting on September 1, the town advertised a reward for information about who had taken "six half Barrels of POWDER, with about thirteen Hundred Flints, and some Lead."

The army's seizure of gunpowder in Charlestown and the fortification of Boston confirmed fears in Wrentham that some parties were up to no good, so the townspeople quickly took their military preparation to the next level. On September 15 they voted to buy two cannon "of the size and bigness most proper and beneficial for the town." The town also found a gunpowder supplier because by May 1775 Wrentham was known to be "well stocked" with that commodity.

In central Massachusetts, Lancaster voted on September 5 to "raise fifty pounds, for to buy ammunition with, to be a town stock." Later that month the town decided to "buy one field piece for the use of the town," and on the 28th, at the same meeting in which the townspeople agreed to send a delegate to the Provincial Congress, they raised their cannon order to "two field pieces instead of one." By December, those guns must have arrived because Lancaster authorized a further expenditure: "to buy 5 hundred wt. of ball suitable for the field pieces."

Lancaster's neighbor Worcester already had some cannon, but they were not mounted in carriages and thus not ready for action. A September 26 town meeting chose a three-man "Comittee To Provide Carriages for four Cannon." It appears that committee arranged for five cannon to be brought out from Boston. On October 17 the town agreed to pay Jonathan Rice and Jonathan Stone a total of £4.12s.10d. for their "time trouble and Expenses in geting the Cannon out of Boston," and £4.13s.4d. to three other men for carting that ordnance from Brookline.

Worcester's five cannon came in two sizes: "three Small" and "two large." The bigger pair would require bigger carriages as well as more gunpowder and heavier shot. The town decided to purchase carriage "for but three (Viz) the three Small Cannon" at a cost of £38 and instructed its committee to "provide timber directly for the two large Cannon." As expenses mounted, however, and the danger people felt in September faded, Worcester voters looked for ways to cut their costs. On November 1 they declined to "purchase ammunition and Shot for ye Cannon," and on January 3 they instructed their selectmen to "dispose of the two Largest Cannon belonging to the Town to some one or other Neighbouring Town."

Closer to Boston, the men of Framingham voted to buy five barrels of gunpowder and five hundred pounds of "bullets or lead" on September 9, and then on September 30 "to purchase a chest of 25 Fire Arms, and two field pieces, of such size as the Committee shall judge proper." On October 3, Cambridge empowered its selectmen "to procure a carriage for the cannon belonging to the town, to purchase another cannon, and to furnish powder and balls for both." Evidently Cambridge had one cannon already, but it was not ready for use. Two weeks later, Watertown voted to mount the "two pieces of Cannon now lodged in the Town." The wording of that item suggests that these artillery pieces, later referred to as "Great Guns," were new arrivals, perhaps removed from batteries around Boston harbor the month before.

On October 13, two days after the Massachusetts Provincial Congress convened in Concord, "Several cannon were purchased and brought" to the town, according to local historian Lemuel Shattuck. On October 24 Concord's voters instructed their selectmen to have those guns mounted and authorized paying £120 for 25 four-pound balls, 200 pounds of grapeshot, and 392 pounds of powder.

Some of those four-pounders came from Concord resident Duncan Ingraham, who in 1778 petitioned the legislature "that he may be paid for four Four-pound Cannon, which were taken for the public Service in *October* 1774." Ingraham was a merchant captain who had settled in Concord with his new wife just the year before. Those cannon might therefore have been property left over from his maritime career. Ingraham was not a Patriot. He refused to participate in boycotts of British imports, he was ready to hold court sessions as a justice of the peace, and he hosted British army officers at dinner. The people of Concord showed their disapproval of this new arrival by hanging a sheep's head and guts on his chaise. They also confiscated his property: on January 3, 1775, Dr. Joseph Lee wrote in his diary, "The mob unloaded Capt. Ingraham's Bords that were to go to Boston," where they might have been used by the army to build barracks. It seems likely that the community seized Ingraham's four cannon for the public good.

A comprehensive look at local records could find other New England communities taking similar initiatives. Still, the military effect was probably limited. All of the cannon that Massachusetts towns collected were iron, probably old guns that had been shipped and trucked across many miles during previous wars. Most needed work before they were ready for use on a battlefield, and even then they would not have been as maneuverable as the Royal Artillery's brass fieldpieces. Nonetheless, the fact that so many thrifty New England towns were ready to spend money on cannon showed how they valued military power.

The Provincial Congress sitting in Concord slowly caught up. On October 24, the congress chose a five-man committee to suggest the "most proper time for this Province to Provide a stock of Powder, Ordnance, and Ordnance Stores." That committee included Jeremiah Lee and Azor Orne of Marblehead, Joseph Palmer of Braintree, Josiah Batchelder of Beverly, and Zephaniah Keith of Easton. Four of those gentlemen were designated by their militia titles. Four came from seaside towns in eastern Massachusetts, places most likely to have artillery or be able to bring in supplies from other ports. Realizing what a dangerous step they were taking, the congress voted to keep all their discussions secret just before they called that committee back in to report. Lee and his committee then stated that "the proper time" to start building an artillery force was *now*.

The congress added four more militia officers to that committee: Thomas Gardner of Cambridge (who had been at the Powder Alarm on September 2), William Heath of Roxbury, James Warren of Plymouth, and Seth Pomeroy of Northampton. Their assignment was to draw up a shopping list of cannon, gunpowder, and other artillery supplies, and a budget. The next afternoon they presented their recommendation: sixteen mounted three-pounders, four mounted six-pounders, four mortars, carriages for twelve battering cannon (which the province presumably already possessed), tons of shot, bombshells, and more. The price: £1,737. Plus £8,000 of gunpowder.

The Provincial Congress did not flinch at that large sum. Its members voted to add £11,000 for muskets, bayonets, and flints. The legislature justified this bold step with a report that said, in part:

> his excellency General Gage . . . has fortified against the country the capital of the province, and thus greatly endangered the lives, liberties and properties of its oppressed citizens; invaded private property, by unlawfully seizing and retaining large quantities of ammunition in the arsenal at Boston, and sundry pieces of ordnance in the same town; committed to the custody of his troops, the arms, ammunition, ordnance, and warlike stores of all sorts, provided at the public expense for the use of the province; and by all possible means endeavored to place the province entirely in a defenceless state; at the same time having neglected and altogether disregarded the assurances from this Congress of the pacific disposition of the inhabitants of the province.

Despite that "pacific disposition," the congress was preparing for war.

On October 27 the body designated members to carry out its plans. The commissaries responsible for gathering that equipment would be David Cheever of Charlestown, Moses Gill of Princeton, Lee of Marblehead, Benjamin Lincoln of Hingham, and Benjamin Hall of Medford. Those men were also referred to as the "committee for supplies." The committee of safety to direct the new military started with three Bostonians—John Hancock, Dr. Joseph Warren, and Dr. Benjamin Church—joined by Palmer, Orne, Richard Devens of Charlestown (another figure at the Powder Alarm), and three others. The congress appointed three generals.

The next day, the Provincial Congress turned to how to pay for all its plans, choosing a "receiver general" who would be the Massachusetts treasurer in all but name. After the first choice declined, the delegates chose Henry Gardner of the small Middlesex County town of Stow. They recommended that all towns in the colony direct taxes to him instead of to the royal treasurer in Boston. On October 29, the legislature recommended that militia companies hold elections for officers, shaking any remaining Loyalists out of command roles. By making a claim on the public revenue stream and military authority, the Provincial Congress took its last steps to become Massachusetts's government. Then the body adjourned for nearly a month.

The job of collecting military supplies came with several big challenges. Those commissaries did not yet have public cash for pay for anything. There was a limited supply and increasing demand. If they arranged for goods to be brought in by sea, their ships would have to evade the Royal Navy and the customs service. Any material in Boston had to be smuggled out past the army. And if the royal authorities caught those men, they could be charged with the most serious of crimes. For example, the congress authorized Dr. Warren, Dr. Church, and Heath "to take care of, and lodge in some safe place in the country, the warlike stores now in the commissary general's office, and that the matter be conducted with the greatest secrecy." Exactly how was still a question.

With the congress adjourned, the committee of safety and committee of supplies met together at a tavern in Cambridge on November 8, wisely deciding that they should "procure all the arms and ammunition they can, at the neighboring provinces." Bringing material across the borders, far from any redcoat soldiers, would be easy. A week later in Charlestown the committees faced a tougher hurdle: the merchant William Powell, a mildly active Patriot, had "seven large pieces of cannon" available in Boston. The delegates voted that Moses Gill should buy those guns "on the best terms he can," and work with Benjamin Hall "to get them out of Boston to some place in the country, in such manner as they may think most prudent."

The next day, evidence suggests, the committee of supplies appointed an artillerist "as the most proper person to collect materials and military stores, for the defence of the country." The members living on Cape Ann approached David Mason, the painter who had co-founded Boston's artillery train more than a decade before. Mason's appointment was not entered into the committee's record, no doubt for his safety. The first time Mason's name appeared in those papers was when the committee summoned likely artillery officers on April 21, 1775, but that entry listed him as being "upon furlough"—and therefore already in service in some way. When Mason died in 1794, within the lifetime of some committee members, Boston newspapers referred to his duties gathering military supplies, so people accepted that history.

Furthermore, Mason left a small notebook, bound in green leather and now held together with stitches and pins, in which he calculated his pay from when he "Entered the Service as [of] 16th Novr. 1774." The notebook recorded payments from David Cheever and the "Treasury," as well as "Mr. [Benjamin] Hall," "Colo. [Jeremiah] Lee," and "Mr. [Elbridge] Gerry," added to the committee of supplies on February 9, 1775.

Another man who paid Mason was "Capt. [Richard] Derby" of Salem. Mason's relationship with the Derby family had begun even before he left Boston. When the painter considered moving out in June 1764, a merchant wrote a letter of reference for him to Richard Derby, Sr. This captain had made a small fortune on trading voyages to Spain and its islands (which was, of course, mostly illegal) before settling as a merchant in 1757. His namesake son, born in 1736, followed his father to sea and then into business, but he also went into politics. Richard Derby, Jr., co-sponsored the launch of the *Essex Gazette* newspaper in 1768, represented Salem in the General Court starting in 1769, and took a seat on the Massachusetts Council in 1773. As Massachusetts's confrontation with the Crown intensified, Richard, Jr., became a member of Salem's committee of correspondence and was bold in defying Gen. Gage during the confrontation over Salem's town meeting in August 1774, as described in Chapter 1.

David Mason had reestablished himself as a craftsman in Salem in 1770. Aged forty-eight, with a wife and six surviving children, he did "all kinds of painting, japanning, varnishing and gilding"; papered rooms; glazed windows; and painted chaises and coaches. When the province's conflict with the British ministry heated up, Mason became active on Salem's political committees. He helped to enforce the tea boycott, confiscating "2 large chests" of the commodity and giving "the school boys . . . much amusement in burning it on the Common."

Mason also developed an interest in "the newly discovered Electrical Fire," or electricity. He presented lectures on the topic in Boston in 1765, in Portsmouth the following January, and finally in Salem in 1771 "At his Dwelling-House near the North Bridge." For the small admission price, usually just one pistareen, an attendee could learn such lessons as "That the Electric Fire is a real Element . . . That it doth not take up any perceptible Time in passing thro' large Portions of Space . . . That our Bodies at all Times contain enough of it to set an House on Fire." They could witness such marvels as "An artificial Spider, animated by the Electric Fire, so as to act like a live One"; "A Leaf of the most weighty of Metals suspended in the Air"; "Fire darting from a Lady's Lips, so that she may defy any Person to salute her"; and "A Battery of eleven Guns discharged by Fire issuing out of a Person's Finger." These demonstrations probably gave Mason a reputation for ingenuity, a quality the committee of supplies needed.

Mason's daughter Susan Smith wrote a memoir of him in June 1842 and sat for an interview that November. They vividly preserve the experiences of an eleven-year-old girl working at home while her father handles mysterious and risky business for the Provincial Congress. Susan feared for her father's safety and her mother's health. She resented neighbors' insinuations and snooping as her family toiled in locked rooms, sewing "5000" gunpowder cartridges for cannon. Because young Susan never accompanied her father on trips away from Salem, however, her descriptions of those activities are less reliable.

Smith stated that her father visited Boston in late 1774 on Provincial Congress business. He may have made that trip, but his daughter was not privy to what he did in the capital. It seems reasonable to suspect that Mason hoped to contact people who possessed cannon, particularly the four that belonged to Boston's militia train. It would be only natural for him to visit his old master: Capt. John Gore. Perhaps he and that painter's son Sam chatted about why the train had disbanded. Mason was also acquainted with Samuel Holbrook, his son's former writing teacher, who had helped to hide two of the company's cannon from the army.

Mason's visit, coming just weeks after four brass cannon vanished, would have raised suspicions in people on the other side of the political divide, like his old colleague Paddock. In March 1842 Mason's daughter wrote that he had to race to the Charlestown ferry just ahead of eight soldiers, and "never dared venture into the town [of Boston] again till the British left it." In a November interview, Smith stated that Mason also took the train's two brass cannon from a stable under guard "in the upper part of Main Street" out to Roxbury in a wagon filled with manure. She had mentioned no such activity months earlier, however, and the story has some holes in it—starting with how Boston had no Main Street. That claim therefore seems unreliable.

Mason's family also understood that in the fall of 1774 he "went with Gen. Lincoln to Simsbury in Connecticut, and contracted for the casting of four thousand cannon balls." Simsbury was the site of an abandoned copper mine converted into a prison and thus an unlikely source for shot. However, there was an active iron forge at Salisbury, Connecticut, and Benjamin Lincoln was on Massachusetts's committee of supplies, so a trip to that town is plausible.

There is no doubt that David Mason was gathering cannon for the Massachusetts Provincial Congress in the winter of 1774–75. His small green notebook shows how he systematically catalogued a collection of artillery pieces, including mortars and cannon of three-, four-, six-, nine-, and twelve-pound caliber. One page, for instance, preserves the "Marks & Number of Guns sent of[f]" to Cambridge on April 22, 1775:

M	No. 1		3¶
D	No. 3	}	
D	No. 5	} Capt Derbys	3¶
S	No. 7	Salem	3¶
S	No. 1	Salem	4¶

(Mason used a stylized P, rendered here as ¶, to mean "pounder.") Another page is headed "Dimensions of Capt Derby Guns," showing that the Derby family supplied Mason with ordnance as well as cash. Yet another gives the "Dimensions of Salem 12 ¶—No. 1,2,3,4." These guns became part of Massachusetts's new artillery force.

The Provincial Congress was not the only New England legislature taking control of artillery. On December 8, the Rhode Island assembly voted to remove almost all the cannon from Fort George off Newport. The Providence militia led by Joseph Nightingale netted "six twenty-four Pounders, eighteen eighteen Pounders, fourteen six Pounders, and six four Pounders [that] formerly belonged to a Providence Sloop." They left behind only "two eighteen-pounders and one six-pounder." In addition, the assembly voted to buy four brass cannon for a new "Train of Artillery, in the County of Providence"; its second-in-command was John Crane, a member of Paddock's company who had left Boston after helping to destroy the East India Company tea.

Five days later, the people of New London, Connecticut, moved their battery cannon "into the Country," just as the people of Charlestown had done three months earlier. As in Newport, the ostensible reason for moving that artillery inland was fear that the French and Indians would swoop down from Canada. In reality, Rhode Island governor Joseph Wanton "very frankly" told Capt. James Wallace of the Royal Navy, the Newport fort was stripped of guns "to prevent their falling into the *hands of the King.*"

Back in Boston, on December 12 Patriots saw signs that a Royal Navy ship was preparing to sail to Portsmouth, where New Hampshire maintained Fort William and Mary. The next day, Paul Revere rode sixty miles on icy roads with that warning. New Hampshire militiamen stormed the fort, overwhelmed the six soldiers inside, and seized most of the gunpowder in its storehouse. The Portsmouth action was the boldest and most dangerous confrontation between Crown and Patriots yet. The militia companies acted in daylight, not at night. For the first time, British regulars fired back at American units: Capt. John Cochran reported shooting "three four pounders." Fortunately, no one was hit. In another sign of rising enmity, New Hampshire's elected politicians did not express regret about the takeover of the fort or hush it up. Rather, militia units went back two days later to take cannon and ammunition. And the leaders of that enterprise included New Hampshire's two Continental Congress delegates, John Sullivan and Nathaniel Folsom.

What happened in Portsmouth harbor was armed rebellion. Had anyone died there, it would certainly be considered the start of the

Revolutionary War. People in other colonies and in Britain would have read about local militia regiments attacking a vastly outnumbered squad of the king's soldiers to seize weapons. The Patriots would then have had a much harder time making the case that they were merely defending their homes and property, that they were not the aggressors.

Back in Massachusetts, the Patriots were still gathering artillery as quietly as possible. In the new year, the Massachusetts committees of safety and supplies claimed ownership of the Boston train's four brass cannon. On January 5, 1775, the committees of safety and supplies voted that Dr. Warren

> wait on Col. Robinson, to desire him to deliver to any person Deacon [David] Cheever shall send, two brass cannon, and two seven inch mortars and beds, and that Mr. William Dawes be desired to deliver to said Cheever, one pair of brass cannon, and that the said Cheever procure carriages for said cannon, or any other cannon that require them.

"Col. Robinson" was Lemuel Robinson, commander of a Suffolk County artillery company and proprietor of the Liberty Tree tavern "near the Lower Mills, in Dorchester." He was thirty-nine-years-old, married with eight children and at least one slave. His new military title had been conferred in the recent militia election. Robinson was also one of Dorchester's delegates to the Provincial Congress. He knew all the political leaders in Boston, his tavern having hosted the big 1769 Sons of Liberty banquet described in Chapter 4. As Paddock's equivalent for a part of the county beyond British military control, Robinson was an appropriate custodian for Boston's artillery. Euphemistic tradition held that the missing cannon were stored at his tavern "under a compost heap."

"Mr. William Dawes" was a twenty-nine-year-old tanner who was active in Boston's militia regiment: in 1772 he was a "Junr. Adjut. [with] Lieuts. Rank." Clearly the committee of safety and supplies believed that he knew where to find two of Paddock's brass cannon in January 1775. Thus, it seems likely that Dawes had either participated in stealing the first pair of the train's cannon or served as liaison between the men who held those guns and the Patriot leadership.

According to one of Dawes's daughters, while helping to carry away two of the train's cannon, "my father accidentally received a painful injury, his sleeve-button getting imbedded in his wrist: for some days he did not venture to seek surgical aid, lest suspicion should at once attach to him." Finally the pain was too much. "He did not dare to show the injured wrist to any one but Dr. Warren," wrote a granddaughter. The physician examined the tanner's wound and asked, "Dawes, how and when was this done?" Dawes refused to answer. Guessing the truth, Warren said, "You are right not to tell me. I had better not know." But the doctor had figured out Dawes's secret. Whether or not that story was true, in January 1775 Warren went to the tanner with the Provincial Congress's request to deliver "one pair of brass cannon" to David Cheever.

By that point more British army regiments had arrived in Boston, meaning that soldiers far outnumbered adult males. The town was also home to a growing number of bitter Loyalists. In particular, there was a Royal Navy veteran in his sixties named Edward Stow. He owned three houses and a wharf at the south end of Orange Street, the last buildings inside Boston before the army fortifications on the Neck. That was in the same neighborhood as Obadiah Whiston's forge, where two of the train's brass guns were stashed. Stow became "the person appointed by Authority to Examine the Carriages going out of Town for Arms and Ammunition." He later told the Loyalists Commission that he had "seized for His Majesty Two Gun Carriages, a Pair of Swivels, and a Cowhorn" or mortar being smuggled out of town in the spring of 1775. In response, on April 3 angry Patriots splashed his house with "Excrement and Feathers." Any artillery leaving Boston would have to get past Edward Stow.

Or around him. According to William Tudor, the pair of brass cannon stolen by Samuel Gore and company and then hidden in Whiston's forge "were put into a boat in the night, and safely transported within the American lines." Unfortunately, Tudor offered no other details. Those guns were probably at Robinson's tavern by the end of the year.

The older pair of brass cannon, the biographer said, lay "concealed in the stable . . . on the south side of Court Street"—called Queen Street in 1775. Sometime in January, "Mr. Williams, a respectable farmer of Roxbury, drove in his own team with a load of hay, which was taken into that stable; the cannon were then put in the bottom of the cart, which was loaded with manure, and in this way they were taken out of town without opposition." There was quite a respectable farmer in Roxbury named Joseph Williams. His daughter Abigail had raised Mehitable, William Dawes's wife.

Still another story, told publicly on July 4, 1835, credited the nineteen-year-old Dorchester farmer George Minot with transporting two four-pounder cannon out of Boston in separate trips "with an ox-team for offals." Lemuel Robinson's wife was born Jerusha Minot, so she may have been related to this farmer. The local historian F. S. Drake, recording or combining local traditions a century after the events, reported that Minot carried two of the Boston train's cannon to Robinson's tavern, along with a quantity of gunpowder, while Jonathan Parker of Roxbury drove out the other two and "deposited them in Muddy Pond Woods." Or, rather, that story gave credit to Minot even though he stated that the driver—the man who risked being caught with stolen artillery while Minot "purposely kept out of the way"—was his family's "colored servant" Cuffee. African day-names such as Cuffee ("born on Friday") were common for enslaved laborers in colonial times, but lost popularity among free black Americans in the early republic. Therefore, the nineteenth-century chronicler who referred to the Minots' driver as Cuffee may simply have been cueing his readers into picturing a generic male slave from Massachusetts's Revolutionary period, not a specific individual.

One more man who claimed to have smuggled artillery for the provincial forces was James Brewer, a pump and block maker about thirty-years-old in 1774. He had been at both the Massacre and the Tea Party. Soon after the war began, the British military confined Brewer on board a Royal Navy ship for unrecorded reasons, then exchanged him and eight other men for some of the British officers and soldiers captured during the retreat from Concord. In July 1775, Brewer joined the Massachusetts artillery regiment. During the war he helped transport specie from Boston to York, Pennsylvania, and served on a privateer. Clearly, James Brewer was willing to take risks for the Patriot cause.

Brewer's confession to artillery-smuggling took the odd form of an invoice dated "Aug. 12, 1783" to the United States, asking to be paid £30 for transporting two "6-inch brass mortars, taken from the British troops when the town of Boston was shut up, & carrid over to Dorcester" in 1775. Brewer's descendants showed this document to members of the Massachusetts Historical Society in 1863 but did not donate it, so the location of the original is unknown. Brewer's invoice was not contemporaneous with the actions he claimed to have done. There is no evidence that the U.S. of A. honored it, or even that he sent it. He obviously had a financial motive for writing out that claim. And yet this poorly supported story cannot be dismissed. In January 1775 two brass mortars were indeed hidden alongside two cannon at Robinson's tavern in Dorchester.

The work to secure almost all that ordnance was not a top-down operation. Men stole, hid, or even smuggled artillery pieces before the Massachusetts Provincial Congress gave instructions to do so. There is no sign that Boston's political leaders knew about the raids on the Charlestown battery and their own town's two gunhouses until after those events had occurred. Indeed, many of the men who had set the Whigs' political strategy for years were not even in town during the crucial weeks of September 1774.

At times, in fact, the people working to collect artillery supplies were at odds with political leaders, as in the conflict outside Joseph Scott's shop. James Brewer reported not only smuggling mortars but burgling Richard Boynton, a deacon and member of the Boston committee of correspondence, to secure 500 pickaxes for the provincial army. "He not being able to get them out of town," Brewer wrote on his invoice, "I, under cover a dark night, broke open the back of his smith's shop, took them, and car[rie]d them out to our army at the risque of my life."

The men who spirited those artillery pieces away from the royal authorities took the initiative on their own, based on a desire to keep weapons they had paid for and tended. The thieves we can identify were men in their twenties and early thirties, some active in politics and the militia but not yet leaders in either area. They were mechanics and farmers, not professionals or sons of the elite. They needed the physical skills and strength to move heavy battery cannon and to break through the wall of Boston's old gunhouse. The South Writing School where the three-pounders were hidden was not a grammar school but a school for boys who hoped to run shops or counting offices.

An even more varied swath of the people appear to have participated in removing the cannon from Boston. That effort depended on militiamen and selectmen, merchants and mechanics, ship captains and farmers, husbands and wives, boys in school and girls at home, and possibly both slave owners and slaves. People seem to have undertaken the riskiest steps through family networks to maintain secrecy and through such close-knit groups as the militia train, but eventually the effort rested on trusting people one did not know. Gathering artillery was not a public event like the tea meetings of late 1773 or the militia alarm on September 2, but it was nonetheless a collective act.

Outside Boston, people could debate the question of mounting and equipping cannon in open town meetings. The most fervent Patriots still outran traditional leaders. In north Braintree (and perhaps Wrentham) rank-and-file Whigs secured the powder supply without waiting for town selectmen or militia commanders. Several towns voted to mount fieldpieces before the Provincial Congress took the same action. As many historians have noted, by late 1774 Massachusetts's urban political elite was damping the passions of the rural populace, not stoking them.

Soon after the towns' elected representatives had formed a new government in the Provincial Congress, however, the people involved in cannon-stealing accepted its authority. The men hiding guns cooperated with agents of the committees of safety and supplies. Turning over the cannon to the congress made sense to Boston mechanics for more than tactical reasons. It was the logical outcome of their justification for having taken those cannon in the first place. Samuel Gore described his group's motivation as "to secure for the country a property which belonged to it." They took the fieldpieces from British appointees and handed them over to the people's representatives.

Around the end of January 1775, all four brass fieldpieces from Paddock's company and those two mortars were under the care of Lemuel Robinson in Dorchester. Eventually those guns became the responsibility of David Mason. On the third page of his green notebook he had made a table listing several cannon, from three to twenty-four pounders, and at the bottom he added:

> 2 Brass 2¶ . . .
>
> 2 d[itt]o. 3 ¶
>
> 2 d[itt]o 6 1/4 mortars

The Provincial Congress now had control of the Boston train's artillery.

According to William Tudor, the evening after the two-pounders had been moved from their hiding-place on Queen Street, soldiers "patrolled the street for several hours." One of Dr. Joseph Warren's medical students, William Eustis, warned him not to go out among the redcoats lest he be arrested. The doctor calmly repeated to Eustis that they had an appointment, pocketed his pistols, and walked out with the young man. If this story is accurate, Warren had the advantage of knowing the cannon were safe outside town.

A few days later, however, the doctor heard unsettling news: the blacksmith Obadiah Whiston was switching sides.

Left: Gen. Thomas Gage, longtime commander of the British army in North America, arrived in Boston in May 1774 with an additional job: Massachusetts's new royal governor. He had personally promised King George III and his ministers in London that he would enforce Parliament's tough new measures. Right: Only thirty-three years old as spring 1775 began, Dr. Joseph Warren was far from Boston's senior resistance organizer. But with Samuel Adams, John Hancock, and Thomas Cushing at the Continental Congress; Dr. Thomas Young leaving town; William Molineux dying; James Otis mad; and James Bowdoin ill, more and more responsibilities fell on the shoulders of Warren and Dr. Benjamin Church. (*Library of Congress*)

Boston Harbor was crowded with Royal Navy ships in 1774, according to this engraving by Paul Revere. Below the word "Boston" in the banner are Fort Hill and the South Battery. Under "Ships," Long Wharf juts out. Under "Harbour" is the North Battery. (*Anne S. K. Brown Collection, Brown University Library*)

Boston Common was the site of town militia drills, but in 1774 it became a British army campsite. At the left of this view by Christian Remick is the town powderhouse. John Hancock's mansion stands at the upper right, in front of the beacon on Beacon Hill. The line of elms at the bottom led to the "Paddock Elms," named after Adino Paddock, who watched over them from his nearby coach-making yard. (*New York Public Library*)

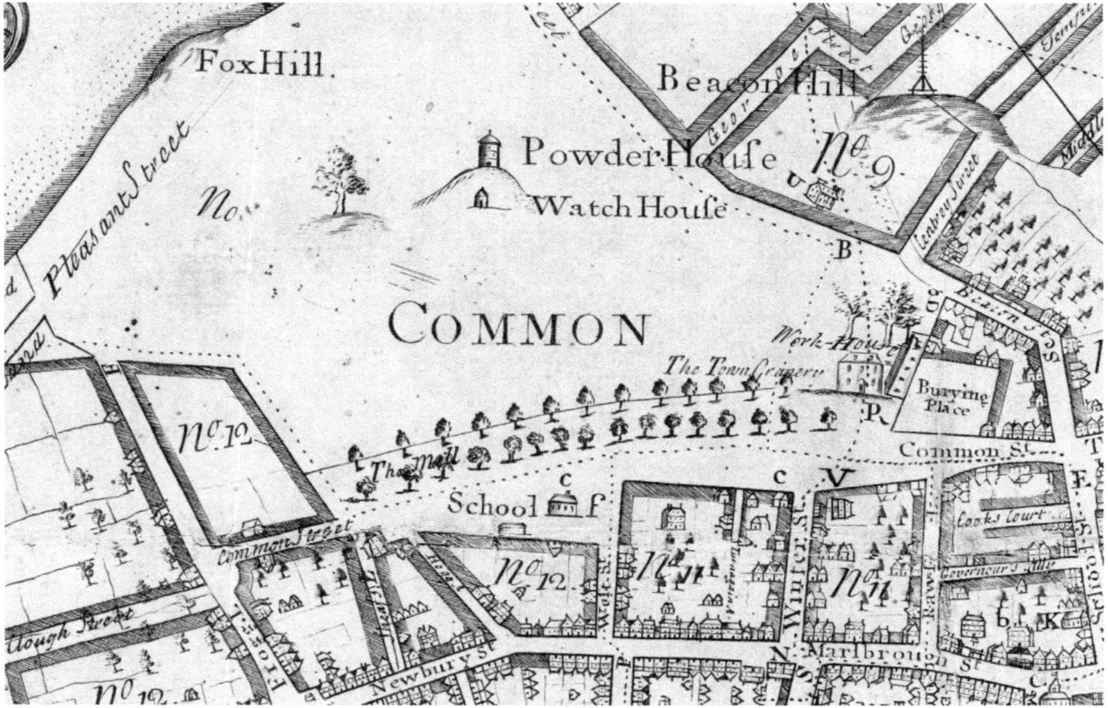

Near the center of this portion of the 1769 map of Boston is the South Writing School, built alongside the Common. Because this map was printed from an engraving originally made in 1722, it does not show the militia gunhouse that shared a fenced yard with that school. (*Library of Congress*)

Thomas Dawes's plan for a new militia gunhouse in 1768 called for a door in the front, facing the Common, and a door three times as wide on the right side. In September 1774 the British army stationed sentries on the street to ensure the two small brass cannon inside did not disappear. (*Boston Public Library*)

John Norman's frontispiece for a 1779 American edition of John Muller's *Treatise on Artillery* shows cannon and mortars mounted on standard military carriages. (*Library of Congress*)

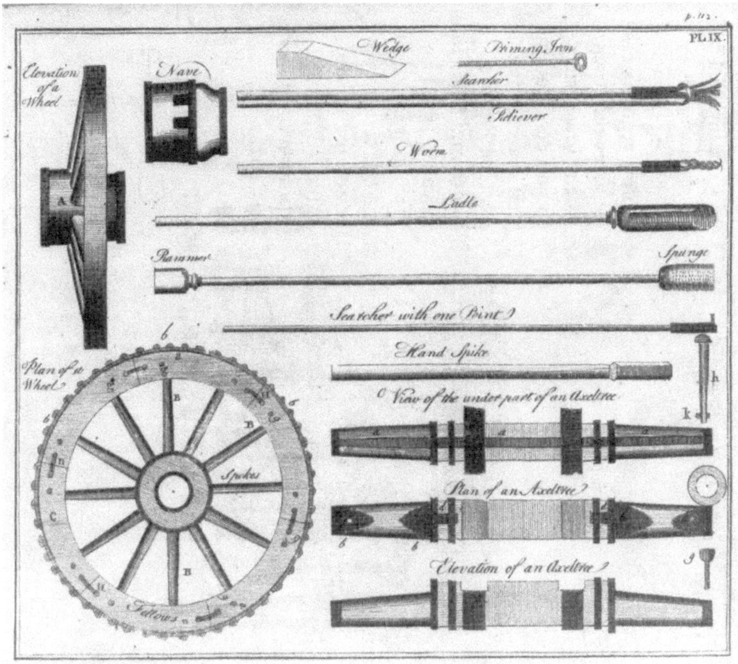

In addition to sturdy carriages, cannon required a variety of tools to fire and maintain them—a challenge for blacksmiths, artillerists, and the Massachusetts officials who had to find funds to pay for that equipment. (*Library of Congress*)

Many of the cannon collected by the Massachusetts Provincial Congress were missing trunnions, the cylindrical knobs on either side that served as an axle for tilting a gun. Cannon without trunnions required a more awkward form of mounting, as shown in this picture of an eighteen-pounder on Boston's Castle Island in 1794. (*New York Public Library*)

Ralph Earl and Amos Doolittle visited Concord in 1775 to produce this engraving of the British regulars taking over the town. At the lower right the officers leading that search mission, Lt. Col. Francis Smith and Maj. John Pitcairn, stand on the high ground of the old cemetery scanning the landscape. (*Albany Museum of History and Art*)

As illustrated in *Harper's Magazine* in 1875, the top goal of the British army march to Concord was to search James Barrett's farm beyond the North Bridge and destroy the military supplies hidden there.

For over a century the "Adams" cannon was mounted on the wall in the circular chamber atop the Bunker Hill Monument, displaying the hole left when it burst during gunnery practice in 1820. (*Jim Mac*)

The "Hancock" cannon sat on a reproduction carriage at Minute Man National Historical Park in 2007. When the same gun was hidden in that town in 1775, it was not mounted nearly as well. (*Dave Pape*)

The touch hole of the "Hancock" cannon, at top, shows signs that this gun was at some point spiked and repaired. (*National Park Service*)

Eight

"To Act the Traitor"

WHILE THE PATRIOTS OF GREATER BOSTON WERE SEIZING cannon wherever they could—in batteries, shops, the militia train's old and new gunhouses—Gen. Gage left little written reaction to those events. In his September 12 letter to Lord Dartmouth, he described the removal of cannon from the Charlestown battery in the vaguest terms, saying that the people were "getting magazines of arms and ammunition in the country and such artillery as they can procure, good and bad." In the following week both the British military and the Patriots scrambled to secure more cannon, but none of the general's surviving reports to London or orders for his troops mentioned those events. It is possible Gage sent his superiors more detail in a secret dispatch that has not survived; the government kept one letter he marked as "Private," so it would presumably have kept others.

Likewise, other British army officers in Boston seem to have been silent on the train's missing fieldpieces and other disappearing cannon. Those incidents do not appear in documents from Gage's seconds-in-command, Col. Percy and Gen. Frederick Haldimand. Junior officers wrote angrily about provincials smuggling muskets and cartridges, and some of them wrote just as angrily about Gen. Gage, but they never discussed missing cannon. News of the gunhouse thefts may have been kept within Col. Samuel Cleaveland's Royal Artillery, the branch of the army apparently responsible for securing those guns. On September 23 Adm. Samuel Graves told the naval board that locals "actually carried off some [cannon] from Charlestown and Boston," but made no clear reference to the train's guns.

The Massachusetts Loyalist who had the most interest in the train's cannon was of course Adino Paddock, nominal commander of that company. In his statement to the Loyalists Commission in December 1783 he said that he "Commanded the Corps of Militia Artillery in that Town from the Year 1763 to 1775." Paddock did not state that after September 1774 his company had no guns and never met. Of course, he had shared responsibility for keeping those cannon secure. Paddock also stated that he had received "the most flattering offers, from the Americans of entering into their Service against the King." Those offers probably came in the late summer of 1774; after that, it was clear which side Paddock was on.

In a postwar memoir, Customs Commissioner Henry Hulton reported that the people "secretly removed several Cannon from Boston, and dragged them into the Country beyond Watertown." This is a rare example of a British civil official stationed in Boston noting the disappearance of the town's artillery. It might actually be a reference to the Charlestown battery since it echoes his letter of September 13 about that event, quoted in Chapter 3.

In contrast, Capt. James Wallace of the Royal Navy reported clearly how Rhode Islanders had "seized upon the King's cannon," but he was not at risk of being blamed for that. Likewise, New Hampshire governor John Wentworth reported on how Patriots had emptied Fort William and Mary (adding an angry remark about the "imbecility of this government"). Wentworth's letters even went to London enclosed with one of Gage's, but the Massachusetts governor never described similar events.

Despite Gage's silence about the disappearance of the Paddock company guns, his September correspondence suggests that it had a powerful effect on his thinking. His next message home, to Secretary of War Barrington on September 25, was quite alarmed:

> The New England Provinces . . . are I may say in Arms, and the Question is now not whether you shall quell Disturbances in Boston, but whether those Provinces shall be conquered. From Appearances no People are more determined for a Civil War, the whole Country from hence to New York armed, training and providing Military Stores.

Instead of reporting the missing cannon, Gen. Gage had bigger ideas. To Secretary of State Dartmouth he floated the proposal of a "Suspension of the Execution of the late Acts" that were riling up the people of Massachusetts. That would gain time to raise and land "an Army near twenty Thousand strong composed of Regulars, a large Body of good Irregulars, such as the German Huntsmen, picked Canadians, &c, and three or four Regiments of Light Horse, these exclusive of a good and sufficient Field Artillery."

The general repeated those ideas in more letters over the following weeks, arguing more and more forcefully. On November 2 he told the Secretary of War: "This Province and the neighboring ones, particularly Conecticut, are preparing for War; if you will resist and not yield, that Resistance should be effectual at the Beginning. If you think ten Thousand Men sufficient, send Twenty, if one Million [pounds] is thought enough, give two; you save both Blood and Treasure in the end."

Instead of galvanizing the ministers in London, Gage's dispatches caused them to lose faith in him. His first letter to propose suspending the Coercive Acts arrived on November 18. After reading it and other dispatches, Lord North readily agreed that "the Province was in actual Rebellion, and must be subdued." But "He did not know what General Gage meant by suspending the Acts: there was no suspending an Act of Parliament." The prime minister also doubted the governor was facing "bodies of people actually in arms" and thus a military foe. William Knox, an undersecretary of state who outlasted multiple secretaries of state from 1770 to 1782, later wrote that the September proposals were "What turned us all so much against Gage."

The moment when Gage could have reported the theft of the Boston militia cannon as part of his argument for stronger measures passed. In early winter he received cool responses to his proposals and pleas—a promise of smaller reinforcements in the spring and an insistence he should be able to quell resistance with the forces he had. The ministers in London were clearly in no mood to hear about how he had let provincials steal four field-pieces under redcoat guard. Reporting that theft now would weaken his position further and raise the question of why he did not share the news earlier. The only way Gen. Gage could avoid that embarrassment would be to retrieve the missing guns before anyone in London heard about them.

Of course, Londoners did hear some things about the arms race in Boston. On December 20, the opposition member of Parliament Edmund Burke brought up those reports in Parliament as he argued against the ministry's American policy. Expressing sympathy for Gen. Gage as a man sent to do an impossible job, Burke declared: "The account we have is, that the general is besieging and besieged; that he had cannon sent to him, but they were stolen; that he himself has made reprisals of a similar nature on the enemy; and that his straw has been burnt, and his brick and mortar [for barracks] destroyed."

It is not clear what incidents Burke had read about, but his allusion to "stolen" cannon did not match the circumstances of the Boston train's guns. Furthermore, by raising the question in this context, Burke made it a political issue. To defend their policy, and the man they had chosen to carry it out, government ministers now had to dismiss those rumors as exaggerated.

As the year turned, Gen. Gage maintained his silence about the train's missing two- and three-pounders, but that does not mean he thought little of those cannon. The general's private intelligence files and the actions he took show that he was very eager to recover those guns. He recruited spies, sent agents to search the countryside, and issued orders for action whenever he received intelligence of brass cannon in provincial hands. Gage was still reluctant to confiscate private property, but there could be no legal complaint if his army seized easily identified stolen ordnance—and the men found with it. (Likewise, "any Gunpowder, or any Sort of Arms or Ammunition" that had been imported since October were illegal, but harder to identify.) This analysis of Gen. Gage's motives is speculative, but it explains his odd mix of silence about the Paddock company's missing cannon and intense interest in locating them.

The Boston Patriots had no doubt that Gen. Gage wanted to find those missing weapons. One step toward that goal, they assumed, was to suborn men involved in stealing them. That was how Dr. Joseph Warren came to fear that blacksmith Obadiah Whiston had been enticed to the British side. On February 10, Warren wrote to Samuel Adams:

> One Whiston, who has hitherto been thought firm in our cause, . . . is now making carriages for the army. He assisted in getting the four field-pieces to Colonel Robinson's, at Dorchester, where they are now. He says the discovery [i.e., disclosure] of this "will make him;" and he threatens to make the discovery. Perhaps resentment and the hope of gain may together prevail with him to act the traitor.

Whiston was already "making carriages for the army," Warren believed. Those were gun-carriages, the sturdy wheeled carts needed to transport and aim fieldpieces. Military contracts were good business—the army paid cash. The smith had said that revealing the guns' whereabouts to the army "would make him," meaning he could be financially independent. It is not clear what Warren meant by the "resentment" that might also have motivated the blacksmith. Without a statement from Whiston himself, we have no way of knowing what motivated him to switch sides—or if he really did. Neither Whiston's name nor any information he would have to offer is in Gen. Gage's intelligence files. But the Patriot leadership could not take a chance.

To prevent the British from seizing the guns at Robinson's tavern, Warren urged Adams and his Provincial Congress colleagues to move them further inland. He wrote: "Dr. Church and I are clear, that it ought not to be one minute in his [Whiston's] power to point out to the general the place in which they are kept; but that they ought to be removed without. Pray do not omit to obtain proper orders concerning them."

Adams quickly forwarded the doctors' recommendation. On February 13, the committees of safety and supplies voted that members Benjamin Lincoln and Benjamin White should "wait on Col. Robinson, and receive from him the four brass field pieces, and three brass mortars, now in his hands, the property of the province, and as soon as may be, remove them to the town of Concord," over a dozen miles from Boston. The committee men assured Robinson and his neighbors, however, that "the said field pieces shall be for the use of the artillery companies in Boston and Dorchester, and if matters are settled without, said field pieces are to be returned to said Robinson." The Dorchester officer evidently did not like the idea of giving up those fine fieldpieces when he had his own artillery company to command.

Back in Boston, the suspect blacksmith was cut out of the Patriots' network. Decades later, his apprentice Joshua Wyeth recalled how he swiftly "became a tory." In March 1776 Whiston and two family members left town with the British army, and in 1778 the state formally banished "Obadiah Whiston, Blacksmith."

Unfortunately for Dr. Warren, in conferring about what sensitive secrets Whiston might reveal with his colleague Dr. Benjamin Church, he had alerted Gen. Gage's best placed spy.

The question of exactly when Dr. Church began supplying sensitive information to British officials has been debated ever since his treachery came to light in late 1775. The crucial point appears to have come that February. Church was a member of the committee of safety and supplies, but he did not attend its first four meetings of the year. He was not present when the committee decided to move the last two brass cannon out of Boston and then to move all four brass cannon and mortars to Concord. But Church did attend the February 21 meeting in Charlestown.

On that same day, Gen. Gage suddenly had a lot of intelligence about the Provincial Congress's military supplies to write down:

> Memorandums 21st. Feby.— The Gun Carriages that are making at Charles Town is by one Kinney—a wheelwright but making principally Wheels for them, at present; many have been carted through Cambridge 'tis said for Worcester—
>
> Gun Carriages are making at Water Town by McCurtain—an Irishman, who has fallen out with the Select Men there, as he will not permit them to be taken away untill the Cash is forthcoming.—Bowman a Smith making Tools at Menotomy.
>
> One Brown who arr'd last night from Conecticut reports that small magazines are forming in the several Towns, of Provisions, de guerre et de bouche but a considerable one at Hartford.—
>
> Horton a Black Smith at Work at Marble Head on Gun Carriges—went from hence a month since.
>
> Gun Carriages making at Salem
>
> Twelve pieces of Brass Cannon mounted, are at Salem, & lodged near the North River, on the back of the Town.— . . .

This information reveals that the Provincial Congress's artillery force had fieldpieces but not field-carriages. David Mason and his colleagues had gathered dozens of two- to six-pounders suitable for the battlefield, and a few large siege guns as well. But many of those cannon were not properly equipped. The mounts used on ships and in shore batteries were not maneuverable. Fieldpieces needed larger wheels to roll over obstacles and be easily turned, and those vehicles had to be sturdy enough to carry the heavy guns and their equipment over long distances and rough terrain. They needed backup parts for quick repairs during campaigns, especially extra wheels. Gun carriages thus required the best work of the province's wheelwrights and blacksmiths. And those men wanted money: when the congress first debated buying artillery in October, it estimated the cost of one carriage for "battering cannon" at £30, the same as a fully equipped four-pounder with carriage.

Furthermore, with so many different types of cannon in the provincial arsenal, carriages had to be custom-made. Page after page of David Mason's notebook is filled with the dimensions of the guns in his care. Mason also wrote down "Generall Constructions for Travelling Carridges," "Directions Left for the wheels for the four Brass-Guns," "Dimensions of an 8 Inch Howitz Carridge," "Dimensions of wheels for field Carridges," and so on. He also billed the province for painting seventeen carriages. It is no surprise, therefore, that when Gen. Gage received his first good intelligence about the location of provincial cannon, they were still in the shop waiting to be put on wheels.

Mounting cannon was also a burden for the towns. On January 2, committee of safety and supplies member John Pigeon presented his neighbors in Newton with two fieldpieces—but the town had to start a subscription to buy carriages. Watertown had discussed field-carriages since October, at one point cutting its school budget to pay for them, but on February 6 citizens voted "that the Committe appointed to mount ye great Guns do not Compleat the Same till after the Congress Rises at it." Perhaps that was why McCurtain the blacksmith had fallen out with them. It took two more weeks before Watertown voted to mount those cannon "as Soon as may be." On March 21 Richard Derby gave two more fieldpieces to Salem, which had to "vote to have them fitted for service."

On top of carriages, artillery companies also needed ropes and harnesses for either horses or men to move those carriages. They needed specialized tools to fire and maintain their cannon: the long poles with rammers or swabs on the ends, iron worms and trail spikes and buckets and fuses and more. Each gun needed cannon balls of the right size, plus grapeshot and other specialized projectiles. The companies not only had to obtain gunpowder, not yet manufactured in North America, but to package it in cloth cartridges of the right size to load swiftly into their guns. Without every one of those things, a cannon was simply a harmless metal tube. Gathering or making all that equipment was a bottleneck for the Patriots, so it is hard to know how many towns that voted to buy cannon or establish artillery companies were actually able to field guns.

Gen. Gage wanted to act before his opponents got far along in their plans. Back in early January, when replies from London made clear that the government was hoping for him to quell the Massachusetts resistance with the resources he had, the general asked army officers "capable of taking sketches of a Country" to contact his adjutant general, Maj. Stephen Kemble. The day after his intelligence memorandum, Gage wrote out instructions for two men who came forward, Capt. William Brown of the 52nd Regiment and Ensign Henry D'Berniere of the 10th.

Those officers were to "go through the counties of *Suffolk* and *Worcester*, taking a sketch of the country as you pass." In particular Brown and D'Berniere were to mark out roads, towns, rivers, passes, fords, heights, woods, travel distances, and sites "proper for encampments." Gage told the officers that "he expected to have occasion to march troops through the country the ensuing spring." It is possible that the general sent out similar scouts in other directions; we know about this mission into Suffolk and Worcester counties only because the officers' instructions and report were left behind during the evacuation of Boston and published by a Patriot printer in 1779.

Brown and D'Berniere left Boston with a servant named John, all three of them disguised as "surveyors," on the morning of Thursday, February 23. Though the general's orders did not mention cannon, their route took them through towns where Patriots were working on building an artillery force, starting with Charlestown and Cambridge. In Watertown the men stopped for midday dinner, and "a black woman" told them she recognized them as from the army. The officers' cover was blown, but they understood that "it was absolutely necessary to push on to *Worcester*," where the Patriots were collecting the most supplies, so they continued west, arriving in that town at five o'clock on Saturday evening.

When those spies passed through Charlestown, the committee of safety and supplies were also in that town in the middle of a four-day conference. They met every day from February 21 to February 24, with Dr. Church listed as attending all those meetings but the last. The first couple of days were taken up with decisions on supplies, such as tents, lead, and peas. On the 23rd, the committee voted to draft and print letters telling the militia commanders "to assemble one fourth part of the militia through the province" if they needed to form the core of an army.

As part of that military preparation, the committee also started assigning the cannon it controlled to various artillery companies. Members voted that these colonels "have each two field pieces put into their hands":

Thomas Gardner of Cambridge
Edward Mitchell of Bridgewater
James Warren of Plymouth
William Heath of Roxbury
Artemas Ward of Shrewsbury
Jedediah Foster of Brookfield
Lemuel Robinson of Dorchester

Warren, Ward, Mitchell, and Foster needed special letters about the cannon they received. Gardner, Heath, and Robinson were evidently prepared for them; their regiments may have had established artillery companies. The committee men did not list Timothy Bigelow of Worcester and James Barrett of Concord, probably because they knew those colonels already had cannon in their possession; they had become responsible for safeguarding many of the Provincial Congress's guns.

In addition, there were two fieldpieces "for the use of the artillery company of Boston, lately commanded by Major Paddock." Dr. Warren was to apply to that company "and know how many of them may be depended on, officers and men, to form an artillery company." Finally, on February 24 the committee voted "That eight field pieces, with the shot and cartridges, and two brass morters with their bombs, be deposited at Leicester," just west of Worcester, with militia colonel Joseph Henshaw.

The next day, Gen. Gage received a summary of those discussions. The committee members who lived in or near Boston were "to observe the motions of the Army." If the troops were to "attempt to penetrate into the Country," those men would alert the colonels in Worcester County and at the ports of Plymouth and Marblehead, south and north of Boston. The committee expected to raise "about 15000" minutemen while Gage commanded about 5,000 redcoats. "[A]ll military stores, [were] to be deposited at Concord and Worcester." As to cannon:

> There are in the Country thirty eight Field pieces and Nineteen Companys of Artillery, most of wh. are at Worcester, a few at Concord and a few at Watertown.
>
> There Whole Magazine of Powder consisting of between Ninety and an Hundred Barrelles is at Concord. There are eight Field pieces in an old store, or Barn, near the landing place at Salem, they are to be removed in a few days, the seizure of them wd. greatly disconcert their schemes.

That intelligence prompted Gen. Gage to take action—his most aggressive move since September 1. He had already learned about "Twelve pieces of Brass Cannon" at Salem. Now, three days later, he had more specific news: those "Field pieces in an old store, or Barn, near the landing place at Salem, . . . are to be removed in a few days." David Mason, the founder of the Boston militia train, lived in that town. Gage might have guessed that the four missing brass cannon were part of that assemblage in Salem. And he had to move fast.

On Sunday, February 26, Lt.-Col. Alexander Leslie and 240 men of the 64th Regiment sailed from Castle William to Marblehead, next to Salem. This expedition was about the same size as the one that Gage had sent to Cambridge in September. Col. Leslie had the further advantage of landing about two o'clock on a cold Sunday afternoon as church services were resuming. (Locals complained that the ship had landed before then but the soldiers kept out of sight below decks until people went into their meetinghouses.) The regulars marched briskly toward Salem, a little over four miles away.

Nevertheless, word of the redcoats traveled faster than they did. In mid-afternoon "two of the selectmen" warned the Provincial Congress's artillerist, David Mason, that "troops were marching into the town . . . to take possession of his guns." Mason had collected seventeen unmounted cannon—iron, not brass, most of them old. He had arranged for a neighbor named Robert Foster to make carriages for them at his smithy just past the drawbridge over Salem's North River. Mason left his meetinghouse and ran toward that bridge. He burst into the nearby North Church and shouted, "The regulars are coming after the guns!"

Though that was an Anglican church, some of the congregants were Patriots and rushed out to help. A Quaker neighbor named David Boyce "was instantly out with his team to assist in carrying the guns" away from the forge as well. Mason and his helpers hurried to bury the cannon in "a piece of thick oak trees, covered with dried leaves and no snow." Local chronicler Joseph Felt described the hidingplace as "about three quarters of a mile from Foster's." As Col. Leslie and his troops came into sight on the road from the center of town, Mason and Foster pulled up the north side of the drawbridge.

The redcoats marched past Mason's house and the church to the bank of the river, and then they could go no farther. Col. Leslie could see Foster's smithy across the river. He yelled for the men on the other side to let the bridge down. Mason and Foster refused. Leslie wondered aloud about ordering his troops to fire, prompting militia captain John Felt to warn that he had no legal authority to do that. Some soldiers moved toward two flat-bottomed gondolas on the riverbank, thinking to float across the river, but locals jumped in to scuttle those boats with axes. That prompted more pushing and shoving. One of those Salem men, Joseph Whicher, even dared a soldier to bayonet him and got his chest slightly pricked—he "was fond of exhibiting" this wound after the war.

Hearing that some of the cannon belonged to Richard Derby, Leslie asked the captain to help resolve the stalemate. Derby's unhelpful response was, "If he can find them, he can have them." Mason was yelling from the other side of the river that "expresses had gone out and, in a few hours, 1000 [militia] men would be on the ground to resist, & that his [Leslie's] men would be cut to pieces, if they fired on the people." Men clambered onto the raised drawbridge to watch, one shouting insults before others shushed him. Leslie shouted back that he had to follow his orders, insisting "he would go over the bridge before he returned, if it were a month first." One witness said he even threatened to commandeer the nearby warehouses as barracks for his troops.

For a moment it looked like this stalemate would end in violence. Nine-year-old Samuel Gray would remember seeing the soldiers "doing something to their muskets." Scared, he and his friends "ran off and lay down under the fish flakes"—the wooden shelves lining the south side of the river where fishermen laid their salted cod to dry. The boys hid in the cold shadows underneath.

After nearly ninety minutes, with the sun going down, the Rev. Thomas Barnard, minister of that nearby church, negotiated a compromise. Mason, knowing most of his cannon had been trucked away, would let down the bridge. Leslie "pledged his honor he would march not above thirty rods beyond it, and then immediately return." He would not look for cannon nearby. No matter how much the locals' resistance had convinced him they were hiding something, this was the best exit the lieutenant colonel could manage.

The day ended as thus arranged, with the men of the 64th Regiment stepping across the North River and then returning to their ship in Marblehead. Once again, the outcome could have been much worse. Militia companies had mustered in Marblehead and other nearby towns but stayed back to avoid exacerbating the situation. The Danvers company even marched into Salem and "went back of Colonel Sprague's distillery, and sat down so as to expose their persons as little as possible, watching the movements at the bridge until all was over." A single angry or accidental gunshot could have started the war with a shoot-out in the middle of one of Massachusetts's largest settlements.

In the aftermath of the raid, the people of Salem wondered who had supplied the army with such accurate information. Mason's family came to suspect that "an old country man" working at Foster's forge—perhaps a recent arrival from Britain—had gone into Boston with the information. Many witnesses saw a Loyalist named John Sargent walking with Leslie toward the smithy, and some even claimed they had seen him "on the top of his house, near the first church, waving his handkerchief and pointing in the direction of the north bridge." Whether or not that was true, Sargent "left the town immediately and never returned." Another suspect was "Samuel Porter, a lawyer, who came hither from Ipswich"; reportedly he "was seen to point his cane towards North Bridge." No one suspected that Gage's initial conduit for information was not someone in Salem, not a recent immigrant or a known Loyalist, but most likely Dr. Church, a member of the committee of safety and supplies.

The day after the confrontation at the North River, little Samuel Gray went back to the area. Unlike Lt.-Col. Leslie, he got into Foster's workshop. He even found a cannon lying on the ground. Being a nine-year-old boy, he stood on it and started asking questions. Why was this gun still there? It was damaged, someone told him, pointing to "a crack in the breech." How many cannon had been there before? People told him there were twelve, he recalled, and that "they were French pieces, and came from Nova Scotia after the late French war." The good guns had now been "distributed in various directions."

Gen. Gage acknowledged some chagrin at that outcome in a letter to Lord Dartmouth: "The Circumstance of the Eight Field Pieces at Salem led us into a Mistake, for supposing them to be brass Guns brought in from Holland or some of the foreign Islands, which Report had also given Reason to suspect." If Gage had indeed received a hint that the Salem cannon were imported, his intelligence papers do not preserve it. But giving that reason for the Salem raid would prompt no hard questions from his superior. In the end,

Gage insisted, the radicals had secured "only some old Ship Guns which had been carried away from Salem some time ago."

Maj. John Pitcairn of the Marines also made light of the unsuccessful raid in a letter to the First Lord of the Admiralty:

> The Colonel landed, and marched with great expedition to Salem: the people beat their drums, rung their alarm bells; but the Colonel saw none in arms but five, and those took care to get out of the way as fast as they could. The people behaved as I suppose they will ever do, made a great noise when they is nobody to oppose them, but the moment they see us in arms and in earnest they will talk very differently. The Colonel found no guns—it is supposed a false information. He marched back to Marblehead and embarked for this place. The moment he left Salem, I am told the people got arms and paraded about, and swore if he had stayed half an hour longer they would have cut him to pieces. If he had continued there till now, none of them would have dared to have appeared in arms.

The people of Salem told a different story. On the night of March 3, the *Essex Gazette* reported, "Twenty seven Pieces of Cannon were removed out of this Town, in order to be out of the Way of Robbers." Their new hidingplace would be in Concord.

Nine

"The Town Is Full of Cannon"

While Lt.-Col. Leslie was negotiating with the people of Salem, his fellow army officers Capt. Brown and Ens. D'Berniere, and their enlisted servant, were still out in Worcester County, sketching the landscape. The raid on Salem naturally put the whole province on alert. On Sunday evening at eight o'clock two men came to the Worcester tavern and told the landlord they knew those strangers were "officers of the army."

That warning cued Brown and D'Berniere to head back toward Boston the next day. In Framingham they found "the company of militia" training not only near their tavern but "before the windows of the room we were in." The officers assured each other that "they did not know who we were, and took little or no notice of us." That may be true, but at the time part of the Massachusetts Patriots' strategy was to show that they were unified and ready for a war in order to prevent one from starting, so the decision to train in front of suspected officers might not have been a coincidence. Brown and D'Berniere traveled east for another day without meeting too many wary people, so they decided it was safe to scout roads to the west again. They made it to Marlborough before running into trouble.

As they entered that town, "the people came out of their houses (tho' it snowed and blew very hard) to look at us." At the home of Loyalist Henry Barnes, they were about to reveal their identities when "he told us we need not be at the pains of telling him, that he knew our situation, that we were very well known (he was afraid) by the town's people." In fact, "a party of liberty people" had been looking for them the night before. Barnes was anxious. During the nonimportation campaign of 1770, he had been called out for resisting the boycott, and locals had tarred and feathered his horse. After only about twenty minutes, Barnes urged the officers to leave for their own safety, and they trudged hours through the snowy night back to Weston. A few days later Barnes became one more Loyalist seeking refuge in Boston; he told Brown and D'Berniere that the local committee had searched his house and the surrounding roads shortly after they left.

Inside Boston, tensions were rising. With both the Continental Congress and the Provincial Congress in recess, all the town's Patriots were home and within the army lines. In early March, Maj. John Pitcairn wrote, Gage met with some of the provincial leaders and "swore to it by the living God, that if there was a single man of the King's troops killed in any of their towns he would burn it to the ground." Still, the general did not arrest any Massachusetts organizers.

There were inflammatory incidents. On March 6, Dr. Joseph Warren delivered the town's annual oration on the Massacre. The Old South Meeting-House was packed with townspeople and "a great number of Officers" who came to show their disapproval of the "most seditious, inflammatory harangue." When officers shouted, "Fie!", locals heard, "Fire!", and there was nearly a fatal crush as people tried to leave. Two days later, soldiers of the 47th Regiment grabbed Thomas Ditson, a Billerica farmer, for enticing soldiers to sell their army muskets. They held him overnight, covered him with tar and feathers, and then paraded him around town in a cart as regimental musicians played.

On March 15 Dr. Thomas Bolton, a young Loyalist from Salem, parodied Warren's oration from the balcony of the British Coffeehouse, speaking of "the ignorance of Hancock, the insolence of Adams, . . . the vicious life and untimely death of Mollineaux, the turged bombast of Warren." With five thousand soldiers in town, Bostonians could not force him to shut up.

While that drama was happening in public, Gen. Gage was privately feeling pressure from London. In March he received Lord Dartmouth's suggestion, written in January, that he "recover into The King's possession those Cannon and Stores which have been taken away in so extraordinary a manner from the Fort at Newport." The general was having enough trouble recovering the cannon taken away from Charlestown, Dorchester, and Boston. The same letter also chided Gage for allowing militia activity to continue inside the town: "you have not only indulged them in having such a Guard, but have also allowed their Militia to train and discipline in Faneuil Hall." What would the Secretary have to say about letting the Boston train members take away their weapons?

Gage was still gathering intelligence. On March 3, he questioned a well-placed informant, probably Dr. Church, about the Provincial Congress's political plans. The body had rejected the idea of "An assumption of the old Charter . . . Because it would amount to a declaration of independency & revolt & thereby preclude the possibility of a peaceable accommodation." But the congress was continuing to prepare its militia for the moment when "hostilities shall have commenced on the part of Government"—i.e., when Gage started a war. In that case, "the first opposition would be irregular empetuous & incessant from the numerous Bodies that would swarm to the place of action & all actuated by an Enthusiasm wild & ungovernable." The next day, the general received more specific answers about the colony's military resources, including how there were "upwards of 20 Artillery Companies dispersed throughout the province each furnished with 2 field pieces. . . . The field pieces are supplied with Carriages & every other Requisite for immediate use."

On March 7, the committee of safety and supplies met in Cambridge. Dr. Church attended. One day later, Gage received a report on the discussion from someone who had seen "the Books of the Committee of Safety." Those records revealed that "the greatest magazine of provisions & ammunition is at Worcester" with a smaller part at Concord, which reflected how the committee had decided to divide up their stock of food in November. The committees had collected only about half the quantities of flour, pork, and peas they had voted to procure.

The next day, Gen. Gage gained a valuable new conduit of information. Someone wrote to him from Concord about artillery. The general's intelligence files contain two reports in the same handwriting dated March 8 and 9. The first is in English, the second in poor French, probably an attempt to minimize the number of people in rural Massachusetts who could read it. They started with nearly the same facts:

> Four brass Cannon, & Two Cohorns or Mortars (so call'd by the Peasantry) Conceal'd at Mr: B, (Lately chose or appointed Minute Colo.) Suppos'd to be deposited in his Cellar.—The Calibre of these pieces of Ordnance is not exactly ascertained, but reported to be only Diminutive.

Concord's colonel, in charge of the new minutemen, was James Barrett, a sixty-five-year-old farmer and representative to the Provincial Congress.

The general's new informant went on to report more artillery in Concord:

> Two pieces of Iron Ordnance (Suppos'd to be 4 or 6 pounders) are mounted, (On carriages said to be very indifferent) in the Courthouse & watch'd at Night, hitherto by a Slender Guard of Minute men.—
>
> Eight more pieces of Iron Ordnance were this day (Le 8 de Mois de Mars) convey'd to C~~oncord~~ from L[eicester?] (where they had been deposited a few days preceeding their Last removal;[)]—Two of the Eight appear to be Smaller <than the rest> & about three or four pounders—These last mentioned

> were met at a small distance from C[oncord] in three Carts there were no appurtenances, but it was said that carriages were made or making at Salem & soon to follow.—
>
> It is conjectured & reported that a Large quantity of Cartridges are now preparing at Ch[arlestow]n; of Different Sizes, & numbered in order to distribute & distinguish properly. . . .

This spy even stated which Concord families were keeping gunpowder, small arms, flour, pork, peas, and other supplies for the provincial military. In some cases the information was very specific:

> It is said with certainty 7 Tons of powder (equal to 13000 net or 280 barells,) is collected at C——d—The greatest part Lodg'd at one Whitings together with some small arms near the entrance into the Vilage on the Road from hence—on the right hand, a White plasterd house, with a Small Yard in front & a Raild fence—a store adjoining the house contains the Powder.

That was the house of Thomas Whiting, a justice of the peace who had acceded to the closing of the courts. The spy clearly aimed to help Gage raid the town, reporting that "Two Capital Roads Lead to C—— one from the Ferry through Cambridge & Lexington—The other through WaterTown & part of Weston—22 miles distant the former only 19."

In the French version written the next day, that informant no longer had any doubt about the laboratory in Charlestown making ammunition cartridges. He or she also reported that information about a recent deserter's escape route had come from the "pretre de Concord, (nommé Emmerson, *un très mauvais sujet*:)"—the minister of Concord, the Rev. William Emerson, "a very bad subject."

Aside from being able to write in poor French and being on speaking terms with Emerson, there is no indication in these letters about who Gage's new correspondent was. Capt. Brown and Ens. D'Berniere prompted suspicion wherever they went, so the spy was probably not an army officer or a new arrival from Britain. On the other hand, while the spy was familiar with Concord, he or she apparently did not know the full name of every suspicious inhabitant, suggesting that the person had not spent a lifetime within that community. Had the general recruited an inhabitant of Concord or a neighboring town who sided with the Crown—Dr. Joseph Lee, Duncan Ingraham, or someone more discreet? Was the informant an American no one suspected of working for the army? An immigrant who had been working in the town long enough to gain people's trust?

The spy's reports focused closely on the movement and locations of military supplies, not on resistance organizers, militia officers, political fissures, or other topics that might be useful to the governor. That pattern suggests the spy was responding to Gen. Gage's desire for that particular information. That in turn suggests that he or she had met with Gage or trusted agents before sending the first reports, explaining why there is no introductory correspondence preserved.

At the very top of those first two reports was the phrase "Four brass Cannon," perhaps an indication of what Gage told his agent he wanted to locate. In any event, those words would have caught the general's attention. There was also a mention of carriages from Salem. Gage could have inferred that David Mason and his comrades had removed the train's fieldpieces from Boston, kept them away from Lt.-Col. Leslie in Salem, and then moved them on to Concord. In fact, those guns had traveled out through Dorchester by a route the general's intelligence documents never mention.

On March 11, the general's new spy had new information about what was at Worcester: at least fifteen tons of gunpowder and considerable quantities of arms in the homes of "un certain *Salisbury*, (marchant) et par Bigelow (*un grand Chef*)"—merchant Stephen Salisbury and new political leader Timothy Bigelow. There were also three iron cannon, three- or four-pounders, in front of Worcester's church. Those guns were "montés sur des roues assez mauvaises"—mounted on wheels rather badly. Gage's informant did not have as much inside information to share about Worcester as about Concord. That dispatch concluded:

> Les cannons de *Cuivre*, qui autrefois etoient entre Les mains de Monsr. Paddick; n'ÿ sont Jamais arrivés; et *Vraisemblablement* sont presentement à Concord.
> (The *brass* cannon, which formerly were in the hands of Mr. Paddick, never arrived there [Worcester]; and *veritably* are now at Concord.)

The spy's information was correct. James Barrett's own undated "account of all the Province Stores Sent to Col James Barretts of Concord Partly in His Own Costody & Partly Elsewhere all under his Care" began:

> Two peices of Cannon Brought From Watertown to ye Towns
> Eight Peices of Cannon Brought to ye Town by Mr Harrington
> Four Peices of Brass Cannon & Two Mortar from Col Robertsons [*sic*]. . . .

There were also musket balls and many barrels of flour and other foods.

The spy's March 11 dispatch also said that a member of the Boston militia train had come out to the countryside to train new artillerists:

> Un certain nommé *Popkins* (un Tailleur) élevé par Le Majr. Paddick (dans la Compagnie *d'artillerie* au moins;) est arrivé depuis quelques Jours *à Worcester*, pour instruire une Compagnie d'artillerie *Milicien*, qui doit être formée Là en peu des Jours.
> (A certain man named *Popkins* (a tailor) trained by Majr. Paddock (in the company *of artillery* at least) arrived days ago *at Worcester* to instruct a *militia* artillery company, which should be formed there in a few days.)

That was John Popkin, a thirty-four-year-old tailor, perhaps recruited by the committee of safety. He would serve the entire war in the American artillery, rising to lieutenant-colonel.

The rural companies had suffered from a lack of trained men. Back on February 27 Artemas Ward of Shrewsbury had written to David Cheever of the committee of supplies with the warning that no one in his militia district could teach his newly designated gunners and matrosses how to handle the two cannon they had been assigned. "There is a person in this town who understands the Exercise," Ward said, "but has of late discovered such Sentiments in Political matters that I dare not trust him."

In all three reports, the Concord spy commented on how badly the provincial cannon were mounted on their gun carriages. Other scouts also reported that the fieldpieces in Concord "were mounted but in so bad a manner that they could not elevate them more than they were, that is, they were fixed in one elevation." In a comment he dated to late April, after the shooting had started, the Patriot minister William Gordon acknowledged that the provincials' cannon "are scarce worth mentioning. They reckon upon sixteen field pieces. It is well if six of them are calculated for much actual service."

The most detailed description of how the provincials had mounted their cannon comes from the American surgeon James Thacher, based on observations during the winter of 1775–76:

> Before our privateers had fortunately captured some prizes with cannon and other ordnance, our army before Boston had, I believe, only four small brass cannon, and a few old honey-comb iron pieces, with their trunnions broken off; and these were ingeniously bedded in timbers in the same manner as that of stocking a musket. These machines were extremely unwieldy and inconvenient, requiring much skill and labor to elevate and depress them.

The trunnions are the knobs that stick out the sides of a cannon and rest on its carriage so that it can pivot up and down.

It is possible that the awkward type of gun carriage that addressed the problem of broken trunnions was invented by Preserved Clapp, a forty-three-year-old doctor from Amherst. In late 1776, after the restoration of some cannon that the British army had left damaged at Castle William, Dr. Clapp lobbied the Massachusetts legislature and the public to be credited as "the real inventor of a carriage, whereby the cannon that had their trunnions broken off, by this new invented carriage the guns are rendered serviceable, which otherwise would have been useless."

On top of the problems of damaged cannon that could only be poorly mounted, Mason was working at the edge of his knowledge as an artillerist. He had left the Boston militia company before Paddock arranged for advanced training from the Royal Artillery. Some of Mason's struggle can be seen in his little green notebook. Under the title "Dimensions of a Brass 3 ¶" he wrote:

> the whole Length 3.10 feet
>
> from hind ¶ Trunions to Base R:g 18 do.
> from ye Edge of Base Ring to ye Centre of the Sceru
>
> [screw hole] 2 Inches -
>
> Diameter Base Ring - 7 Inches
>
> Do. Second Reinforce 6 Inches
>
> Diameter of the Chase - 2.913
>
> Do. of the Shott - 2.775
>
> The base ring, reinforce, and chase are names for different sections of the cannon barrel, back to front.

The first five dimensions on Mason's list match the cannon later dubbed the "Hancock," so long as we read "3.10 feet" as "3 feet, 10 inches." Mason measured to the inch, but the base ring and reinforce are both a notable fraction-of-an-inch wider than his whole numbers. Mason's last two numbers are clearly different from the rest, stated to the third decimal place. The label "Diameter of the Chase" is also inaccurate. That measurement should be the diameter of the whole cannon at its mouth end, or five inches. Mason appears to have written down what he thought was the diameter of the mouth or bore only.

Those anomalous numbers—2.913 and 2.775—exactly match the Royal Artillery's 1764 specifications for the bore of a standard light three-pounder and its shot. It appears that Mason measured the length and breadth of the Boston fieldpieces in several ways to order carriages for them, but when it came to size of the bore and the ball, he assumed those guns matched the British army standard and copied the corresponding measurements out of an official source.

Unfortunately, the Boston train's three-pounders were not Royal Artillery light three-pounders. The standard guns were forty-two inches long. The guns Mason was working with were forty-six inches long. Bostonians understood those two cannon to have been newly made in 1768, "cast from two old Pieces which were purchased some time since by the General Court." It is possible the manufacturer actually shipped back an older pair of brass cannon that no longer fit the Royal Artillery's specifications, after decorating them with the Massachusetts arms for its new customer. Mason apparently made the assumption that their bore and shot would match the Royal Artillery standard and copied those numbers into his notebook without checking.

Gazing at Massachusetts's old, poorly mounted field artillery in late 1775, Continental army medic James Thacher thought, "Had the enemy been made acquainted with our situation, the consequences might have been exceedingly distressing." But Gen. Gage *was* acquainted three times with the problems of the Patriots' artillery. He knew that, although the Provincial Congress was equipping its militia regiments with fieldpieces, the effectiveness of those weapons in battle would be limited. Nevertheless, the general continued to track those cannon, and particularly the brass cannon from Boston. Even if those guns were not much of a threat to Gage's men, they may yet have been a threat to his career.

Having read his spy's conclusion that the Boston train guns were at Concord, Gage ordered Capt. Brown and Ens. D'Berniere out to "examine the road and situation of the town; and also to get what information we could relative to what quantity of artillery and provisions." They set out from Boston on March 20. Their report said: "We were informed that they had fourteen pieces of cannon (ten iron and four brass) and two cohorns, . . . their iron cannon they kept in a house in town, their brass they had concealed in some place behind the town, in a wood."

The officers dined at the house of Daniel Bliss, a Loyalist lawyer. He might have been their source for this information, but he was not the Concord spy because, after a warning from the Patriots that "they would not let him go out of town alive," Bliss took advantage of Brown and D'Berniere's protection and returned with them to Boston.

Local traditions suggest that provincials had started to read any British excursion into the countryside as an attempt to find artillery. Brown and D'Berniere had been detected in Watertown during a mission in late February, and locals interpreted their goal as the town's cannon: "some British officers came to Watertown to search; but they searched in vain, the pieces being effectually concealed in a barn." On the morning of March 30, Percy marched his brigade down Boston Neck, and the farmers of Roxbury remembered the event this way: "redcoats were at Jamaica Plain, searching for the missing cannons. This company was part of a battalion of five hundred men who were scattered in various directions for the same purpose."

In fact, Percy's brigade did spot some provincial artillery that day, in plain sight. Lt. John Barker wrote that "at Watertown about 9 miles off, they got 2 pieces of Cannon to the Bridge and loaded 'em but nobody wou'd stay to fire them." Similarly, Lt. Frederick Mackenzie would later note that when "The 38th & 52ed Regiments marched once to Watertown, . . . Cannon were fired" for an alarm. These were probably the pair of "Great Guns" the town had finally mounted for its militia the month before. The British column did not try to seize any of those cannon, however. Gen. Gage hoped that uneventful marches, which he had ordered periodically since December, would accustom the people of nearby towns to seeing troops.

But lulling the countryside into complacency was only an intermediate goal. Gage was focused on the weapons in Concord. On March 22 the Provincial Congress convened in that town. Four days later, the general received a report on its business, saying one topic of conversation was "a number of letters from England"—the Patriots had their own sources of inside information. The next day, the congress asked delegates to tell its steering committee "the number of field pieces, whether the property of the province, towns, or private persons, that have fallen within their knowledge." Gen. Gage learned that that committee had "ordered the Committee of Safety to remove all the Cannon Stores &c from Concord to the Town of Leicester—these consist of 8 field pieces 2 Mortars 70 half Barrels Gun powder" and more. The informant at the congress added that those supplies "at present they lay scattered in different places up & down the Town & could not easily be come at by a party to be either taken or destroyed."

In the last week of March, the Provincial Congress was discussing "the rules and regulations for a constitutional army." March 30 was the day Col. Percy led the march into Roxbury and his officers spotted cannon on the bridge at Watertown. That prompted more urgent legislative action out in Concord, according to Dr. Church:

> The marching of the first Brigade last Thursday greatly alarmed the Congress, and accelerated their determination for on the day the Comittee appointed to consider of the state of the Province reported to to [*sic*] the Congress that it was their opinion, that should any body of troops, wth. Artillery and Baggage, march out of Boston, The Country should instantly be alarmed, and called together to oppose their March to the last extremity.

All 169 members of the congress present appeared to accept that recommendation.

While the congress was meeting in Concord, Gage's spy continued to collect information. On April 6, he or she reported that three or four men in militia uniforms had come from Connecticut to consult with the Massachusetts Patriots. More supplies were arriving in town, not just military material but "trois Grandes Caisses, contennant *Selon toute apparance*, Les archives de La Ville de Boston"—three big chests containing, to all appearances, the archives of the city of Boston.

As for artillery, that report said there was thought of building a fort on a hill near the center of Concord to protect the guns, other military supplies, and any prisoners the provincials would have. The men in charge would be "Le Coll. B—— et L'Engenieur *Mason*"—Col. James Barrett and David Mason. Twelve cannon were mounted around the courthouse at the center of town with a constant guard, day and night. There were also "trois canons de *24 lb* calibre, dans La Cour de La prison"—three big twenty-four-pounders in the courtyard of the prison.

But those were all iron cannon. Once again the Concord spy gave Gage a glimpse of the Boston train's guns: "Les quatres Canons de *Cuivre* et un Mortier sont placés dans Le Cave óu dans La *Grange* de Monsr. B——t *Leur nouveau Colonel*." The four brass cannon and a mortar were in the cellar or barn of Barrett, the new colonel. A great deal of other ammunition and provisions had been dispersed throughout almost all the houses in the village, particularly the homes of Ebenezer Hubbard, Samuel Jones, and men named Butler and Bond. This report ended with the note that a couple of local guides would be available, again hinting that the writer was ready for Gage to send troops.

James Warren, a prominent Provincial Congress delegate from Plymouth, was also gazing around Concord. On April 6 he wrote to his wife Mercy:

> All things wear a warlike appearance here. This Town is full of Cannon, ammunition, stores, etc., and the Army long for them and they want nothing but strength to Induce an attempt on them. The people are ready and determine to defend this Country Inch by Inch. The Inhabitants of Boston begin to move. The Selectmen and Committee of Correspondence are to be with us. . . .

In a postscript on April 7 he added: "The Inhabitants of Boston are on the move. H— and A— go no more into that Garrison, the female connections of the first come out early this morning and measures are being taken relative to those of the last." John

Hancock's aunt Lydia and his fiancée Dorothy Quincy joined him and Samuel Adams in the countryside, away from the king's army.

There was one last move in the New England arms race. On April 8, Gen. Gage sent a small force by ship to secure "all the Artillery and spare arms" in Fort Pownall in Penobscot Bay, now Maine. Three days later he received a report from his source within the Provincial Congress—obviously Dr. Church—that the "Guns at fort Pownall [were] intended to be seized & the fort destroyed." The Crown thus managed to keep "Sixteen Peices of Cannon," all six- and four-pounders, out of Patriot hands. This preemptive move by the British military would be the last small success of Gage's American career.

As their scheduled session neared its close, the Provincial Congress began to debate the crucial step of forming an army. This was a step up from a militia. An army consisted of not just citizens turning out in an emergency but full-time soldiers paid to drill and patrol. On April 11 the weighty committee on the state of the province proposed paying the minute companies—a quarter of all the militiamen in Massachusetts—to train extra time, in effect turning them into army soldiers. That had implications both political and financial. "After a long debate" the congress declined that option.

The next day, the committee on the state of the province recommended "engaging six companies of the train, and keeping them constantly in exercise, and paying them." That was not exactly forming an army, but it would create an artillery branch "in readiness to enter the service of the colony, when an army shall be raised." The cost would be only a fraction of the expense of paying all the minutemen. The congress delegates could stomach that expense and voted yes. Thus, Massachusetts decided to build an army around its artillery corps.

Two days later, the Provincial Congress adjourned until May. Dr. Church sent the governor another message about the legislature's plans for an army of 18,000 men with "Six Companies of Matrosses" (180 men) as its core. Church did not attend the meetings of the committees of safety and supplies that followed, but they moved ahead with creating an artillery corps as directed. On April 17, those delegates voted "that Col. Barrett be desired to raise an artillery company" in Concord. They also decided to invite Jabez Hatch to restart the Boston train; he had been its second-in-command. If he declined, they would invite Thomas Crafts to take charge, and after that they would resort to Lemuel Robinson "as captain of the company in Dorchester." They decided to send "the four six pounders" to Col. William Prescott in Groton, "the two seven inch brass mortars" to Acton. On the 18th, the committee made its final determination about the Boston train's guns: "the two brass two pounders, and two brass three pounders, [would] be under the care of the Boston company of artillery, and of Capt. Robinson's."

Meanwhile, on April 14, Gen. Gage received orders from London written January 27. On behalf of the royal government, Lord Dartmouth did not merely authorize military action against the rebellion; he told the general that he had to act. The ministry specified that "the first & essential step . . . would be to arrest the principal actors and abettors in the Provincial Congress," even if "such a proceeding should be, according to your own idea of it, a signal for hostilities."

The Concord spy's last report in poor French was dated the same day. It said that at the end of the previous week Paul Revere had brought a letter from Dr. Warren warning that "dans peu des Jours, *un Corps des troupes reglés*, devait marche pour investir, et prendre possession de Concord"—in a few days, a body of regulars would march to take possession of Concord. In a panic, the congress had ordered Barrett to empty the town house of the twelve cannon and all the ammunition. Medicine and powder barrels were sent to different houses, including Barrett's, "où Les Canons de Cuivre Restent encore cachés"—where the brass cannon were still hidden. But for how much longer? It was once again time for Gen. Gage to act.

Ten

"If You Meet with Any Brass Artillery"

LORD DARTMOUTH HAD TOLD GEN. GAGE TO ARREST THE leaders of the Massachusetts resistance. He wrote that that was "the first & essential step." He said the general should detain those rebels even if it prompted "hostilities," meaning a violent uprising. Yet Gage did not make any arrests.

The general may have seen practical problems with seizing Patriot leaders that the government ministers, writing in January from three thousand miles away, could not. The militia uprising and court closings back in September had shown Gage that, contrary to years of assumptions by Crown officials and supporters, the rural populace was not being led around by malcontent politicians in Boston. The farmers were taking action on their own, so detaining men like Samuel Adams would have limited benefits.

Nonetheless, an order was an order, and Gage set aside this order from his superiors. As of April 15, it would have been possible to arrest some of the "principal actors and abettors in the Provincial Congress." Dr. Joseph Warren was in Boston, as was Continental Congress delegate Thomas Cushing. Of the fourteen members of the committees of safety and supplies who attended meetings in April, Devens and Cheever lived in Charlestown, Heath in Roxbury, Gardner and Watson in Cambridge, Palmer in Watertown, White in Brookline, and Pigeon in Newton—all towns close to Boston. Orne, Lee, and Gerry were based in Marblehead and Lincoln in Hingham, but on the morning of April 18 those four men and more were at a committee meeting in west Cambridge. Even Hancock and Adams, trying to keep out of Gage's reach, were significantly closer than the provincial stores at Concord and Worcester.

There is no evidence that Gen. Gage had that information about the delegates' locations, however. His intelligence files contain only a few incidental reports on individual Patriot leaders. His most recent list of committee of safety and supplies members came from Church on February 24; he never asked the doctor for an update. The general had told Brown and D'Berniere to gather information on roads and weapons, not local leaders. In effect, Gen. Gage had decided at the start of the year to track the congress's supplies. Again, that approach might have made sense. Arresting a few leaders would not pacify Massachusetts. Gunpowder barrels and iron cannon weighing hundreds of pounds were less mobile than people (though, as it turned out, Patriots had less trouble moving fieldpieces from Concord than moving Hancock from Lexington). But as a result of his approach, on April 15 Gage did not have the information his troops would need to arrest the "principal actors and abettors" aside from those living in Boston.

Even the intelligence that Gage had collected about the Patriot military supplies was tightly focused. The congress's "military magazine, or laboratory," in Charlestown was much closer than Concord, and Gage's officers had seen cannon in Watertown, but his files show no attempts to follow up on those leads. By late February Gage knew where the Provincial Congress had artillery pieces: "most . . . are at Worcester, a few at Concord and a few at Watertown." But the general never received house-by-house inventories about the material stored in and around Worcester. Indeed, much of his intelligence about Worcester came from the Concord spy's visit there, checking to see if the Boston train's guns had arrived. It looks like Gen. Gage decided in March to focus on Concord, so when the time for action arrived he had detailed information about only one town.

Destroying the Provincial Congress's arms at Concord, Gen. Gage knew, would require a bold march deep into unfriendly territory. It was seventeen miles from Boston to the center of Concord and another two across the North Bridge to Barrett's farm. Each of those miles meant his troops would be more tired and more exposed to rebel attacks, as would every quarter-hour the men spent searching for weaponry or destroying it. But at Concord, and only at Concord, the army might find the four brass fieldpieces from the Boston train. If they succeeded in doing that, their mission would erase the embarrassment of having let those guns get away.

How much those cannon weighed on Gen. Gage as he made his plans is speculative. But when he listed what Lt.-Col. Francis Smith's column should look for, the first items were "Four Brass Cannon and two Mortars or Cohorns . . . in the Cellar or out Houses of Mr. Barrett a little on the other side the Bridge where is also lodged a Quantity of Powder & Lead." To get through Concord to Barrett's farm, the regulars would have to move past other cannon: "Ten Iron Cannon before the Town-House and two within it," and "Three Guns 24 Pounders, lodged in the Prison yard." There were also "Cannon hid in a wood a mile & a half from the Center of the Village between the River and Malden [Walden] Pond." But the brass cannon were at the top of Gage's list.

The general also listed other houses Lt.-Col. Smith's troops should search: "Messrs Hubbard, near the Meeting, Butler, Jones the Tailors, near Hubbards, two men of the name of Bond, and particularly at Mr. Whitneys who lives on the Right Hand near the Entrance of the Town, at a House plaistered white a small yard in Front and a railed Fence." All that information came from the Concord spy's letters on March 9 and April 6. In some cases, the spy had provided first names as well; given how many families shared surnames in colonial New England towns, Gage should probably have passed that additional data on to allow Smith's men to find the right house quicker.

Sometime on April 18, however, Gage received what must have been frustrating news:

> The military Stores are removed—The Field pieces four Excepted which are now in Concord Town House are committed to the care of several Towns in the vicinity—The Powder is sent to Leicester excepting a few Barrels that were left with Capt Barrett to make up into cartridges together with a Quantity of Balls in proportion.

Almost all the supplies left in the other Concord houses were "Provisions," not weapons. That information most likely came from Dr. Church because it went on to describe the inner workings of the committee of safety and supplies.

Following the committee's orders, James Barrett had started moving the congress's most important military supplies out of the center of Concord and off his farm to neighboring towns and woods. The colonel's grandson James, then fourteen, later recalled how he and other boys "With oxen and cart, . . . removed the stores deposited at the house of his grandfather into the woods, and concealed them, a cart-load in a place, under pine boughs." To speed the movement, "the lads would march on each side of the oxen and goad them into a trot." In 1835 local historian Lemuel Shattuck stated, "Four cannon were carried to Stow." A tradition from that town says that those guns, possibly the fieldpieces from the Boston train, "were hidden in the woods north of the lower village, not far from the residence of Henry Gardner." As the Provincial Congress's receiver-general, Gardner was used to taking responsibility for its treasures.

As time grew short, Barrett and his family looked for places to hide material on their farm. Local historian Ezra Ripley wrote in 1832:

> Mrs. Barrett had concealed the small articles that belong to cannon, with musket balls, flints cutlasses, &c., in casks in the garret, and had put over them a quantity of feathers which prevented discovery.

In another half-century, descendants were telling a more elaborate story, as recorded by Margaret Sidney:

> the men in the Barrett family ploughed up the land south of the old barn, in what is now the kitchen garden, a space of about thirty feet square, and while one led the oxen, the others followed and dropped into the furrow the muskets that were stored in the house—then went back and turned the earth over them, thus concealing them.

Such stories domesticated the process of hiding the congress's property, turning it into a family project linked to the everyday tasks of a preindustrial farm. The quaintness of that trickery might camouflage what the Barretts were doing: hiding weapons of war from the government.

Despite knowing that the Barretts and their helpers were moving the Provincial Congress's "military Stores," Gen. Gage proceeded with his plan for an expedition to Concord. The pressure from London to act was strong. So is bureaucratic inertia—once the general had begun preparations, he may have felt a need to see them through. And another possible factor was how Gage read where the locals had moved the fieldpieces, "four Excepted which are now in Concord Town House." The general's informants in Concord had consistently described the four brass fieldpieces being stored together. Might those be the four still in town? The odds were not great, but the desire to recover those stolen cannon might have given Gage just enough motive to carry on.

The general revised his instructions for Lt.-Col. Smith about what his troops should look for. Gage still held out hope that the regulars would find artillery, and brass guns in particular, but his final draft was much less specific:

> Having received Intelligence, that a Quantity of Ammunition, Provision, Artillery, Tents and small Arms, have been collected at Concord, for the Avowed Purpose of raising and supporting a Rebellion against His Majesty, you will March with the Corps of

Grenadiers and light Infantry, put under your Command, with the utmost expedition and Secrecy to Concord, where your will seize and destroy all the Artillery, Ammunition, Provisions, Tents, Small Arms, and all Military Stores whatever. But you will take care that the Soldiers do not plunder the Inhabitants, or hurt private property.

You have a Draught of Concord, on which is marked, the Houses, Barns, &c., which contain the above Military Stores. You will order a Trunion to be knocked off each Gun, but if its found impracticable on any, they must by spiked, and the Carriages distroyed. The Powder and flower, must be shook out of the Barrells into the River, the Tents burnt, Pork or Beef destroyed in the best way you can devise, And the men may put Balls or lead in their pockets, throwing them by degrees into Ponds, Ditches &c., but not Quantity together, so that they may be recovered afterwards.

If you meet with any Brass Artillery, you will order their Muzzles to be beat in so as to render them useless.

You will observe by the Draught that it will be necessary to secure the two Bridges as soon as possible, you will therefore Order a party of the best Marchers, to go on with expedition for that purpose.

A small party on Horseback is ordered out to stop all advice of your March getting to Concord before you, and a small number of Artillery go out in Chaises to wait for you on the Road, with Sledge Hammers, Spikes & c.

You will open your business, and return with the Troops, as soon as possible, which I must leave to your own Judgment and Discretion.

On the night of April 18, 1775, companies of British soldiers were rowed quietly out of Boston. This time they numbered around 800, or about three times the forces sent to Charlestown and Salem. Brown, D'Berniere, and some Loyalists who knew the Massachusetts countryside accompanied them as guides. This column was also preceded by that "small party on Horseback"—army officers patrolling the roads between Charlestown and Concord to prevent Patriot couriers and travelers from spreading the alarm.

Ironically, those mounted patrols provoked the alarm they were supposed to prevent. Two members of the committee of safety and supplies, Richard Devens and Abraham Watson, were returning from a meeting at the Black Horse Tavern in west Cambridge after sunset when they met "a great number of B[ritish]. O[fficers]. and their servants on horseback" on the road. The two men decided to turn around to warn their committee colleagues, which meant riding back through the crowd of military men. At the tavern, Elbridge Gerry quickly sent John Hancock in Lexington a warning of "eight or nine officers, . . . suspected of some evil design." At nine o'clock in the evening Hancock wrote back, "it is said the officers are gone Concord Road, & I will send word thither."

Ordinary citizens were taking similar action on their own. Solomon Brown of Lexington spotted those officers as they all rode west from Boston, and he saw "by the occasional blowing aside of their top coats" that "they were armed." When he reached his hometown, Brown alerted his militia sergeant, William Munroe, who set up a guard outside the Lexington parsonage, where Hancock and Adams were staying. The sight of "a party of officers" also alerted Elijah Sanderson. Militia captain John Parker sent Nathan Munroe riding to Bedford and Concord over a different road with the news. That must have spurred the Barretts and their neighbors to work even faster.

The Boston Patriots had been on high alert for over a week by that point. Gen. Gage suspected that "two vessels [arriving] at Marblehead, on the 8th of April," brought a warning about the government's instructions to start arresting people. The next day, reportedly between two sessions of his Sunday service, the Rev. Samuel Cooper decided that it was the right time to travel in the country for his health. His brother William, the town clerk, probably went out with the town records. Samuel Adams and John Hancock had already decided to stay in Lexington. Thomas Cushing and his family left Boston on April 16. *Massachusetts Spy* printer Isaiah Thomas packed up a press and type and sent it out the same day, following on the night of the 18th.

That Massachusetts Patriots' worry about being taken prisoner produced two significant results. First, it left Dr. Joseph Warren as their one major organizer in Boston. As a member of the committee of safety and supplies, Dr. Warren had the authority and the knowledge to direct the Patriots' actions. He had contacts all over town and exclusive sources of information. Even seasoned activists waited for Dr. Warren's instructions before setting their plans in motion. If Gen. Gage had arrested the young physician on the afternoon of April 18, he might have put a significant crimp in the Patriots' ability to respond to events. But the general was either wary of overstepping his authority or concentrating his attention elsewhere. That left Dr. Warren free to gather his own intelligence and send out warnings—his first messenger being the young tanner and militia adjutant William Dawes, the second the politically active silversmith Paul Revere.

The second result of Massachusetts Patriots' worry about arrests is that some organizers assumed the British soldiers were coming straight for them. That anxiety played out as both tragedy and farce. In west Cambridge, the three Marblehead members of the committee of safety and supplies—Jeremiah Lee, Azor Orne, and Elbridge Gerry—woke up to find the column of soldiers passing right by their tavern. They rushed downstairs in their night clothes and dashed out a back door. There they flung themselves down on the cold ground of "a cornfield, where the old stalks still remained," until all the soldiers had passed. Lee, at age fifty-four, "never recovered from the effects of the exposure. He was attacked, soon after, by a severe fever, and died, May 10th, 1775."

No accounts of the day from 1775, published or unpublished, British or American, describe soldiers stopping to search the Black Horse Tavern in west Cambridge on their way west. Lt.-Col. Smith's orders did not authorize such a stop or say anything about detaining committee members. The mounted officers who had gone out earlier had not stopped Devens and Watson, even as those men drove past them twice. The mission of the British expedition was to reach Concord as quickly as possible.

The first published account of British soldiers entering the Marblehead men's inn and looking inside their bedroom appeared more than fifty years later in James T. Austin's biography of Gerry (which omitted Lee entirely). That account stated with some surprise that the soldiers did not take Gerry's watch from under his pillow—in other words, they left no evidence of going into that room. That search appears to be a later addition to the event, inserted to make the men's flight into the cold appear more reasonable and less fearful.

The same anxiety about arrests shaped events further west in Lexington. The presence of Samuel Adams and John Hancock—thought to be Gen. Gage's top quarry—put the town on extra-high alert. Militia sergeant Munroe and his guard were already outside. When Revere and Dawes arrived with news that the regulars were on the march, that raised the alarm even higher. Adams, Dorothy Quincy, the Rev. Jonas Clarke, and Revere spent hours convincing Hancock that he had to leave Lexington before those soldiers arrived. Clarke later wrote that they feared "sudden arrest, if not assassination." Scores of militiamen mustered in the early morning of April 19 and later lined up on the town common as those troops appeared from the east. That crowd might not have been so large and anxious if the men of Lexington were not so keenly aware that their minister was hosting two of the colony's Continental Congress delegates.

To be sure, the Massachusetts Patriots also recognized that Gen. Gage might target the supplies at Concord. Paul Revere visited that town earlier in the week to confer with Barrett about the possibility. As the expedition set off from Boston on the night of April 18, Col. Percy reported hearing a local gentleman state that its aim was "The cannon at Concord." But Dr. Warren knew that Barrett had already received orders to move those artillery pieces. When he sent out warnings on the night of April 18, Warren told Dawes and Revere to ride only as far as Lexington. Those men decided on their own to proceed to Concord.

The sad irony is that if the Marblehead delegates had remained in their warm bedroom, the king's soldiers would have marched right by their tavern. Jeremiah Lee—who had chaired the Provincial Congress committee that had recommended creating a military

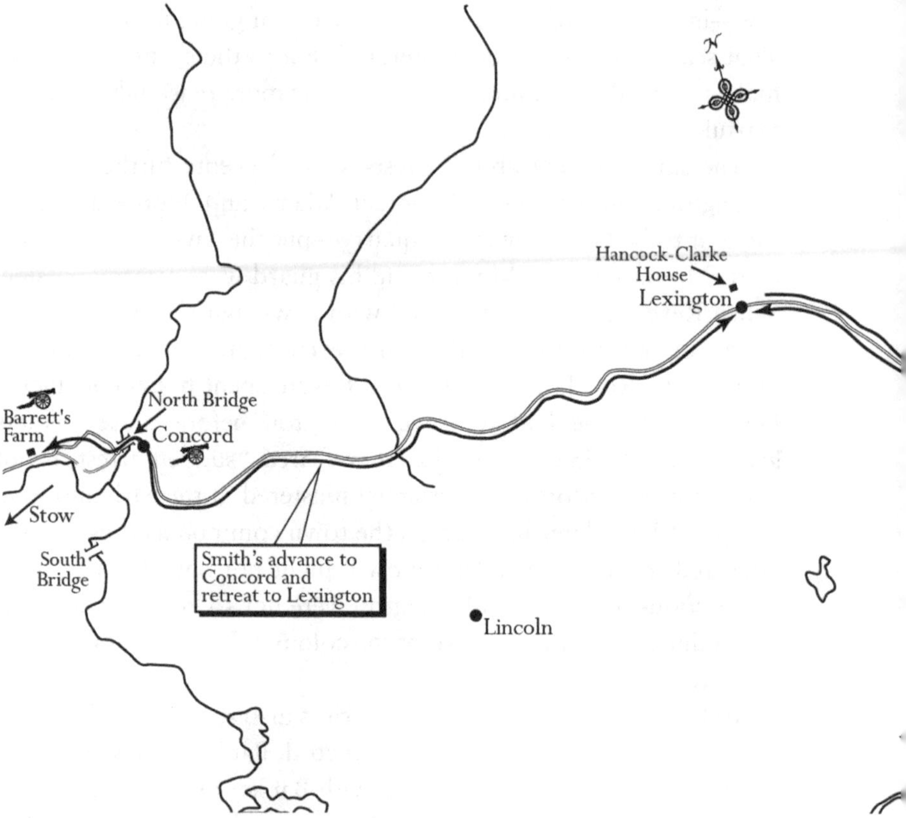

MAP 3. The Road to Concord, April 18–19, 1775. The fieldpieces symbolize places known to have cannon.

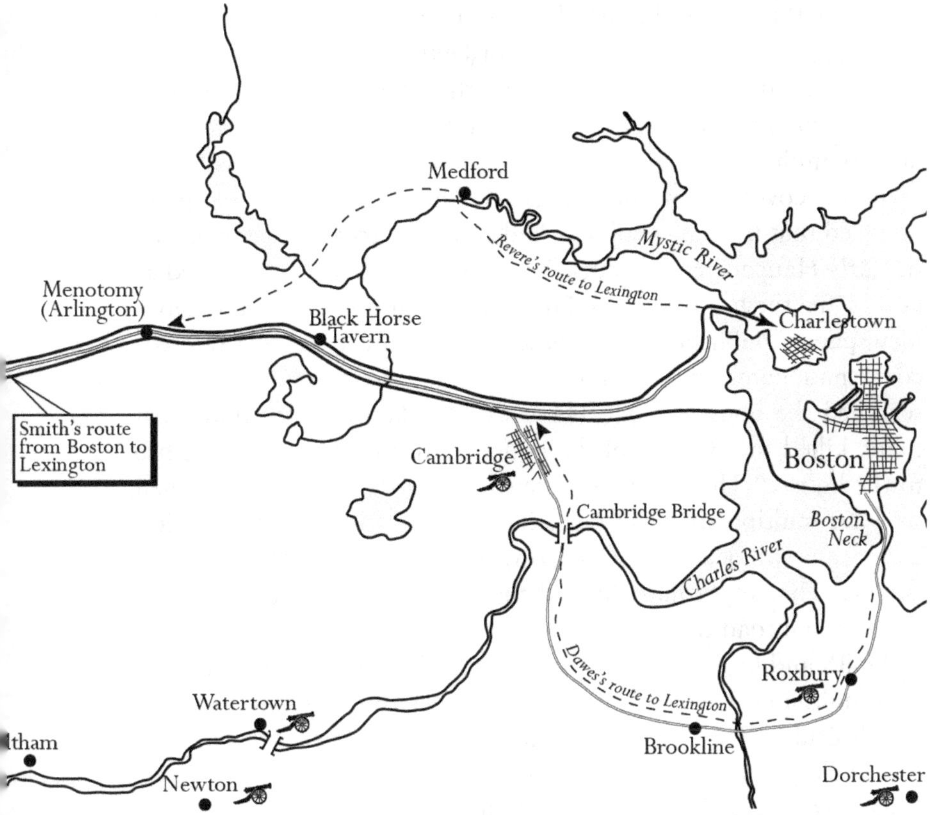
Medford
Mystic River
Revere's route to Lexington
Menotomy (Arlington)
Black Horse Tavern
Charlestown
Smith's route from Boston to Lexington
Cambridge
Boston
Cambridge Bridge
Boston Neck
Charles River
Dawes's route to Lexington
Roxbury
Watertown
tham
Brookline
Newton
Dorchester

force, served on the committee of supplies, brought in material on his ships, and supplied David Mason with money—did not have to take sick and die. Likewise, Hancock could have stayed in the parsonage, either eating his breakfast salmon or gripping his sword and ready to resist arrest. The men of Lexington could have sullenly watched from their doorways as the regulars passed through their town. Lt.-Col. Smith's mission was solely to search for and destroy military supplies in Concord.

In its coverage of the events of April 19, the Patriot press assumed that the king's soldiers had come out to arrest people, particularly Hancock and Adams. Those two gentlemen were hailed as heroes as they traveled to Philadelphia in the following days. Newspapers published a false description of atrocities that the redcoats had committed at the Lexington parsonage: "when they searched the house for Mr. Hancock & Adams, & not find them there, killed the Woman of the house & all the children & set fire to the house." Those stories were so strong that even today, when we have multiple drafts of Gen. Gage's orders and his private files, Americans still believe that the army was out to arrest Hancock and Adams. That myth had clouded the real reason that the redcoats were on the road to Concord.

Smith and his column reached their goal about eight o'clock, the local militia companies withdrawing before them to a hill past the North Bridge. The redcoats set out to search the places on the map that their general had supplied, based on his intelligence sources. Gage's letter to Lord Dartmouth about the expedition stated vaguely that his soldiers "proceeded to Concord where they destroyed all the Military Stores they could find." In an almanac printed at the end of the year, the Rev. William Gordon of Roxbury was more specific about what the troops found:

> The detachment while at Concord disabled two 24 pounders, destroyed their two carriages, and seven wheels for the same, with their limbers; sixteen wheels for brass 3 pounders, and two carriages, with limber and wheels for two 4 pounders, 500 pounds of ball thrown into the river, wells and other places, and broke in pieces 60 barrels of flour, half of which was saved.

As of April 6, those two twenty-four-pounders and a third had been in the courtyard of the Concord jail. Their large size probably made them harder to move than the other cannon in town.

Following his orders, Lt.-Col. Smith sent three companies of soldiers to search James Barrett's farm, across the North Bridge. D'Berniere guided them to the "house where there was some cannon and other stores hid." Three more companies of redcoats went as far as the bridge to make sure the first three could come back. Meanwhile, in the center of Concord other companies set about burning the artillery carriage wheels that they found there. The smoke from that fire, which momentarily spread to a town building, agitated the militia units massed above the bridge. Adjutant Joseph Hosmer asked senior officers, "Will you let them burn the town down?" Incensed, the militiamen advanced on the outnumbered soldiers at the bridge. The nervous redcoats fired, and the provincials fired back. Men on both sides died. That was the second fatal skirmish of the day, and it even more clearly grew out of Gen. Gage's orders to search for and destroy provincial artillery.

The cannon that the Massachusetts Provincial Congress and the towns had gathered and guarded so proudly over the preceding seven months played no part in the fighting that followed. In Newton a shot from "one of John Pigeon's guns" was merely the signal for men to assemble. Some militia artillery companies marched as infantry. But none of those companies, even those from towns close to the line of march such as Cambridge and Watertown, brought out cannon to fire back at the Royal Artillery.

In fact, for all the Massachusetts Patriots' pride in their new artillery force, they may not have had even one cannon entirely ready for action when the war began. On April 21, the committee of safety and supplies ordered David Mason to: "provide one field piece, with every implement necessary for action, and proceed forthwith to provide for the remainder, till the whole are in a thorough state of preparation, unless otherwise ordered: the cannon to be provided for are eight three-pounders, and three six-pounders."

The loss of some carriage wheels at Concord may have set back Mason's work, but more likely it had never been complete because of technical difficulties and how often those weapons had to be moved. Thus, although the Massachusetts artillery force was crucial to starting the war, what those cannon represented on April 19 turned out to be more significant than what they could actually do.

As important as that provincial artillery had been, however, both sides had powerful reasons not to publicize it. The Massachusetts Provincial Congress was trying to reinforce a "myth of injured innocence," as David Hackett Fischer termed it. The congress's detailed report on the outbreak of the war therefore played down the alarm system and the alliances its leaders had prepared. That effort would hardly benefit from an admission that those innocent Massachusetts yeomen had accumulated a large artillery force. The Provincial Congress's report therefore described what the regulars had been looking for only as "a quantity of stores," "the province stores," or, in Col. Barrett's words, "some magazines belonging to the province."

Likewise, Gen. Gage referred to the goal of the march to Concord only as "a Magazine of Military Stores, deposited there for the Use of an Army to be assembled," or "a large quantity of Military Stores." He had equally strong but personal reasons to play down what he knew about the Provincial Congress's artillery when he reported to his superiors in London. The Concord expedition was the third or fourth time the provincials had made off with weapons just before his forces came to take them. As a result of the vague official statements from both sides of the battle, most accounts of the start of the Revolutionary War have said little about Massachusetts's cannon.

Gen. Gage continued to track the Boston train's guns for the first few weeks of fighting. On May 12, Maj. John Small, who had good contacts among American officers from the previous war, passed on intelligence that "All the Cannon Excepting the four that were Paddocks are removed from Concord to Cambridge togeather with ye small Arms & Ammunition." By then, provincial sources had stopped mentioning the Boston militia train's guns separately from the rest of the Massachusetts artillery force. Once the New Englanders saw they were fighting a siege, they knew they needed heavy artillery more than small, maneuverable field guns. After the four brass cannon were mounted and equipped, they were presumably assigned to Robinson's artillerists in Roxbury, as promised, and played little role in the subsequent months.

The siege of Boston ended in March 1776 with the evacuation of the British army and nearly one thousand Loyalist supporters. Bostonians held a town meeting on March 29, and among other business they named a committee to "wait on General Washington, & to acquaint him that it is the Desire of the Town, that the Four Pieces of Cannon which are in the Continental Train of Artillery, & belonging to the Town of Boston, may not be carried out of this Colony, if his Excellency should apprehend the general Interest of the Colony will permit their remaining here."

The committee was led by the militia train's former third-in-command, Thomas Crafts, Jr., who was setting up a Massachusetts artillery force after he had refused a Continental army commission as major because it did not rank high enough. With him were Paul Revere, who would eventually succeed Crafts as head of this state unit, and the colonel of the Boston militia regiment, Thomas Marshall. They wanted cannon for the local troops. Furthermore, with the war largely about property rights and defining the powers of different levels of government, it was only logical for the town of Boston to claim its property back from the Continental army.

Gen. George Washington, however, had a wider war to win. As commander-in-chief he had already sent his new artillery commander, Henry Knox, and most of the American artillery south to prepare defenses in New York. There is no record of Washington's reply to the Boston committee, but the militia train's four brass cannon remained with the Continental army.

Massachusetts did not forget about those four cannon, however. At the end of the war, the states had to sort out their property with the national government. In March 1783 Stephen Higginson, a new delegate to the Continental Congress, wrote to his colleague John Lowell: "Genl. Knox has two of the four ps. of brass Cannon lent to [*sic*] Our State, the Secretary of War [Benjamin Lincoln] had better be requested to return them, & the Continent charged with the two that are lost." That request took a while, and five years later John Hancock, now governor of Massachusetts, wrote to Knox, now secretary of war: "You will please to deliver to Capt. Thomas Barnard, Commander of the New York packet [ship], the two brass field pieces with the apparatus, belonging to this Commonwealth, said field-pieces having been loaned to the United States, during the late war."

On May 19 Knox told the confederation Congress:

> That there are, in the Arsenals of the United States, two brass Cannon, which constituted one moiety of the field artillery with which the late was commenced on the part of America, and which were constantly in service throughout the war—that the said cannon are the property of the Commonwealth of Massachusetts, and the Governour thereof hath requested that they be returned.

The Congress did not simply authorize Knox to send those two fieldpieces back to his home town. It resolved "That the Secretary at War cause a suitable inscription to be placed on the said cannon."

The War Department quickly put those guns on a ship to Boston. On June 5 the *American Herald* reported that the "two pieces of brass artillery" had arrived. In addition, Knox had written to Gov. Hancock from New York to say that when he came back to his home in town that month "he will agree with Mr. [Joseph] *Callender*, to engrave such facts on the cannon, as shall be directed." As for what made those cannon notable, the newspaper said:

> They were, while under a British guard in this town, taken off the carriages and safely conveyed to Dorchester; and have been used in 17 engagements during the late war, one of them having been taken by the enemy, and retaken several times. . . . we shall therefore ere long, be able to give our readers a more particular history of the peregrinations of those extraordinary daughters of Bellona.

Unfortunately, the newspapers appear to have never published the full story of the Boston train's three-pounders during the war—what Continental unit used them, which seventeen battles they had been part of, how they were lost and "retaken several times." One of the surviving weapons shows signs of having been spiked and then restored, which certainly indicates a close call. As for the train's other two cannon, those lost to the British, they were no longer discussed.

The engraving that Knox ordered took nearly a year. On May 26, 1789, the *Salem Mercury* reported that "Mr. Joseph Callender has just finished the inscription ordered by Congress. . . . The inscription is finely executed in relievo—the HANCOCK, one. The ADAMS, the other." From then on, those two little cannon could always be identified as the "Hancock" and the "Adams." Those names were a final jab at the British army, which had missed those guns at Concord just as Americans thought they had missed the two Patriots at Lexington.

Beyond those names, the cannon were now engraved with this proud story:

SACRED TO LIBERTY.
THIS IS ONE OF FOUR CANNON
WHICH CONSTITUTED THE WHOLE TRAIN
OF FIELD ARTILLERY
POSSESSED BY THE BRITISH COLONIES OF
NORTH AMERICA
AT THE COMMENCEMENT OF THE WAR
ON THE 19 OF APRIL 1775.
THIS CANNON AND ITS FELLOW
BELONGING TO A NUMBER OF CITIZENS OF
BOSTON
WERE USED IN MANY ENGAGEMENTS
DURING THE WAR.

THE OTHER TWO, THE PROPERTY OF THE
GOVERNMENT OF MASSACHUSETTS
WERE TAKEN BY THE ENEMY.
BY ORDER OF THE UNITED STATES
IN CONGRESS ASSEMBLED
MAY 19, 1788.

EPILOGUE

"Through All Our History, to the Last"

Henry Knox's statement that "four cannon . . . constituted the whole train of Field Artillery, possessed by the British colonies of North America, at the commencement of the war" is obviously contradicted by all the events described in the preceding chapters. The Massachusetts Provincial Congress counted thirty-eight fieldpieces under its direction when the war began. The four Boston militia guns were the only *brass* fieldpieces belonging to Massachusetts, but Rhode Island soon sent four brass cannon to the siege lines around Boston. And other colonies controlled artillery as well.

That inscription on the "Hancock" and "Adams" was the first of many myths told about those small cannon over the next century. Those myths, as well as the gradual release and rediscovery of more accurate information, provide a revealing map of how New Englanders looked back on the American Revolution.

The story that Knox told reinforced the "myth of injured innocence," the new nation's self-portrait as people innocently taking up arms to protect their property and rights after being attacked by an oppressive government. By describing the "Hancock" and

"Adams" as much rarer than they really were, Knox's inscription also made the Bostonians who secured those guns more important, the Americans who stood up to the better equipped British military more courageous. And, incidentally, that version of history rendered Henry Knox more significant, since he brought the Continental army around Boston many more cannon in the winter of 1776.

Massachusetts did not set aside those two brass fieldpieces in a museum or monument as valued relics of the Revolutionary War. Instead, they appear to have gone into a state militia armory, much like other cannon. In the early 1800s the state lent them to the Ancient and Honorable Artillery Company. On October 2, 1820, company members were using the "Hancock" and "Adams" for "experimental gunnery" when the "left piece"—the "Adams"—burst. The explosion injured nobody but left a fist-sized hole in the brass barrel. A report to the Massachusetts Council the next year expressed hope that the gun could be recast "to perpetuate the two pieces of ordnance to which a memorial so interesting to the people of the Commonwealth is attached." That period's idea of perpetuation was not to preserve the "Adams" from further harm but to melt it down and re-create it. Instead, both guns went back into storage.

Those weapons' reemergence into the historical record in 1823 came in the context of another attempt to shape how Americans remembered their past. In 1817 William Wirt, a Jeffersonian official from Virginia, published a popular biography of Patrick Henry. John Adams was not pleased with how the book made Virginia the first mover in the struggle for American independence. "Virginian geese are always swans," the former president was prone to grumble. In January 1818 Adams told the biographer, "I envy none of the well merited glories of Virginia, or any of her sages or heroes. But, sir, I am jealous, very jealous, of the honour of Massachusetts."

Specifically, Adams promoted the memory of Massachusetts's James Otis, Jr., whose argument against the writs of assistance before the Massachusetts Supreme Court in 1761 predated Patrick

Henry's speech against the Stamp Act by four years. In a March 1817 letter to his old law clerk William Tudor, the former president described Otis's oration in highly dramatic terms and declared that "American independence was then and there born." After Wirt's book, Adams allowed that letter to be published. He also encouraged Tudor's namesake son, editor of the *North American Review*, to write the biography of Otis that he had imagined.

William Tudor, Jr.'s *Life of James Otis, of Massachusetts* appeared in 1823. While he was working on that book, Tudor was also a key organizer in Massachusetts's effort to build a massive monument at the site of the Battle of Bunker Hill. He gathered stirring stories about Revolutionary Massachusetts in the early 1770s, including Samuel Gore's recollection of saving the train's guns. The fiftieth anniversary of independence was approaching, and the young men who had fought the Revolution were nearing the ends of their lives. There was growing public interest in those veterans' stories, bringing them out of the shadows of anonymous collective activity. The story of the artillery theft that appeared in *The Life of James Otis* reflected the patriotic values of that time. It also sidestepped the awkward question of Obadiah Whiston, either a turncoat or unjustly accused.

After some delays, the Bunker Hill Monument was completed in 1842. The state chose to mount the "Hancock" and "Adams" in a place of honor inside that granite obelisk, Boston's most prominent Revolutionary War memorial. Visitors could climb the stairs of that tall tower and see the two brass fieldpieces in the round chamber at the top. Not surprisingly, people soon concluded that the "Hancock" and "Adams" were somehow linked to the Battle of Bunker Hill. In fact, of the six field-pieces that American artillery companies brought onto the Charlestown Peninsula during that battle, the British captured five, all four-pounders. The Massachusetts artillery regiment still had its "four small brass cannon" that fall.

The public reappearance of the "Hancock" and "Adams" in the Bunker Hill Monument apparently shaped how Susan Smith, the daughter of David Mason, shared more information about her father's work gathering artillery for the Massachusetts Provincial Congress between November 1774 and April 1775, as discussed in Chapter 9. Smith's narrative of her father's work before the war reveals how Americans were remembering their Revolutionary forefathers not just as innocent victims but as "bold, active, and defiant defenders of home and hearth," in Fischer's words. It had become safe, even desirable, to discuss how Massachusetts had *prepared* for war.

The historian who most shaped how nineteenth-century Americans heard the story of the "Hancock" and "Adams" was James Spear Loring, author of *The Hundred Boston Orators* in 1852. In his chapter on John Hancock, Loring described the theft of the gun dubbed the "Hancock," quoting what Samuel Gore had told Tudor—without, however, citing Tudor's book. Loring also provided full names for the conspirators whom Gore had remembered only as "Balch, Gridley, Whiston, and two or three more," plus "*Master* Holbrook." Unfortunately, those identifications do not stand up. For example, Loring wrote that "Gridley" was Jeremiah Gridley, who died in 1767. It appears that Loring's method was simply to look for the period's most prominent man with the matching last name. Nonetheless, many chroniclers of Boston repeated Loring's identifications.

In 1851 an entirely new version of the removal of the Boston cannon credited Dr. Elisha Story with leading the effort. That tale appeared in a book by a grandson of the doctor in 1851. It said that the British had "stationed two brass field-pieces on the Common" to intimidate the townspeople, and Dr. Story had held a pistol to the head of a redcoat guard while his friends made off with the weapons.That tale was more than improbable, and Dr. Story's office records show that he had moved out of Boston before the train's two cannon disappeared.

The tale about Dr. Story came from his daughter, "Mrs. E[lizabeth]. White." As "E.S.W.," she also set down family lore about how her maternal grandfather, John Pedrick of Marblehead, had warned the people of Salem that Lt-Col. Leslie and his troops were on their way, as recounted in Chapter 8. Pedrick was actually a supporter of the royal government before and after that date. Another story from the same source described White's mother being courted by a British army officer who died at Bunker Hill—except that no officer of the stated name died in that battle. All those family fables appear to have come from Pedrick's daughter Mehitable, who became Dr. Story's second wife. A grandson had this to say about Mehitable Story:

> she was a great talker, telling manifold stories of the Revolution, and of the men and deeds of the past age. Her mind had a romantic turn, and with a sort of half-superstition she used to recount the legendary tales of her native town, never quite believing nor quite disbelieving them.

Some descendants were thus wary of Mehitable Story's "legendary tales," but others repeated them. Though some historians had doubts, others drew on those anecdotes for vivid details that more reliable historical records sadly do not supply.

Likewise, in 1827 someone rewrote Ens. D'Berniere's report of scouting the roads to Worcester to amplify the exciting moments. Presented as an authentic account taken from the papers of a Revolutionary War veteran, *A Journal Kept by Mr. John Howe* narrated the hike through the eyes of a twenty-two-year-old working for the British. This retelling switched the date of that mission to April 5, 1775, and brought Lt.-Col. Smith along for comic relief. The book went on to say that in May young "Howe" suddenly defected to the Americans for no clear reason, and it ended with stories of smuggling goods across the Canadian border during the War of 1812. The "John Howe Journal" was periodically reprinted over the following decades, sometimes with the dubious parts stripped out, and many authors have taken it as an authentic source.

In 1865 the Massachusetts Historical Society published John Andrews's letters, including his anecdote of the British army discovering that both of Boston's gunhouses had been burgled in September 1774. That story closely matched the episode that readers could now find in many local histories, tracing back through

Loring to Tudor and Gore. However, very few authors used Andrews's letter to pin that story to a particular date. The local historians of that time focused on individuals' heroism, more interested in identifying all the men who might be responsible for stealing the brass cannon than in clarifying the event's timetable. That vagueness meant that descendants and biographers could continue to link virtually anyone to the daring deed.

As a result, by the end of the century there was a long line of Bostonians linked to the "Hancock" and the "Adams," telling mutually contradictory narratives. The descendants of William Dawes made their claim in 1878 in a privately published book, as discussed in Chapter 9. An item in the *Massachusetts Historical Society Proceedings* for October 1880 retold the story of burglarizing the gunhouse on the Common, setting it during the first army occupation of Boston in 1768. Citing no sources, the author credited the theft to "Nathaniel Langdon . . . , with others of [Paddock's] company." In 1898, Abram English Brown wrote in *John Hancock: His Book* that Hancock instigated the theft in February 1775. Starting with Noah Brooks in 1900, biographers of Henry Knox have hinted that he was involved in securing the weapons of the Boston militia artillery after the war had begun in April 1775.

Thus, as the twentieth century began, Bostonians could read half a dozen mutually contradictory stories of rescuing the "Hancock" and "Adams." Those tales dated the gun's removal from Boston anytime from 1768 to mid-1775, and they credited at least a dozen men with performing the feat. The accumulation of so many different versions of history cast doubt on the veracity of the whole story. Cynicism, or at least skepticism, about such undocumented heroism produced a tidal change in the writing of American history around World War I. With so many claims and so little evidence, the legend of the "Hancock" and "Adams" collapsed under all the weight chroniclers had balanced on top of those two small guns. For most of the century the tale of stealing the Boston train's cannon, if told at all, was usually an anecdote used to enliven the pre-Revolutionary lives of William Dawes or Henry Knox.

Another important development of that era was the release of British documents about the start of the war, particularly the papers of Gen. Thomas Gage at the Clements Library in Michigan. Until then, American historians had been largely confined to British officials' public statements. Allen French's work with the Gage Papers brought more attention to the general's efforts to gather information before the war. After that, fewer authors retold how the brass cannon disappeared from Boston, but more probed the end of those guns' journey in Concord.

Again, there were speculative statements about who was involved. In *Turncoats, Traitors and Heroes* (1959), John Bakeless named the general's spy in Concord as "John Hall." That was an idea of Frank E. McKone of New Hampshire, who saw Hall everywhere: accompanying Brown and D'Berniere on their hikes from Boston, sending Gen. Gage reports from Concord, marching with Timothy Bigelow's Worcester company on April 19, and deserting from the British army to join the Americans in Cambridge. Aside from the common name "John Hall" and a perceived similarity of handwriting, McKone did not have hard evidence to support his theory.

This book is an attempt to bring the story of the "Hancock" and "Adams" back into how historians describe the start of the Revolutionary War in New England. Its roots lie in a Bicentennial-era interest in "ordinary" people and the Revolution "from the ground up," as explored by such authors as Alfred F. Young, Dirk Hoerder, and Robert Gross. Equally, this book is a testament to how computer networks and databases enable historians to share and search for information on a scale that would have left earlier generations of scholars flabbergasted—at least for a few minutes, before they hurried to take advantage of those resources themselves.

One day that growing cloud of information might reveal more about the Massachusetts artillery force. For example, a document might surface to show that Gen. Gage's staff did alert the authorities in London about the theft of the Boston train guns, to little response. In that case, the hypothesis that he was so anxious to retrieve them because he wanted to avoid having to share that embarrassing news would become untenable. Someone might find documents that reveal exactly who was sending Gage such detailed information on Concord. There is surely more to this story.

The start of the War for Independence in New England on April 19, 1775, will always interest Americans, so there will always be new books to compare with the previous wave. Recent years have brought us the British imperial perspective of Nick Bunker's *Empire on the Edge*, the emphasis on New England organizing in Ray and Marie Raphael's *The Spirit of '74*, the technical analysis of Derek W. Beck's *Igniting the American Revolution*, and more. Decades from now, scholars may look back on all the titles of this time and see common trends—perhaps an emphasis on communication networks or the fragility of empire. We are writing, after all, when Americans are all too aware of how a search for military weapons can lead to a long and costly war.

Among those various approaches, this book's tight focus on one story within the larger historical movement might seem narrow. But part of the "microhistory" approach is the conviction that individual aspirations and actions mattered, even within mass movements. Samuel Gore was just one link in the Patriots' network, but he made a significant choice to help spirit two cannon out of a militia gunhouse in September 1774—a choice tinged as much by local pride and family circumstances as by ideology. Gen. Thomas Gage could not repair the fundamental rift between the British Parliament and its North American colonies, but the choices he made as governor of Massachusetts, perhaps swayed by personal interests, affected how events played out.

In that spirit, it seems appropriate to relate how some of those people's stories ended:

On the evening of April 19, 1775, Gen. Thomas Gage's hand shook as he wrote to Col. Percy in Charlestown, assuring his subordinate that reinforcements were on their way to protect the exhausted soldiers back from Concord and Lexington. Gage remained the commander-in-chief of British forces in North America and royal governor of Massachusetts for another six months, finally recalled to London in September 1775. He retired with his American-born wife Margaret to Firle Place in the Sussex Downs, where they had two more children. Gage died in 1787, partially vindicated by the fact that no other British general had done any better at pacifying the British colonies than he had.

DR. JOSEPH WARREN slipped out of Boston early on the morning of April 19 and helped Gen. William Heath direct some of the fight between Massachusetts militia and the British troops withdrawing toward Boston. He was nearly shot that day. As president of the Provincial Congress of Massachusetts, Warren oversaw its response to the battle—issuing reports that told the Patriot side of the story, reorganizing the militia into an army, seeking support from other colonies. The congress named him a major general for his boldness and leadership, not because of any military experience. Before taking up that commission, he volunteered to fight at Bunker Hill on June 17, 1775, and was killed during the American retreat.

THOMAS OLIVER continued to serve as the royal lieutenant governor of Massachusetts, presiding over the last meetings of the mandamus Council in October 1775. He and his family evacuated with the king's troops the following March. After his first wife's death, Oliver remarried in Antigua in 1781 and then settled in Bristol, England. He lived until 1815, having received his salary from the Crown for over forty years.

Eager to be in the thick of political activity, DR. THOMAS YOUNG moved from Newport to Philadelphia in 1775. With other radicals, he helped to rewrite Pennsylvania's constitution on democratic lines. Keeping in touch with his old friend Ethan Allen, Young coined the name "Vermont" for the newly independent territory west of New Hampshire. He died in 1777 of a fever contracted while treating American soldiers.

DAVID MASON became the third-ranking officer in the artillery regiment of the Massachusetts army in April 1775 with the rank of major. During the Continental army shelling of Boston on March 2,

1776, in preparation for the advance onto the Dorchester Heights, Mason was in Roxbury firing a thirteen-inch mortar nicknamed the "Congress." After only two or three shots, it exploded, wounding him badly. Once he had partially recovered, and been promoted to the rank of lieutenant colonel, Mason became director of the Continental army laboratory in Springfield. He died in Boston in 1794.

ADINO PADDOCK helped to organize a Loyalist militia inside Boston during the siege. He then moved to London with his friend Capt. John Gore. While Gore eventually returned to his family in Boston, Paddock accepted a British government position on the Isle of Jersey, where he formed and trained a militia artillery company. Nineteenth-century Bostonians remembered Paddock for the "Paddock elms," a line of trees planted across from his coach-making yard beside the Common, which he looked after.

During the war SAMUEL GORE joined the reformed Cadets and served briefly in a campaign to drive the British out of Newport. Afterwards, he expanded his father's paint business while his younger brother Christopher prospered in the law, diplomacy, and finally politics, serving one term as governor of Massachusetts. In partnership with a brother-in-law, Samuel Gore bankrolled and managed factories for window glass in Boston and Chelmsford. These businesses made him a wealthy man until the company suddenly went bankrupt in 1827. In his seventies, Gore ended up living with a daughter and son-in-law on land the state had confiscated from his father's friend Adino Paddock.

OBADIAH WHISTON sailed away from Boston with the British army in March 1776 and dropped out of the historical records. His wife Priscilla and their two sons remained in Boston or returned to the town by the 1790s, however. And his grandson Francis C. Whiston helped to lay the cornerstone for the Bunker Hill Monument.

After helping to spread the alarm on April 18–19, 1775, WILLIAM DAWES's top priority was to bring his family out of Boston. During the war he worked as a commissary in Worcester before returning to Boston. In 1786 the men of western Massachusetts were keeping their courts closed, a movement that led to the Shays' Rebellion. Bostonians responded by forming volunteer militia companies. Dawes bustled around town enlisting men in the Ancient and Honorable Artillery Company, which had been inactive since 1775. Among those new members were Samuel Gore and Andrew Cunningham. Dawes died in 1799.

As one of Concord's justices of the peace, DUNCAN INGRAHAM participated in gathering testimony about the battle of April 19 for the Massachusetts Provincial Congress. During the war he was suspected of being a Tory but also served briefly during a militia call-up. In 1791 Ingraham won a term as Concord's representative to the General Court. Four years later, he remarried and moved out of town.

DR. BENJAMIN CHURCH became the head of the Continental army's medical wing in the summer of 1775. At the end of September a baker from Newport brought Gen. George Washington a suspicious letter that his former wife had asked him to send into Boston for her. Washington interrogated that woman and eventually learned that the letter had come from her lover, Dr. Church. The doctor lost his military positions and was locked up, but he insisted he was innocent and the army and the state of Massachusetts lacked the proof to hang him as a spy. In 1778 Massachusetts banished Church. He boarded a ship for Martinique, and it disappeared at sea. Not until the twentieth century did historians find conclusive evidence of Dr. Church's secret communication with Gen. Gage.

RICHARD DERBY, JR., and his brother Elias Haskett Derby spent most of the first day of the war arguing with their militia colonel, Timothy Pickering, that their Salem regiment should march faster to confront the British column. They did not make it. A younger brother, John, sailed one of Richard's ships to Britain as fast as possible in May 1775 to ensure that the Patriot side of the battle they missed got into the British newspapers first. During the war the family became even richer by financing privateers, and after the war they became fabulously rich in the China trade.

On April 19, 1775, Lemuel Robinson mustered the Dorchester minutemen. By the end of the day, they were helping to seal off the Boston Neck. When Massachusetts made the move to replace its militia units with an army to serve until the end of the year, Robinson was assigned to enlist troops for a regiment under Gen. William Heath. Instead, he signed up people to serve under him as colonel, and as a result was pushed out of the army. He retained his seat in the Provincial Congress and then the General Court, but passed away in 1777.

The "Hancock" and "Adams" remained together at the top of the Bunker Hill Monument into the late twentieth century until the former's mount became loose. Today, after some years being misplaced under a pile of bicycles in a police station and more in storage, the "Hancock" is on display at the Concord visitor center of Minute Man National Historical Park. As of this writing, the "Adams" is being carefully conserved by the National Park Service.

The Concord spy has not yet been identified.

NOTES

Abbreviations used in the citations:

AAS	American Antiquarian Society
BPL	Boston Public Library
BTR	*Boston Town Records*, formally *Reports of the Record Commissioners of the City of Boston* and published in 39 volumes between 1881 and 1909
CSM	Colonial Society of Massachusetts
EIHC	*Essex Institute Historical Collections*
JEPCM	*Journals of Each Provincial Congress of Massachusetts in 1774 and 1775*, William Lincoln, editor (Boston: Dutton & Wentworth, 1838)
JHRM	*Journals of the House of Representatives of Massachusetts*
MHS	Massachusetts Historical Society
NDAR	*Naval Documents of the American Revolution*
NEHGR	*New England Historical and Genealogical Register*
NEHGS	New England Historic Genealogical Society
NYHSC	*New-York Historical Society Collections*
NYPL	New York Public Library
PEI	*Proceedings of the Essex Institute*

INTRODUCTION: "THE COMMENCEMENT OF THE WAR"

p **xii.** "to march": Lt. Col. Francis Smith to Gen. Thomas Gage, April 22, 1775, *MHS Proceedings*, 14:350.

"Committee of Supplies": Allen French, *The Siege of Boston* (New York: Macmillan, 1911), 139. As British army sources became available, French wrote many more insightful books about the start of the war.

p **xiii.** "This Town": James Warren to Mercy Warren, April 6, 1775, "Warren-Adams Papers," *MHS Collections*, 72 (1917), 46.

CHAPTER ONE: "ORDERED OUT BY THE CAPT. GENERAL"

p **1.** Expedition to Charlestown: John Andrews to William Barrell, September 1, 1774, "Letters of John Andrews, Esq., of Boston, 1772-1776," Winthrop Sargent, editor, *MHS Proceedings*, 8 (1866), 350-1. Thomas Newell, "Diary of Mr. Thomas Newell," September 1, 1774, *MHS Proceedings*, 15 (1878), 357. The only book that focuses solely on this event is Robert P. Richmond, *Powder Alarm 1774* (Princeton, N.J.: Auerbach Publishers, 1971), which relied on published sources.

"a small common": William Glanville Evelyn, *Memoir and Letters of Capt. W. Glanville Evelyn, of the 4th Regiment ("King's Own") from North America, 1774-1776*, G. D. Scull, editor (Oxford: James Parker, 1879), 27.

p 2. Cost of tea: Charles Bahne, "How Much Was the Tea in the Tea Party Worth?", boston1775.blogspot.com/2009/12/how-much-was-tea-in-tea-party-worth.html.

p 3. Rising tide: *Bickerstaff's Boston Almanack* for 1774 calculated the tide to peak that morning at 7:56 A.M.

Officials with soldiers: John Andrews's September 1 letter states that Phips, Goldthwait, and "Judge Oliver" conducted the soldiers from Temple's farm to the powder house; *MHS Proceedings*, 8:350-1. "Judge Oliver" probably meant Lt. Gov. Thomas Oliver, whose actions during this crisis were described in detail by many people, including himself (see Chapter 2), yet no one else said that he worked with the troops on September 1.

Joseph Goldthwait: Robert Goldthwait Carter, "Joseph Goldthwait, the Barrack Master of Boston," *Collections and Proceedings of the Maine Historical Society*, 2nd series, 9 (1898), 349-82. No source but Andrews mentions Goldthwait, but he worked for the British military both before and after this date, so his presence makes sense.

David Phips: *Sibley's Harvard Graduates*, 11:53-6. Doris Whipple Jones-Baker, "Col. Elisha Jones of Weston and the Crisis of Colonial Government in Massachusetts, 1773-1776" (Ph.D. dissertation, University College London, 1978), 213-4, which cites a statement by Phips himself, says he went into Boston on the night of August 31 and came out again with the troops.

Charlestown powder house: "Records Relating to the Old Powder House," *Historic Leaves* (Somerville Historical Society), 7 (1908-09), 62-5.

p 4. Troops at Castle William: John R. Alden, *General Gage in America* (Baton Rouge, La.: Louisiana State University Press, 1948), 115.

Boston population: Figures for 1765 in J. H. Benton, Jr., *Early Census Making in Massachusetts, 1643-1765* (Boston: Charles E. Goodspeed, 1905), 74-5.

Tough measures: The Boston Port Bill was one of Parliament's Coercive Acts, designed to force better behavior out of Boston. The others consisted of a revised Quartering Act, authorizing royally appointed magistrates to seize "uninhabited buildings" for use as army barracks, and the Administration of Justice in Massachusetts Act, letting the royal government transfer trials of government employees arrested for doing their duty to the imperial government to a jurisdiction in England. Gage never ended up invoking either. There are several myths associated with these laws, but the most common is that colonists called them "the Intolerable Acts." That term did not appear until the late 1800s, when it became common in U.S. textbooks.

p 5. Boston population in 1765: Benton, *Early Census Making in Massachusetts,* 74-5. In that year Boston was home to slightly under three thousand white men over the age of sixteen.
"manifestly inconsistent": *JHRM*, 50:262.
"your Administration": Albert Matthews, editor, "Documents Relating to the Last Meetings of the Massachusetts Royal Council, 1774-1776," *CSM Publications*, 32 (1933-37), 470.

p 6. "a Meeting of Committees": *JHRM*, 50:288.
Delegates to First Continental Congress: The original list also included Council member James Bowdoin, but he eventually declined the appointment because of illness. *JHRM*, 50:290.
Gage and Massachusetts Government Act: Alden, *General Gage*, 210.
Mandamus Councilors: *CSM Publications*, 32:471-3.
"a number of people": Gage to Dartmouth, August 27, 1774, *Parliamentary Register*, 1:45-6.

p 7. "a written notification": Leonard to Gage, August 22, 1774, *CSM Publications*, 32:482.
Pistols outside Loring house: *CSM Publications*, 32:480-1.
"In Worcester": Gage to Dartmouth, August 27, 1774, *Parliamentary Register*, 1:45-6.

p 8. Committees of correspondence: For their importance, see Richard Brown, *Revolutionary Politics in Massachusetts: The Boston Committee of Correspondence and the Towns* (Cambridge, Mass.: Harvard University Press, 1970).
"I came to execute": Ronald N. Tagney, *The World Turned Upside Down: Essex County During America's Turbulent Years, 1763-1790* (West Newbury, Mass.: Essex County History, 1990), 90-1.
Gage and Salem committee: Tagney, *World Turned*, 91. Derby had just taken a seat on the Council in May; *JHRM*, 50:250-2.

p 9. "The people behaved": *Parliamentary Register*, 1:46-7.
"you wou'd be able": Alden, *General Gage*, 212. This letter is not in *The Correspondence of General Thomas Gage*, Clarence Edwin Carter, editor (New Haven: Yale University Press, 1933).
William Brattle: *Sibley's Harvard Graduates*, 7:10-23.
Brattle as demonstrator: Francis Bernard to John Pownall, November 5, 1765, *Papers of Francis Bernard*, Colin Nicolson, editor (Boston: CSM, 2012), 2:398.
"Mr. Brattle presents": *Boston Gazette*, September 5, 1774, dating this letter August 27. *The Boston Evening-Post*, September 5, 1774, dated it August 20. Brattle later implied that he was simply responding to Gage's request for a "Return" of the "several Military Stores in your charge, at Cambridge," but his letter went well beyond an inventory. *Boston News-Letter*, September 8, 1774.

p 12. "enormous quantities": Andrews, July 22, 1774, *MHS Proceedings*,

8:333, where the keeper's name is transcribed as "Slyde." Byfield Lyde: *Sibley's Harvard Graduates*, 7:206-14. As "Loyd" in *BTR*, 19:207.

David Phips: *Sibley's Harvard Graduates*, 11:53-6.

Thaddeus Mason: *Sibley's Harvard Graduates*, 8:449-55.

Eight wagons: Benjamin Hallowell to Grey Cooper, September 5, 1774, in Colonial Office, Great Britain, *Documents of the American Revolution 1770-1783*, K. G. Davies, editor (Dublin: Irish University Press, 1975), 8:187-8.

Borrowed horse: *Boston Post-Boy*, September 12, 1774.

"Very hot dry": John Tudor, *Deacon Tudor's Diary*, William Tudor, editor (Boston: Wallace Spooner, 1896), 49.

p 13. "*Temple's* barn": Andrews, September 1, 1774, *MHS Proceedings*, 8:350-1.

"the Mob desired": John Nutting, memorial, in AO 13/51, Massachusetts New Claims, N, 236-8, National Archives, U.K. Samuel Francis Batchelder, "Adventures of John Nutting, Cambridge Loyalist," *Cambridge Historical Society Publications*, 6 (1910), 63.

Cannon moved to Boston: Some authors have concluded that the soldiers moved the cannon south across the Charles River and over land into Boston. The period sources I have seen do not specify one route or another, but after consideration the water route seems more secure.

"now conveying": *Boston News-Letter*, September 1, 1774. The same day's *Massachusetts Spy*, a Patriot newspaper, stated that the powder would be moved into Boston's powder house, suggested that the town of Charlestown's supply was being seized as well, and emphasized the secrecy of the action.

p 14. "The Governor": Andrews, September 1, 1774, *MHS Proceedings*, 8:350-1.

"Tratorous plot": Abigail Adams to John Adams, September 2, 1774, *Adams Family Correspondence*, 1:146.

"it is affirmed": *Boston News-Letter*, September 8, 1774.

Jonathan Sewall: *Sibley's Harvard Graduates*, 12:306-25. Carol Berkin, *Jonathan Sewall: Odyssey of an American Loyalist* (New York: Columbia University Press, 1974).

p 15. "he was advised": Edmund Quincy to Katherine Quincy [September 1774], Miscellaneous Bound Manuscripts, MHS. It is unclear who advised Sewall to leave Cambridge and whether that warning followed the discovery of the Brattle letter in Boston.

Sewall and bipolar disorder: Sewall's political and legal activity came in bursts. He sat out the Boston Massacre trial in 1770 without explanation and entered deep depressions in 1778 and 1783; *Sibley's Harvard Graduates*, 12:306-25. Other members of Sewall's family showed histories of depression as well.

"a damned liar": Anonymous account of a Sewall family friend printed in Leslie F. S. Upton, editor, *Revolutionary Versus Loyalist: The First American*

Civil War, 1774-1784 (Waltham, Mass.: Blaisdell Publishing Company, 1968), 4-6.

Ward Chipman's gunshot: Dirk Hoerder, *Crowd Action in Revolutionary Massachusetts, 1765-1780* (New York: Academic Press, 1977), 288. Richard Frothingham, *The Life and Times of Joseph Warren* (Boston: Little, Brown, 1865), 356. Ward Chipman: *Sibley's Harvard Graduates*, 16:369-79.

p 16. "Im sorry to understand": Edmund Quincy to Katherine Quincy, [September 1774], Miscellaneous Bound Manuscripts, MHS.

"were mostly boys": *Boston Gazette*, September 5, 1774.

CHAPTER TWO: "AN EXTENSIVE INSURRECTION THRO' THE PROVINCE"

p 17. Merchant McNeil: On September 4, Dr. Benjamin Church met "one Capt. McNeal from Ireland"; Church to Samuel Adams, September 4, 1774, Samuel Adams Papers, NYPL. Archibald McNeil was a Loyalist baker proscribed in 1778.

"[A]bout midnight": Ezra Stiles, *The Literary Diary of Ezra Stiles, D.D., Ll.D.*, Franklin Bowditch Dexter, editor (New York: Scribner's, 1901), 1:479. Stiles's account provides the title for this chapter.

"Brattle at Cambridge": Titus Hosmer to Silas Deane, September 4?, 1774, *Collections of the Connecticut Historical Society*, 2 (1860), 154.

p 18. "that the Ships": Rev. Stephen Williams diary transcript, September 4, 1774, 8:311, transcript at the Richard Salter Storrs Library, Longmeadow, Massachusetts, www.longmeadowlibrary.org/stephen-williams-diary-available-online/. See also *American Archives*, 4th series, 1:942.

"fifty men": Stiles, *Literary Diary*, 1:480-1.

p 20. "No Taxation": J. L. Bell, "No Taxation without Representation," *Journal of the American Revolution*, 1 (2013), 10-3.

p 21. Lexington tea burning: *Massachusetts Spy*, December 16, 1773.

Berkshire County courts: For a timeline and analysis of this movement, see Ray Raphael and Marie Raphael, *The Spirit of '74: How the American Revolution Began* (New York: New Press, 2015), xiii-xviii.

p 22. Fear of disarming the militia: The September 3, 1774, *Providence Gazette* reported complaints from "several" unnamed towns in Massachusetts and Killingly, Connecticut, that they were missing military supplies. This was apparently what Ezra Stiles was recalling when he wrote that "Medfield and it was said some other Towns" were missing gunpowder; Stiles, *Literary Diary*, 1:477. However, the town of Wrentham (discussed in Chapter 9) is the only confirmed example. It is unlikely that secret Crown agents took those supplies, mainly because such people almost certainly did not exist.

Massachusetts militia laws: John Shy, "A New Look at the Colonial Militia," *William and Mary Quarterly*, 20 (1963), 175-85. John R. Galvin, *The Minute Men: The First Fight* (Washington, D.C.: Brassey's, 1989).

"the soldiers of the Militia": Shirley to Josiah Willard, November 19, 1747, *Correspondence of William Shirley* (New York: Macmillan, 1912), 1:406.

"the Militia, the only force": Francis Bernard to the Board of Trade, August 15, 1765, *Papers of Francis Bernard*, Colin Nicolson, editor (Boston: CSM, 2012), 2:303. In the same letter Bernard wrote about the colonel of the Boston militia regiment declining to order his drummers to summon men, saying, "as soon as the drum was heard, the drummer would be knocked down, & the drum broke; he added, that probably all the drummers of the Regiment were in the Mob."

p 23. Size of crowds: Jonathan Smith, "Toryism in Worcester County during the War for Independence," *MHS Proceedings*, 48 (1915), 17-8.

"About five hundred persons": Albert Matthews, editor, "Documents Relating to the Last Meetings of the Massachusetts Royal Council, 1774-1776," *CSM Publications*, 32 (1933-37), 32:482.

Ethnicity in Massachusetts: Jon Butler, *Becoming America: The Revolution before 1776* (Cambridge, Mass.: Harvard University Press, 2000), 21.

p 24. "the County of Middlesex": *Boston Gazette*, September 5, 1774.

"yet they were down": John Andrews to William Barrell, September 3, 1774, "Letters of John Andrews, Esq., of Boston, 1772-1776," Winthrop Sargent, editor, *MHS Proceedings*, 8 (1866), 353.

Towns that reached Cambridge: Dirk Hoerder, *Crowd Action in Revolutionary Massachusetts, 1765-1780* (New York: Academic Press, 1977), 288-9, citing a document in the Sewall Papers, Public Archives of Canada.

Dr. Joseph Lee: Grindall Reynolds, "The Story of a Concord Farm and Its Owners" (Lecture at the Concord Lyceum, February 1, 1883), 15-7. William Lee, *John Leigh of Agawam Massachusetts, 1634-1671: and His Descendants of the Name of Lee* (Albany: Joel Munsell's Sons, 1888), 141-65.

Judge Joseph Lee: *Sibley's Harvard Graduates*, 8:592-8.

"that the country was assembling": Lemuel Shattuck, *A History of the Town of Concord* (Boston: Russell, Odiorne & Co., 1835), 89.

Samuel Danforth: *Sibley's Harvard Graduates*, 6:80-6.

p 25. "I rejoice therefore": *Papers of Benjamin Franklin,* ed. William B. Willcox (New Haven and London: Yale University Press, 1976), 20:324-5.

"refus'd to accept": Andrews, September 1, 1774, *MHS Proceedings*, 8:351.

"make them return": Thomas Oliver to Dartmouth, September 3, 1774, *CSM Publications*, 32:485. In a narrative dated September 7, 1774, Oliver identified the men who came to him as "inhabitants of Charlestown"; Vere Langford Oliver, *The History of the Island of Antigua* (London: Mitchell & Hughes, 1896), 2:349.

Thomas Oliver: Oliver Elton, "Lieutenant-Governor Thomas Oliver, 1734-1815," *CSM Publications*, 28 (1935), 37-66.

Thomas Oliver's family connections: According to the September 1, 1774, *Massachusetts Spy*, Thomas Oliver's post would have gone to Peter Oliver, the Massachusetts chief justice and brother of the previous lieutenant governor, except for "a mistake in the insertion of the christian name." Alternatively, officials in London might have assumed that Thomas Oliver was related to those brothers, but the families had no connection. Thomas Oliver was related to a London politician named Richard Oliver, and the January 10, 1775, *Essex Gazette* suggested his appointment was a favor to that man. However, since Richard Oliver was one of the very few Members of Parliament to oppose the Boston Port Bill, that seems most unlikely; Peter D. G. Thomas, *John Wilkes: A Friend to Liberty* (Oxford: Clarendon Press, 1996), 163.

"were to pass": The quotations in this paragraph come from Oliver's accounts printed in *CSM Publications*, 32:485, and Oliver, *Antigua*, 2:349.

p 26. "left their fire-arms": *Boston Gazette*, September 5, 1774.

"most of the people": Stiles, *Literary Diary*, 1:482.

Cambridge common elms: J. Gardner Bartlett, "The Washington Elm, Cambridge," *Old Time New England*, 14 (1924), 145-6.

"under their regular leaders": Andrews, September 2, 1774, *MHS Proceedings*, 8:351. Hoerder, *Crowd Action*, 288-9.

"the troops were on their march": Oliver to Dartmouth, September 3, 1774, *CSM Publications*, 32:485.

Elizabeth Oliver's neighborhood: This neighborhood was dubbed "Tory Row" in Samuel A. Drake's *Historic Fields and Mansions of Middlesex* (1873). Elizabeth Oliver was also a niece of Sheriff David Phips.

Meeting at Lee's house: Hoerder, *Crowd Action*, 289.

p 27. "about three thousand": Andrews, September 2, 1774, *MHS Proceedings*, 8:351.

Local committees of correspondence: *Boston Gazette*, September 5, 1774.

"requesting me": Warren to Samuel Adams, September 4, 1774, Samuel Adams Papers, NYPL, printed in Richard Frothingham, *The Life and Times of Joseph Warren* (Boston: Little, Brown, 1865), 355-7.

Boston committee members: Hoerder, *Crowd Action*, 289.

John Bradford: During the war Bradford became the Continental government's prize agent for the port of Boston; see, for example, *Papers of George Washington: Revolutionary War Series*, 4:397-8. See also Vincent Carretta, *Phillis Wheatley: Biography of a Genius in Bondage* (Athens: University of Georgia Press, 2011), 38-9.

Dr. Thomas Young: Pauline Maier, "Reason and Revolution: The Radicalism of Dr. Thomas Young," *American Quarterly* (Summer 1976), reprinted in *The Old Revolutionaries: Political Lives in the Age of Samuel Adams* (New York: Alfred A. Knopf, 1980). David F. Hawke, "Dr. Thomas Young—'Eternal Fisher in Troubled Waters': Notes for a Biography," *New-York Historical Society Quarterly*, 54 (1970), 6-29. Henry H. Edes, "Memoir of Dr. Thomas Young, 1731-1777," *CSM Publications*, 11 (1906-07), 2-54. Ray Raphael, *Founders: The People Who Brought You a Nation* (New York: New Press, 2013).

Joseph Greenleaf: Isaiah Thomas, *History of Printing in America*, 2nd edition (Worcester: AAS, 1874), 1:174-5; 2:255-6.

William Cooper: The most detailed discussion of him seems to be in Charles W. Akers's biography of his brother, *The Divine Politician: Samuel Cooper and the American Revolution in Boston* (Boston: Northeastern University Press, 1982).

p 28. "He said he was going": Warren to Samuel Adams, September 4, 1774, Samuel Adams Papers, NYPL.

"Judge Danforth was addressing": Young to Samuel Adams, September 4, 1774, Samuel Adams Papers, NYPL.

"having now arrived": *Massachusetts Spy*, September 8, 1774.

p 29. Nathaniel Cudworth: Alfred Sereno Hudson, *The History of Sudbury, Massachusetts, 1638-1889* (Sudbury, Mass.: Sudbury, 1889), 369. The September 5, 1774, *Boston Gazette* shows that Cudworth attested to Lee and Phips's statements as well, identifying himself as "Cl." or clerk of the gathering.

"what I wrote": Hoerder, *Crowd Action*, 289.

Gamage's letter: *Boston Gazette*, September 5, 1774.

Boston committee's speeches: Hoerder, *Crowd Action*, 289.

"[A] Vote was called for": *Boston Gazette*, September 5, 1774. Hoerder, *Crowd Action*, 290.

p 30. "hardly": *Massachusetts Spy*, September 8, 1774.

Cooper's suggestion: Hoerder, *Crowd Action*, 290.

"kept their particular stations": Young to Adams, September 4, 1774, Samuel Adams Papers, NYPL.

"They were dress'd": Edward Hill to John Adams, [September] 4, 1774, *Papers of John Adams*, Robert J. Taylor, editor (Cambridge, Mass.: Harvard University Press, 1977), 2:143.

"the vast number": William Parker Cutler and Julia Perkins Cutler, *Life, Journals and Correspondence of Rev. Manasseh Cutler, Ll.D.* (Cincinnati: Robert Clarke, 1888), 1:46.

"reported to the body": *Massachusetts Spy*, September 8, 1774.

Thaddeus Mason's resignation: *Boston Gazette*, September 5, 1774.

"no troops": Oliver to Dartmouth, September 3, 1774, *CSM Publications*, 32:485-6.

p 31. Oliver's arguments and promise: Oliver, *Antigua*, 349. Oliver to Dartmouth, September 3, 1774, *CSM Publications*, 32:485-6. *Massachusetts Spy*, September 8, 1774.

"preparing to deliver it": *Massachusetts Spy*, September 8, 1774.

Fistfight with Graves: Allen French, "The Hallowell-Graves Fisticuffs, 1775," *MHS Proceedings*, 63 (1930), 22-51.

Customs Commissioners: Commissioner Henry Hulton wrote on September 8, 1774, "The people suffered my chaise to go quietly along, but soon pursued Mr. Hallowell"; Hulton to Samuel ?, September 8, 1774, Henry Hulton letterbook, 1:106-7, Houghton Library, Harvard. By permission of the Houghton Library, Harvard University. Hallowell suggested the difference was because Hulton took the right road around Cambridge Common while he took the left road closer to the crowd—which was his choice; Hallowell to Grey Cooper, September 5, 1774, in Colonial Office, Great Britain, *Documents of the American Revolution, 1770-1783*, K. G. Davies, editor (Dublin: Irish University Press, 1975), 8:188. Hoerder, *Crowd Action*, 290-1, says three of the five Commissioners went through Cambridge that afternoon.

"No Insult": Hallowell to Gage, September 8, 1774, vol. 123, Gage Papers, Clements Library.

"One Thomas": Hallowell to Grey Cooper, September 5, 1774, in Colonial Office, *Documents of the American Revolution*, 8:188.

p 32. "The sight": *Boston Gazette*, September 5, 1774.

"began a parley": *Massachusetts Spy*, September 8, 1775.

"6 or 8 wou'd not": Hallowell to Gage, September 8, 1774, Gage Papers, Clements Library.

"one gentleman": *Massachusetts Spy*, September 8, 1775.

"a brace of pistols": Hulton letterbook, 1:106-7, Houghton Library, Harvard.

"Stop the Murderer": Hallowell to Gage, September 8, 1774, Gage Papers, Clements Library. Patriots claimed Hallowell had tried to shoot Bradshaw.

p 33. looting the chaise: Hallowell to Gage, September 8, 1774, Gage Papers, Clements Library.

"sent out all day": Stiles, *Literary Diary*, 1:482.

"very fleet horse": *Massachusetts Spy*, September 8, 1774.

Men retrieving guns: *Massachusetts Spy*, September 8, 1774. Stiles, *Literary Diary*, 1:482.

"to take up the bridge": Andrews, September 2, 1774, *MHS Proceedings*, 8:352-3.

"light horsemen": *Massachusetts Spy*, September 8, 1774.

"large companies": Oliver, *Antigua*, 2:349.

"resolved to leave": *Massachusetts Spy*, September 8, 1774.

"I chose to get out": Oliver to Dartmouth, September 3, 1774, *CSM Publications*, 32:486.

"provided some": *Massachusetts Spy*, September 8, 1774.

"a manifest infringement": *Massachusetts Spy*, September 8, 1774.

p 34. "ingratitude & false dealings": Oliver to Dartmouth, September 3, 1774, *CSM Publications*, 32:486.

"the Multitude . . . formed": Stiles, *Literary Diary*, 1:481.

"absolutely refused": Oliver to Dartmouth, September 3, 1774, *CSM Publications*, 32:486.

"some Gentlemen": Stiles, *Literary Diary*, 1:481.

"pressed up to my windows": Oliver, *Antigua*, 2:349.

"calling for vengeance": Oliver to Dartmouth, September 3, 1774, *CSM Publications*, 32:486.

p 35. "immediately handed along": Stiles, *Literary Diary*, 1:481.

"found great difficulty": Oliver to Dartmouth, September 3, 1774, *CSM Publications*, 32:486-7.

"I had several messages": Oliver, *Antigua*, 2:350.
Time confrontation ended: Stiles, *Literary Diary*, 1:481.
"came on hard Thunder": John Tudor, *Deacon Tudor's Diary,* William Tudor, editor (Boston: Wallace Spooner, 1896), 49. See also Thomas Newell, "Diary of Mr. Thomas Newell," September 2, 1774, *MHS Proceedings*, 15 (1878), 357.
"to beg I wou'd": Gage to Dartmouth, September 2, 1774, *The Correspondence of General Thomas Gage with the Secretaries of State, and with the War Office and the Treasury, 1763-1775*, Clarence Edwin Carter, editor (New Haven: Yale University Press, 1933), 1:372.
"all Hurry, Activity": Stiles, *Literary Diary*, 1:482.

p 36. "Affairs in this Province": Gage to Haldimand, September 1, 1774, vol. 122, Gage Papers, Clements Library.
"Tho' I saw Things were bad": Gage to Dartmouth, September 2, 1774, *Correspondence of Gen. Thomas Gage*, 1:369.
"a Day or two after": Hugh Edward Egerton, *The Royal Commission on the Losses and Services of American Loyalists, 1783 to 1785* (Oxford: Roxburghe Club, 1915), 230-1.
"to take a Tour": Charlestown Committee of Correspondence, September 16, 1774, Miscellaneous Bound Manuscripts, MHS.
"The people from Hampshire County": Warren to Adams, September 4, 1773, Samuel Adams Papers, NYPL.
"The western Post": Young to Adams, September 4, 1773, Samuel Adams Papers, NYPL.

p 37. Putnam's alert: Stiles, *Literary Diary*, 1:484.
News in New York: Haldimand to Gage, September 5, 1774, vol. 123, Gage Papers, Clements Library.
"Intimation of the Bombardment": John Adams diary, September 6, 1774, *Diary and Autobiography of John Adams*, L. H. Butterfield, editor (Cambridge, Mass.: Harvard University Press, 1961), 2:124.
Spread of news: Ezra Stiles believed the alarm provoked a reaction in the Iroquois communities near Sir William Johnson's seat in northern New York, but the September 8, 1775, letter to Gen. Gage from Johnson's son and successor Guy Johnson did not mention that news; vol. 123, Gage Papers, Clements Library.
"In the afternoon": Joseph Plumb Martin, *A Narrative of a Revolutionary Soldier* (New York: Signet Classic, 2001), 7-8.

p 38. "Powder Alarm": The first author to use the phrase appears to have been Richard Frothingham in *Life and Times of Joseph Warren* (1865), 352.
"shews that New England": Stiles, *Literary Diary*, 1:457.
"Had the troops marched": Warren to Adams, September 4, 1773, Samuel Adams Papers, NYPL.
"That treacherous": Young to Adams, September 4, 1773, Samuel Adams Papers, NYPL.
"not a Boston Rabble": Gage to Dartmouth, September 2, 1774, Colonial Office, *Documents of the American Revolution*, 8:182. Oliver was credited

with saying the people in Cambridge "were not a mad mob, but the freeholders of the county"; *Boston Gazette*, September 5, 1774.

"In short, this country": Hugh, Earl Percy (later Duke of Northumberland), *Letters of Hugh Earl Percy from Boston and New York, 1774-1776*, Charles K. Bolton, editor (Boston: Charles E. Goodspeed, 1902), 37.

CHAPTER THREE: "BEHOLD, THE GUNS WERE GONE!"

p 39. "their determination": John Andrews to William Barrell, September 2, 1774, "Letters of John Andrews, Esq., of Boston, 1772-1776," Winthrop Sargent, editor, *MHS Proceedings*, 8 (1864-65), 352.

"the Guard upon the Neck": Andrews, September 2, 1774, *MHS Proceedings*, 8:352.

"Four large field-pieces": Thomas Newell, "Diary of Mr. Thomas Newell," September 3, 1774, *MHS Proceedings*, 15 (1877), 357-8.

Gage summoning more troops: Gage to [Lt.-Col. Valentine Jones?] at Quebec, September 4, 1774, vol. 122, and Gage to Gen. Frederick Haldimand, September 5, 1774, vol. 123, Gage Papers, Clements Library.

"Boston Garison": Abigail Adams to John Adams, September 22, 1774, *Adams Family Correspondence*, L. H. Butterfield et al., editors, 6 vols. (Cambridge, Mass.: Harvard University Press, 1963), 1:161.

"frigate of 20 guns": Newell, "Diary," September 3, 1774, *MHS Proceedings*, 15:357. *Boston Gazette*, September 5, 1774.

Ferry boats: Andrews, September 7, 1774, *MHS Proceedings*, 8:356.

"They have haul'd": Andrews, September 4, 1774, *MHS Proceedings*, 8:354.

"to Examine": Brookline, *Muddy River and Brookline Records, 1634-1838* (n.p.: J. E. Farwell, 1875), 248.

"the Selectmen Secure": *Watertown Records* (Watertown, Mass.: Watertown, 1928), 5:110-1.

p 41. "In consequence of the powders": Abigail Adams to John Adams, September 14, 1774, *Adams Family Correspondence*, 1:151-2.

"Guns are so scarce": William Tudor to John Adams, September 17, 1774, *Papers of John Adams*, Robert J. Taylor, editor (Cambridge, Mass.: Harvard University Press, 1977), 2:167.

"irreparable": "The Montresor Journals," G. D. Scull, editor, *NYHSC*, 14 (1881), 400-1.

p 42. "A Scotch Captain": Andrews, September 8, 1774, *MHS Proceedings*, 8:356-7.

"stable dirt": Richard Frothingham, *The History of Charlestown, Massachusetts* (Charlestown, Mass.: Charles P. Emmons, 1845), 306.

"traversing the streets": Andrews, September 12, 1774, *MHS Proceedings*, 8:359.

"Am just inform'd": Andrews, September 13, 1774, *MHS Proceedings*, 8:360.

p 43. "a conspiracy of the Negroes": Abigail Adams to John Adams, September 22, 1774, *Adams Family Correspondence*, 1:161-2.

Slaves during Revolutionary turmoil: See the early chapters of Elise Lemire, *Black Walden: Slavery and Its Aftermath in Concord, Massachusetts* (Philadelphia: University of Pennsylvania Press, 2009).

"What is the reason": Andrews, September 12, 1774, *MHS Proceedings*, 8:359-60.

"The greate gun": Dorchester Antiquarian and Historical Society, *History of the Town of Dorchester, Massachusetts* (Boston: Ebenezer Clapp, Jr., 1859), 364. T. M. Harris, "Chronological and Topographical Account of Dorchester," *MHS Collections*, series 1, 9 (1804), 163.

"The Country People": Gage to Dartmouth, September 12, 1774, *The Correspondence of General Thomas Gage with the Secretaries of State, and with the War Office and the Treasury, 1763-1775*, Clarence Edwin Carter, editor (New Haven: Yale University Press, 1933), 1:374.

p 44. "A few days ago": Percy's letter referred to the crowd gathered at Worcester on September 6 to stop judges from holding court. This was a political milestone, but Percy viewed the event mainly through a military lens. Hugh Earl Percy (later Duke of Northumberland), *Letters of Hugh Earl Percy from Boston and New York, 1774-1776*, Charles K. Bolton, editor (Boston: Charles E. Goodspeed, 1902), 37. Ray Raphael found that the Rev. Ebenezer Parkman's count of men mustering in Worcester was 4,622, not 7,000—but still an impressively large number; www.rayraphael.com/documents_2/parkman_diary.htm, as of January 5, 2015. Ray Raphael and Marie Raphael, *The Spirit of '74: How the American Revolution Began* (New York: New Press, 2015), 111-2.

"The people for their part": Hulton to J——— Esq., September 13, 1774, Henry Hulton Letterbook, 1:108, Houghton Library, Harvard. By permission of the Houghton Library, Harvard University.

Montresor had counted: "Montresor Journals," *NYHSC*, 14:400.

Occupied the South Battery: Andrews, September 28, 1774, *MHS Proceedings*, 8:370.

North Battery company: Richard Frothingham, *History of the Siege of Boston, and of the Battles of Lexington, Concord, and Bunker Hill*, 4th edition (Boston: Little, Brown, 1873), 49.

"intentions of a number": Andrews, September 15, 1774, *MHS Proceedings*, 8:361.

"ready for an engagement": Andrews, September 15, 1774, *MHS Proceedings*, 8:361-2. Newell, "Diary," September 15, 1774, *MHS Proceedings*, 15:358.

"Ridiculous Maneuvre": John Rowe, manuscript diary, 11:1906, MHS.

"cleared again": *Boston Post-Boy*, September 19, 1774.

"they have been drilled": Palmer to Paine, September 15, 1774, *Papers of Robert Treat Paine*, Stephen T. Riley and Edward W. Hanson, editors (Boston: MHS, 2005), 3:3.

p 45. Boston train: This company was an official arm of the militia, separate from the private Ancient and Honorable Artillery Company that still exists today. In the 1770s the Ancient and Honorable Artillery Company was a club and "school for officers" and those who wanted to be officers in the regular militia. Despite its name, it did not use artillery. Its roll thus helps to indicate men active in Boston-area militia regiments, but as an organization it played little role in pre-Revolutionary politics and none in artillery training. Oliver Ayer Roberts, *History of the Military Company of the Massachusetts, Now Called The Ancient and Honorable Artillery Company of Massachusetts, 1637-1888* (Boston: Alfred Mudge & Son, 1897), 2:105, 110, 432-3, 459.

"Artillery training": Newell, "Diary," September 5, 1774, *MHS Proceedings*, 15:537.

David Mason: For biographical information, see "Memoirs of Col. David Mason," *New-York Review, and Atheneum Magazine*, 1 (1825), 301-10; Susan Smith, "Biographical Sketch of Col. David Mason of Salem," *EIHC*, 48 (1912), 197-216; Susan Smith, "Memoir of Col. David Mason—by his daughter Susan Smith, relict of Professor Smith of Hanover, N.H.—Novr, 1842, in her 80th year," Shaw Family Papers (reel 4, frames 272-80), Library of Congress; and Roberts, *Ancient & Honorable Artillery*, 2:68-70.

Adino Paddock: For biographical information, see Roberts, *Ancient & Honorable Artillery*, 2:112-3; Carl Bridenbaugh, *The Colonial Craftsman* (Chicago: University of Chicago Press, 1950), 90, 158-60; and James H. Stark, *The Loyalists of Massachusetts and the Other Side of the American Revolution* (Boston: W. B. Clarke, 1910), 305-7.

Gore painting coaches: See John Gore's advertisements in the *Boston News-Letter*, May 7, 1767; October 13, 1768; and December 21, 1769. His November 11, 1765, invoice to John Hancock for painting his aunt Lydia's "Chariot Body & Carrage" is in the "John Hancock" volume, Mellen Chamberlain Collection, Boston Public Library.

Mason at Fort William Henry: *Massachusetts Acts and Resolves*, 1755-56, chap. 476. *NEHGR*, 97:118.

"6 pieces of cannon": Smith "David Mason," *EIHC*, 48:200-1. *New-York Review*, 1:303-4.

p 46. "The fire was fast": Smith "David Mason," *EIHC*, 48:202. *Boston Town Records*, 29:88, lists the losses in the South Battery.

"very fine Appearance": John Boyle, "Boyle's Journal of Occurrences in Boston, 1759-1778," *NEHGR*, 84 (1930), 84:159.

"the new Artillery Company": *Boston Post-Boy*, June 6, 1763.

p 48. "He was an ambitious": Smith "David Mason," *EIHC*, 48:203.

"Mason was . . . so low": Thomas Crafts, Jr., to John Adams, December 16, 1775, *Papers of John Adams*, 3:367.

Paddock's workyard: Robert Moses Lawrence, *The Site of St. Paul's Cathedral, Boston, and Its Neighborhood* (Boston: Richard G. Badger, 1916), 266.

Company of Royal Artillery: Henry Burbeck to Samuel Swett, March 8, 1848, copy, Bryant-Mason-Smith Family Papers, held at MHS.

p 49. Voted to buy four field-pieces: *JHRM*, 43 (1766), 197-8.

"In the Brigantine Abigail": *Boston News-Letter*, February 11, 1768. *Boston Gazette*, February 15, 1768.

Carriages designed by William Burbeck: Henry Burbeck to Charles Davies, April 13, 1847, Willard (Knox) Papers, MHS. Burbeck to Eliot, September 1847, William Perkins Papers, MHS.

"under a large Elm tree": Burbeck to Charles Davies, April 13, 1847, Willard (Knox) Papers, MHS.

"upon the Towns Land": Town vote on May 6, 1768, *Boston Town Records*, 2:248.

Gunhouse dimensions: The town asked builder Thomas Dawes and carpenters and roofers for cost estimates based on two lengths, but it is not clear from these papers which dimension the town chose. Boston Town Papers (bound), 7:230, 236-7, 242, BPL.

"His Excellency the governour's troop": *Boston Chronicle*, May 30–June 6, 1768, supplement.

p 50. "The Artillery Company divided": *Boston Post-Boy*, June 6, 1768.

"The Company of Artillery": *Boston News-Letter*, September 17, 1772.

p 51. "Fifes and Drums": *Boston Gazette*, June 7, 1773. Raoul François Camus, "Military Music of Colonial Boston," in "Music in Colonial Massachusetts, 1630-1820—I: Music in Public Spaces," *CSM Publications*, 53 (1980), 94.

"Major Paddock apply'd": *BTR*, 23:173.

"was composed": Gov. William Eustis was quoted in James Thacher, *A Military Journal During the American Revolutionary War, from 1775 to 1783* (Boston: Cottons & Barnard, 1827), 428-9. Eustis served as surgeon for a Continental army artillery regiment whose core consisted of men from the Boston train.

p 52. "The Cadet Company": Burbeck to Eliot, September 1847, William Perkins Papers, MHS.

"formed of Mechanics": Burbeck to Eliot, September 1847, William Perkins Papers, MHS. Knox's first biographer stated that he was a member of the Boston train before the grenadier company, but this was an assumption based on Knox's later command of the Continental army artillery; Francis S. Drake, *Life and Correspondence of Henry Knox* (Boston: Samuel G. Drake, 1873), 14-6. Later authors repeated that statement; Noah Brooks, *Henry Knox: A Soldier of the Revolution* (New York: Putnam's, 1900), 19, 22. Henry Burbeck did not list Knox among the Paddock company privates who became Continental army artillerists; list in the William Perkins Papers, MHS. As a demonstration of how valuable a militia rank could be for a rising young man, Knox's appearance in uniform during a grenadier parade caught the eye of Lucy Flucker, daughter of the high-ranking province secretary. Within two years they married.

Sixteen accidents: Adrian B. Caruana, *Grasshoppers and Butterflies: The Light 3 Pounders of Pattison and Townshend*, Historical Arms Series #39 (Bloomfield, Ont.: Museum Restoration Service, 1999), 26-7, 30-1.

p 53. New artillery companies: *JHRM*, 49 (1772-73), 166. New field-pieces: *Massachusetts Acts and Resolves*, 1773, Chap. 1.

"made their first public appearance": *Boston News-Letter*, October 21, 1773. Robinson's company was also called "Train belonging to the Suffolk First Regiment"; Frothingham, *Siege of Boston*, 49.

"elegant COACH": *Boston News-Letter*, November 23, 1769.

Paddock declared his loyalty: "Addressers to the late Gov. Hutchinson and Protesters against the Solemn League and Covenant," *MHS Proceedings*, 11 (1869-70), 392-5.

"Loyall Nine": Dirk Hoerder, *Crowd Action in Revolutionary Massachusetts, 1765-1780* (New York: Academic Press, 1977), 93.

Cadets had dissolved: Cadets to Hancock, August 18, 1774, First Massachusetts Corps of Cadets Papers, Boston University Special Collections.

"ceased meeting": Henry Burbeck to Charles Davies, April 13, 1847, Willard (Knox) Papers.

p 54. Estate of Francis Johonnot: Annie Haven Thwing, *The Crooked and Narrow Streets of Boston: 1630-1822*, 2nd edition (Boston: Charles E. Lauriat, 1925), 159. Henry Wilder Foote, *Annals of King's Chapel*, 2 vols. (Boston: Little, Brown: 1896), 2:310-6, 607-8.

The half-moon set: Lunar and solar data from MacAstronomica software, version 1.5.1.

"dark stormy night": Burbeck to Charles Davies, April 13, 1847, Willard (Knox) Papers.

"Ever since ye. cannon": Andrews, September 16, 1774, *MHS Proceedings*, 8:362.

"Our People in the Country": Palmer to Paine, September 15, 1775, *Papers of Robert Treat Paine*, 3:3.

p 55. "near, very near the common": Newell seems to have heard a late and compressed account of these thefts on Saturday, September 17; Newell, "Diary," *MHS Proceedings*, 15:358.

Tents of the 4th Regiment: The regiment camped on the Common until mid-November. William Glanville Evelyn, *Memoir and Letters of Capt. W. Glanville Evelyn, of the 4th Regiment ("King's Own") from North America, 1774-1776*, G. D. Scull, editor (Oxford: James Parker & Co., 1879), 39-41; Boyle, "Boyle's Journal of Occurrences," *NEHGR*, 84:381.

"yard inclosed": William Tudor, *The Life of James Otis, of Massachusetts* (Boston: Wells and Lilly, 1823), 452-3.

Welcomed paying students: Robert Francis Seybolt, *The Private Schools of Colonial Boston* (Cambridge, Mass.: Harvard University Press, 1935), 62-3.

"At the fixed hour": Andrews, September 16, 1774, *MHS Proceedings*, 8:362.

CHAPTER FOUR: "TOWNSPEOPLE TOOK FOUR BRASS CANNON"

p 56. "Its amazing to me": Andrews to Barrell, September 16, 1774, *MHS Proceedings*, 8:362.

Small three-pounders: Caruana, *Grasshoppers and Butterflies: The Light 3 Pounders of Pattison and Townshend*, Historical Arms Series #39 (Bloomfield, Ont.: Museum Restoration Service, 1999), 3, 4, 11, 22. John Andrews may have been thinking of heavier ship's guns or the type of three-pounder called a "Desaguliers," at 600 pounds.

p 57. Samuel Gore as businessman: Joseph T. Buckingham, compiler, *Annals of the Massachusetts Charitable Mechanics Association* (Boston: Crocker and Brewster, 1853), 24-5.

Loyalism as a political issue: Helen R. Pinkney, *Christopher Gore: Federalist of Massachusetts, 1758-1827* (Waltham, Mass.: Gore Place Society, 1969), 116.

Round-up of suspected Tories: *JHRM*, 51:89. Samuel Gore's brother-in-law Thomas Crafts was one of the people doing the rounding up, so Gore was probably never arrested, just quizzed to confirm that his loyalty had not shifted.

Gore's military service: *Massachusetts Soldiers and Sailors of the Revolutionary War*, 17 vols. (Boston: Wright & Potter, 1896-1908), 6:641.

"Mr. G. was one": *Columbian Centinel*, November 26, 1831. This notice was missed in the *Index of Obituaries in Massachusetts Centinel and Columbian Centinel, 1784 to 1840* (Boston: G. K. Hall, 1961).

"my impression was and is": Henry Burbeck to Samuel Swett, March 8, 1848, copy, Bryant-Mason-Smith Family Papers.

p 58. Gore family genealogy: Gore Family Genealogy at Gore Place, Waltham. An earlier, thinner version appears in William H. Whitmore, "Genealogy of the Families of Payne and Gore," *MHS Proceedings*, 13 (1873-75), 417-24.

Copley's portrait of the Gore children: This painting is now at Winterthur in Wilmington, Delaware. See Carrie Rebora, Paul Staiti, Erica E. Hirshler, Theodore E. Stebbins, Jr., and Carol Troyen, *John Singleton Copley in America* (New York: Metropolitan Museum of Art, 1995), 170-2.

Gore and Copley: Copley's youngest brother Henry Pelham (model for "Boy with a Squirrel") was a classmate of Samuel Gore. The Gores and the Copley-Pelham clan did business together both before the Revolution and afterward: *Boston News-Letter*, November 23, 1769; John Haven Dexter, *Memoranda of the Town of Boston in the 18th & 19th Centuries*, Robert J. Dunkle and Ann Smith Lainhart, compilers (Boston: NEHGS, 1997), 221.

Gore family background: Pinkney, *Christopher Gore*, 4-5.

Notebook on heraldry: Now at the NEHGS. Reprinted imperfectly in William H. Whitmore, *The Elements of Heraldry* (Boston: Lee & Shepard, 1866), and incompletely in Theodore Chase and Laurel K. Gabel, *Gravestone Chronicles II: More Eighteenth-Century Carvers and an Exploration of Gravestone Heraldica* (Boston: NEHGS, 1997).

"The Painter's Arms": The Bostonian Society owns the 1790s version of this shop sign hung by Samuel Gore.

"Coach & Carpet Painting": *Boston News-Letter*, November 5 and 26, 1767.

David Mason: Susan Smith, "Biographical Sketch of Col. David Mason of Salem," *EIHC*, 48 (1912), 198.

p **59.** "Watercolours ready prepared": George Francis Dow, *The Arts and Crafts in New England, 1704-1775: Gleanings from Boston Newspapers,* (Topsfield, Mass.: Wayside Press, 1927), 239-40. *Boston News-Letter*, January 9, 1766.

Customers in Philadelphia: Carl Bridenbaugh, *Cities in Revolt: Urban Life in America, 1743-1776* (New York: Knopf, 1955), 345.

Rose to command a company: *Massachusetts Officers in the French and Indian Wars, 1748-1763*, K. David Goss and David Zarowin, editors ([Boston]: Society of Colonial Wars in the Commonwealth of Massachusetts & NEHGS, 1985).

Brattle Street Meeting-house: *The Manifesto Church: Records of the Church in Brattle Square, Boston: 1699-1872* (Boston: Benevolent Fraternity of Churches, 1902), 101, opp. 40.

Gore as Overseer of the Poor: *Boston Town Records*, 16:207. There was a big turnover of Overseers in 1767. *The Eighteenth-Century Records of the Boston Overseers of the Poor*, Eric G. Nellis and Anne Decker Cecere, editors, in *CSM Publications,* volume 69 (2007).

p **60.** Capt. Gore's taxable property: Bettye Hobbs Pruitt, *The Massachusetts Tax Valuation List of 1771* (Boston: G. K. Hall, 1978), 30-5. For comparison, master goldsmith Paul Revere's annual net income from 1761 to 1770 fluctuated greatly, but averaged about £85: Jayne E. Triber, *A True Republican: The Life of Paul Revere* (Amherst: University of Massachusetts Press, 1998), 35, 163.

"his business brought him": AO 13/73, Massachusetts Temporary Assistance, G(I), 641, National Archives, UK.

Reading schools: Walter Herbert Small, *Early New England Schools* (Boston: Ginn & Co., 1914), 184-5. George R. T. Hewes, as told to "A Bostonian" [Benjamin Bussey Thatcher], *Traits of the Tea Party* (New York: Harper & Brothers, 1836), 20.

New-England Primer: Paul Leicester Ford, editor, *The New-England Primer* (New York: Teachers College Press, 1962).

Queen Street Writing School in 1753: *Boston Town Records*, 29:243.

John Gore, Jr., at South Latin School: Henry F. Jenks, *Catalogue of the Boston Latin School* (Boston: Boston Latin School Association, 1886), 2:iv, 77.

p **61.** Entering South Latin School: Jenks, *Boston Latin*, 1:35-6; Walter Herbert Small, *Early New England Schools* (Boston: Ginn & Co., 1914), 293; Wm. B. Fowle, editor, "Schools of the Olden Time in Boston," *The Common School Journal*, new series, 8 (1850), 311.

School seating: Jenks, *Boston Latin*, 1:35-6, 2:78-9. John Lovell, "A List of the Boys who were educated at the South Latin School in Boston from 1734 to 1774," Isaac P. Davis, transcriber, Ms. N-314, MHS.

Entering class of 1758: Jenks, *Boston Latin*, 2:78-9. Two boys in this class attended the college at Princeton, New Jersey, having prepared elsewhere.

Latin School dropouts: Noah Brooks, *Henry Knox: A Soldier of the Revolution* (New York: Putnam's, 1900), 4. Benjamin Franklin, *The Autobiography and Other Writings* (New York: Penguin Books, 1986), 8-9. William Phillips in Jenks, *Boston Latin*, 2:78-9.
Transfers between schools: *Boston Town Records*, 29:318-9, compared to lists of scholars in Jenks, *Boston Latin*.
Writing Schools: E. Jennifer Monaghan, "Readers Writing: The Curriculum of the Writing Schools of Eighteenth-Century Boston," *Visible Language*, 21 (1987), 167-214.

p 62. Arithmetic problems: Ray Nash, *American Writing Masters and Copybooks: History and Bibliography through Colonial Times* (Boston: Colonial Society of Massachusetts, 1959), 11. Small, *Early New England Schools*, 356, 363.
George Searle: Harold Bowditch, "Early Water-Color Paintings of New England Coats of Arms," *Colonial Society of Massachusetts Publications*, 35 (1942-46), 186-7. Chase & Gabel, *Gravestone Chronicles II*, 585.
John Johnston: Frederick W. Coburn, "The Johnstons of Boston," *Art in America*, 21 (1932-33), 134.
Christopher Gore's schooling: Jenks, *Boston Latin*, 2:87, 92.
Stamp Act protest: Dirk Hoerder, *Crowd Action in Revolutionary Massachusetts, 1765-1780* (New York: Academic Press, 1977), 97-8.
"a man of immense stature": Joseph M. Crafts and William F. Crafts, *The Crafts Family* (Northampton, Mass.: Gazette Printing, 1897), 121.

p 63. Loyall Nine membership: Sharp-eyed readers will note that this does not add up to nine men. The sources on this group list different sets of nine men; Hoerder, *Crowd Action*, 93.
"The whole affair": Henry Bass to Samuel P. Savage, December 19, 1765, *MHS Proceedings*, 44:688-9.
Liberty Tree: For this landmark's role in both focusing and taming protests from 1765 to 1775, see "Liberty Tree: Made in America," in Alfred F. Young, *Liberty Tree: Ordinary People and the American Revolution* (New York: New York University Press, 2006), 325-77.
"Pope Night": This term appeared on the broadside headlined "South End Forever. North End Forever. Extraordinary Verses on Pope-Night" and others.

p 64. March 1768 effigies: Hoerder, *Crowd Action*, 158.
"M.Y.": Hoerder, *Crowd Action*, 94.
Albany Sons of Liberty: "Constitution," *American Historian and Quarterly Genealogical Record*, 1 (April 1876), 146-7.
"two or three hundred little boys": Hoerder, *Crowd Action*, 98.
"According to common Custom": Peter Oliver, *Peter Oliver's Origin and Progress of the American Rebellion: A Tory View*, Douglass Adair and John A. Schutz, editors (San Marino, Cal.: Huntington Library, 1961), 89.
"see how those Boys fight": Oliver, *Peter Oliver's Origin*, 73.
"the Boys came": George G. Wolkins, "Daniel Malcom and the Writs of Assistance," *MHS Proceedings*, 58 (1924-5), 46.

p 65. "that they knew where he lived": Wolkins, "Daniel Malcom," *MHS Proceedings*, 58:47.

"the Scholars . . . from the Latin School": Wolkins, "Daniel Malcom," *MHS Proceedings*, 58:56.

"Boys and Children": Hoerder, *Crowd Action*, 104. More generally, see William Pencak, *War, Politics, and Revolution in Provincial Massachusetts* (Boston: Northeastern University Press, 1981), 121-2.

"their usual sayings": John Mein to Joseph Harrison, November 5, 1769, New England Papers, 10:3:51, Sparks Manuscripts, Houghton Library, Harvard University.

Gore and Paddock friendship: John Gore to J. B. and W. Newdick, May 8, 1776, John Gore Letterbook, The Bostonian Society. After Paddock's son drowned in the Charles River, Christopher Gore served as one of his pall-bearers; Pinkney, *Christopher Gore*, 11.

Crafts's rank in the train: *Boston News-Letter*, September 17, 1772.

John Johnston in the train: Henry Burbeck, "List of names that were privates in Major *Adino* Paddocks Company of Artillery," William Perkins Papers, MHS.

p 66. "opposite Liberty-Tree": *Boston Evening-Post*, May 16, 1768. Dexter, *Memoranda of the Town of Boston*, 221.

John Gore, Jr., elected: *BTR*, 17:234.

John Gore and Sarah Foster: Whitmore, "Genealogy," *MHS Proceedings*, 13:424. Caner was supporting his niece; E. Alfred Jones, *The Loyalists of Massachusetts: Their Memorials, Petitions, and Claims* (London: Saint Catherine Press, 1930), 77. Caner's father, like Capt. Gore's, had been a carpenter; Henry Wilder Foote, *Annals of King's Chapel* (Boston: Little, Brown: 1896), 2:2-16.

Caner's politics: Wallace Brown, *The King's Friends: The Composition and Motives of the American Loyalist Claimants* (Providence: Brown University Press, 1965), 27. Arthur M. Schlesinger, *Prelude to Independence: The Newspaper War on Britain, 1764-1776* (New York: Alfred A. Knopf, 1958), 129. Henry Caner, *Letter-Book of the Rev. Henry Caner*, Kenneth Walter Cameron, editor (Hartford: Transcendental Books, 1972).

John and Sarah Gore's first child: *New England Historical and Genealogical Register*, 92:19. This child had the same first name as his brother born in 1770, so he died in infancy.

p 67. "dress'd wholly": Triber, *A True Republican*, 59.

"Just imported": Dow, *Arts and Crafts*, 242-3.

"the Produce & Manufacture": *Boston News-Letter*, November 23, 1769.

"a general Assortment": *Boston Evening-Post*, May 16, 1768.

"North-American Manufactures": Arthur Meier Schlesinger, *The Colonial Merchants and the American Revolution, 1763-1776* (New York: Frederick Ungar, 1957), 123.

"We had two Tables": John Adams diary, August 14, 1769, *Diary and Autobiography of John Adams*, L. H. Butterfield, editor (Cambridge, Mass.: Harvard University Press, 1961), 1:341.

Diners in Dorchester: "An Alphabetical List of the Sons of Liberty who dined at Liberty Tree, Dorchester, August 14, 1769," *MHS Proceedings*, 11:140-2.

p 68. Nathaniel Balch: John Adams diary, August 14, 1769, *Diary and Autobiography of John Adams*, 1:341-2. See also "Journal of Josiah Quincy, Jr., 1773," *MHS Proceedings*, 49 (1915-16), 444, and Samuel Breck, *Recollections of Samuel Breck*, H. E. Scudder, editor (Philadelphia: Porter & Coates, 1877), 108.

Gores' work for Hancock: Gore invoice, November 11, 1765, "John Hancock" volume, Mellen Chamberlain Collection, BPL.

"300 Coaches & Chaises": John Boyle, "Boyle's Journal of Occurrences in Boston, 1759-1778," August 14, 1769, *NEHGR*, 84 (1930), 259.

Brawl on King Street: John E. Alden, "John Mein: Scourge of Patriots," *CSM Publications*, 34 (1937-42), 587-8.

p 69. First tar-and-feathering: Hiller B. Zobel, *The Boston Massacre* (New York: W. W. Norton, 1970), 159-60.

"obstinate and inveterate Enemies": "At a Meeting of the Merchants & Traders, at *Faneuil*-Hall" handbill, January 23, 1770, New England Papers, 10:3:62, Sparks Manuscripts, Houghton Library, Harvard University.

"4 barrels Painters colours": *Boston Chronicle*, January 18-22, 1770.

p 70. Spinning-bees: Laurel T. Ulrich, "'Daughters of Liberty': Religious Women in Revolutionary New England," in Ronald Hoffman and Peter J. Albert, editors, *Women in the Age of the American Revolution* (Charlottesville: University Press of Virginia, 1989), 216-7. The other spinning bee not at a minister's house came at the end of 1770 in the home of Martin Gay. Some genealogists suggest that Gay was Capt. Gore's brother-in-law, so the two events would actually have taken place in the same family.

p 71. "One Day last Week": *Boston Gazette*, February 26, 1770, supplement.

School closing: Jenks, *Boston Latin*, 1:36-7.

"insulting Every body": "Narrative of Proceedings at Boston From February 7th to March 14th 1770," Sparks Manuscripts, 10:3:70-1. *Boston Evening-Post*, February 26, 1770.

"was Repulsed": "Narrative of Proceedings," Sparks Manuscripts, 10:3:70-1.

"a Company of young tragedians": *Boston Chronicle*, January 29–February 1, 1770.

"besmeared . . . with tar & feathers": "Narrative of Proceedings," Sparks Manuscripts, 10:3:69.

p 72. "Limon Peels": Fight at Richardson's house based on *Legal Papers of John Adams*, L. Kinvin Wroth and Hiller B. Zobel, editors (Cambridge, Mass.: Harvard University Press, 1965), 2:420, 417.

"light rubbish": *Boston Evening-Post*, February 26, 1770.

Sammy Gore's role: The March 1, 1770, *Boston News-Letter* reported that Sammy Gore "happened to be there as a Spectator" and that Christopher Seider "upon hearing a Noise, as he was going from School, ran down with the rest of the Boys." However, newspapers in the first week after the event did not make such exculpatory remarks.

"about the bigness": *Boston Evening-Post*, February 26, 1770.

"stooping to take up": *Legal Papers of John Adams*, 2:418. For Seider's age, see his baptismal record in *NEHGR*, 138:229.

Thursday newspapers: Contrast the reports in the *Boston Chronicle*, February 19-22, 1770, and *Boston News-Letter*, February 22, 1770.

p 73. Seider family: Wilford W. Whitaker and Gary T. Horlacher, *Broad Bay Germans: 18th Century German-Speaking Settlers of Present-Day Waldoboro, Maine* (Rockport, Me.: Picton Press, 1998), 282-3.

Seider's death: *Boston Evening-Post*, February 26, 1770.

"thro' both thighs": *Boston Evening-Post*, February 26, 1770.

"his Life was endanger'd": *Boston Gazette*, February 26, 1770, supplement.

"in all probability": *Boston Evening-Post*, February 26, 1770.

"tell the story": Hewes and [Thatcher], *Traits of the Tea Party*, 91. The barber or Thatcher misidentified the scarred man as Christopher Gore rather than Samuel.

Decision not to sue Richardson: Future Gore in-law Edward Payne stated this reason for not suing for his injuries after the Boston Massacre; Oliver, *Peter Oliver's Origin*, 91-2.

"this little hero": *Boston Evening-Post*, February 26, 1770.

Barber's apprentices: *A Short Narrative of the Horrid Massacre* (Boston: Edes & Gill, 1770), deposition #38.

p 74. Theophilus Lillie's move: Pruitt, *Massachusetts Tax Valuation List*, 342-3.

Lawyers for Richardson trial: Zobel, *Boston Massacre*, 219-23.

Richardson trial: *Legal Papers of John Adams*, 2:404-5.

p 75. "for Shame, for shame Gentlemen!": Oliver, *Peter Oliver's Origin*, 86.

Richardson sentencing: *Legal Papers of John Adams*, 2:410.

John Hancock's lawsuit: Alden, "Mein," *CSM Publications,* 34:590-1.

Baby named John: *Manifesto Church*, 186. John and Sarah Gore had switched to the more socially prestigious Brattle Street meeting-house by this time.

"This Morning (Tuesday)": "Boyle's Journal of Occurrences," September 3, 1771, *NEHGR*, 84:271.

p 76. Sam Gore's nickname: Capt. Gore spelled this "Samme": Gore letter-book, Bostonian Society.

"John Gore and Son": *Boston News-Letter*, April 9, 1772.

Ebenezer Richardson: J. L. Bell, "'A Wretch of Wretches Prov'd with Child': From Local Scandal to Revolutionary Outrage," *New England Ancestors*, 6.1 (Winter 2005), 22-4.

Hancock and the Cadets: William M. Fowler, Jr., *The Baron of Beacon Hill: A Biography of John Hancock* (Boston: Houghton Mifflin, 1980), 136, 145.

Hutchinson letters: Bernard Bailyn, *The Ordeal of Thomas Hutchinson* (Cambridge, Mass.: Harvard University Press, 1974), 239-40.

p 77. "quit the ranks": Ephraim Eliot account of controversy, vol. 3., First Massachusetts Corps of Cadets Papers, Special Collections, Boston University.

North End Caucus: Elbridge Henry Goss, *The Life of Colonel Paul Revere* (Boston: J. G. Cupples, 1891), 2:635-6. *Boston News-Letter and City Record*, November 25, 1826.

Moses Grant as artillerist: *Massachusetts Soldiers and Sailors*, 6:734.

Hutchinson's investment: Bailyn, *Ordeal of Thomas Hutchinson*, 154.

p 78. Dock patrols: "Minutes of the Tea Meetings, 1773," *MHS Proceedings*, 20:11.

"like Sentinels in a garrison": Benjamin Woods Labaree, *The Boston Tea Party* (New York: Oxford University Press, 1964), 134.

"Paddock, whose sympathies": John Austin Stevens, "Biographical Sketch of Ebenezer Stevens, Lieut.-Col. of Artillery in the Continental Army," *Magazine of American History*, 7 (1877), 589.

"they had now done": L. F. S. Upton, "Proceedings of Ye Body Respecting the Tea," *William and Mary Quarterly*, 3rd series, 22 (1965), 297-8.

p 79. "Some of them stopped": Stevens, "Ebenezer Stevens," *Magazine of American History*, 7:859.

Hewes disguising himself: George R. T. Hewes [as told to James Hawkes], *A Retrospect of the Boston Tea-Party* (New York: S. S. Bliss, 1834), 38. Hewes and [Thatcher], *Traits of the Tea Party*, 180.

Lendell Pitts: Hewes and [Thatcher], *Traits of the Tea Party*, 181-4. Hewes and [Hawkes], *A Retrospect of the Boston Tea-Party*, 39, 79. *Boston Gazette*, June 7, 1773. Another of Gore's Latin School classmates, Thomas Melvill, was also recognized early as a veteran of the Tea Party.

Memory of the Tea Party: Alfred Young, *The Shoemaker and the Tea Party: Memory and the American Revolution* (Boston: Beacon Press, 1999), 85-194. Benjamin L. Carp, *Defiance of the Patriots: The Boston Tea Party and the Making of America* (New Haven: Yale University Press, 2010), 218-33.

"one of the number": *Columbian Centinel*, November 26, 1831.

"an aged Bostonian": Hewes and [Thatcher], *Traits of the Tea Party*, 261-2.

p 80. "He always lived": AO 13/73, Massachusetts Temporary Assistance, G(I), 641, National Archives, UK.

"for signing the Address": "Boyle's Journal of Occurrences," September 8, 1774, *NEHGR*, 84:379.

Capt. Gore voted out: *BTR*, 19:217.

Gore family letters: Gore letterbook, Bostonian Society.

Contributions for Boston's poor: John Cary, *Joseph Warren: Physician, Politician, Patriot* (Urbana, Ill.: University of Illinois Press, 1964), 138. Dr. Thomas Young to Samuel Adams, August 23, 1774, Samuel Adams Papers, NYPL.

p 81. Gore marriage: "Boyle's Journal of Occurrences," March 10, 1774, *NEHGR*, 84:373.

"Artillery training": Thomas Newell, "Diary of Mr. Thomas Newell," September 3, 1774, *MHS Proceedings*, 15 (1877), 537.

"was heard to express": William Tudor, *The Life of James Otis, of Massachusetts* (Boston: Wells and Lilly, 1823), 452-3.
"a few individuals": Tudor, *James Otis*, 452.

CHAPTER FIVE: "NOT ONE LISPED A WORD"

p 83. Collection of toys: D. C. Colesworthy, *John Tileston's School, Boston, 1778-1789: 1761-1766: Also, his Diary from 1761 to 1766* (Boston: Antiquarian Book Store, 1887), 46.
Desks and forms: At the South Latin School, the teachers' two desks sat at opposite corners. One form was assigned to each age level, with an extra for boys skipping ahead; Henry F. Jenks, *Catalogue of the Boston Latin School* (Boston: Boston Latin School Association, 1886), 1:36.
Quills: Colesworthy, John Tileston's School, 75, 78-9.
Writing exercises: Ray Nash, *American Writing Masters and Copybooks: History and Bibliography Through Colonial Times* (Boston: Colonial Society of Massachusetts, 1959). George Bickham, *The Universal Penman* (New York: Dover Publications, 1949).
Samuel Holbrook: Robert Francis Seybolt, *The Public Schoolmasters of Colonial Boston* (Cambridge, Mass.: Harvard University Press, 1939), 15, 20; Seybolt, *The Public Schools of Colonial Boston, 1635-1775* (Cambridge, Mass.: Harvard University Press, 1935), 26; Seybolt, *The Private Schools of Colonial Boston* (Cambridge, Mass.: Harvard University Press, 1935), 41; and Victor Channing Sanborn, "Four Boston Families: Holbrook, Yendell, Vail, Whitman," *NEHGR*, 58 (1904), 305-9.
Two hundred boys: extrapolated from figures for 1769-1773 in Seybolt, *Public Schools*, 64, 95. For some daily attendance figures, see Colesworthy, *John Tileston's School*, 72-6.

p 84. Andrew Cunningham: Seybolt, *Public Schoolmasters*, 20. An impressive sample of Cunningham's calligraphy is preserved with the Abiah Holbrook Papers at the Houghton Library, Harvard University.
Andrew Cunningham's father: James Cunningham was also a painter and might thus have known the Gore family well. Oliver Ayer Roberts, *History of the Military Company of the Massachusetts, Now Called The Ancient and Honorable Artillery Company of Massachusetts, 1637-1888*, 4 vols. (Boston: Alfred Mudge & Son, 1897), 2:105-6.
"large box": William Tudor, *The Life of James Otis, of Massachusetts* (Boston: Wells and Lilly, 1823), 453.
"Immediately after the roll call": Tudor, *James Otis*, 453-4.
"*innocent* spectator": Tudor, *James Otis*, 453-4.

p 85. "calling over to his sister": Isaac Smith, Sr., to Isaac Smith, Jr., 30 June 1775, *MHS Proceedings*, 16 (1878), 291. John Gore, who "during the blockade of Boston . . . served in the police," may have exercised some influence with the authorities to get his son released; E. Alfred Jones, *The Loyalists of Massachusetts: Their Memorials, Petitions, and Claims* (London: Saint Catherine Press, 1930), 150.

Private writing lessons for girls: Seybolt, *Public Schoolmasters*, 73-5. One of Holbrook's female students in this decade was Anna Green Winslow; *Diary of Anna Green Winslow: A Boston School Girl of 1771*, Alice Morse Earle, editor (Boston: Houghton-Mifflin, 1894), 12, 22, 35, 52.

"only about half of all white boys": In 1765 Boston's white male population under age 16 was estimated at 4,109; J. H. Benton, Jr., *Early Census Making in Massachusetts, 1643-1765* (Boston: Charles E. Goodspeed, 1905), 74-5. Assuming those boys were evenly distributed across the years, seven-sixteenths of them, or about 1,800, would have been of school age. Yet only 908 boys were in the public schools that year; *BTR*, 16:181.

p **86.** apprentices or servants: Apprenticeship contracts usually called for masters to make sure their young charges learned to read and, for boys, write and do rudimentary math "up to the Rule of Three." Some masters paid for private lessons while others handled this responsibility at home. See Robert Francis Seybolt, *Apprenticeship and Apprenticeship Education in Colonial New England and New York* (New York: Teachers College, Columbia University, 1917).

Latin School curriculum: Pauline Holmes, *A Tercentenary History of the Boston Public Latin School, 1635-1935* (Cambridge, Mass.: Harvard University Press, 1935), has the most thorough analysis of grammar-school textbooks. Wm. B. Fowle, editor, "Schools of the Olden Time in Boston," *The Common School Journal*, new series, 8 (1850), is most thorough about what was not taught. Jenks, *Boston Latin*, 1:36-7.

Enrollment figures: *BTR*, 16:282-5. In 1765, only 9% of all eligible boys in Boston were in the grammar schools.

Teachers' salaries: Seybolt, *Public Schoolmasters*, 21-29; *BTR*, 16:212, 282-3.

Dropout rate: Data from Jenks, *Boston Latin*. Analysis in J. L. Bell, "Classes, Forms, and Divisions in Boston's Pre-Revolutionary Schools," paper delivered at the Dublin Seminar for New England Folklife, June 2015.

"Carter's boys": Harrison Gray Otis [to Benjamin Apthorp Gould], December 18, 1844, quoted in Jenks, *Boston Latin*, 1:39. Did the Latin School boys really get the best of these encounters? The Queen Street boys far outnumbered them.

p **87.** Worcester: See Ray Raphael and Marie Raphael, *The Spirit of '74: How the American Revolution Began* (New York: New Press, 2015).

Joseph Balch: *BTR*, 24:232. Galusha B. Balch, *Genealogy of the Balch Families in America* (Salem, Mass.: Eben Putnam, 1897), 67-8. *Massachusetts Soldiers and Sailors of the Revolutionary War*, 17 vols. (Boston: Wright & Potter, 1896-1908), 1:511. *Acts and Resolves of Rhode Island*, "An Act for embodying, supplying, and paying, the Army of Observation . . . ," May 1775.

p **88.** Richard Gridley's smithy: Dirk Hoerder, *Crowd Action in Revolutionary Massachusetts, 1765-1780* (New York: Academic Press, 1977), 208.

Obadiah Whiston: *BTR*, 21:143. "Baptisms in the First Church at

Dorchester, Mass., 1748-1792," *NEHGR*, 68 (1914), 216. (Note the shift from O.S. to N.S. dating.)

Street lamp work: Boston Town Records, loose papers, March 1774, BPL.

"Baptists by profession": "Revolutionary Reminiscence," *Western Monthly Review*, 1 (1828), 147.

Dispute between Pierpoint and Ness: Hoerder, *Crowd Action*, 208.

"Obadiah Whiston a Black Smith": Deposition of Ens. John Ness, August 23, 1770, in Frederick Lewis Gay Transcripts, State Papers, 12:54-60, at MHS. Other depositions in this collection mention Whiston by name, some blaming him for throwing the brick. See Hiller Zobel, *The Boston Massacre* (New York: W. W. Norton, 1970), 139-40.

"Here is the fellow": Zobel, *Boston Massacre*, 141-2.

p. 89. "Met an Engine": *Legal Papers of John Adams*, L. Kinvin Wroth and Hiller B. Zobel, editors (Cambridge, Mass.: Harvard University Press, 1965), 3:58. *A Short Narrative of the Horrid Massacre* (Boston: Edes & Gill, 1770), deposition #74.

Whiston real estate: Suffolk Deeds 125:232, per Thwing File, MHS.

Whiston family: Obadiah Whiston and Priscilla Winship were married by the Rev. Samuel Stillman of Boston's First Baptist Church on August 4, 1771; *BTR*, 30:64. Obadiah and Priscilla Whiston had two sons, Francis and Obadiah; in a baffling twist of the records, they are said to have been born on November 31, 1761, and March 31, 1763, respectively; *BTR*, 24:302, 307. If there was a collation or transcription error and the boys' births were about ten years after these published dates, Whiston's life would fit a common pattern: married at age 23 or 22, a father shortly thereafter, and a second child within two years.

"This evening two officers": John Andrews to William Barrell, August 21, 1774, "Letters of John Andrews, Esq., of Boston, 1772-1776," Winthrop Sargent, editor, *MHS Proceedings*, 8 (1866), 345.

p 90. Whiston's blacksmith shop: Tudor, *James Otis*, 452-7.

Col. Richard Gridley: Thanks to David B. Ingram and the Thwing File at MHS for help sorting out the many Gridleys. Daniel V. T. Huntoon wrote several articles about Col. Richard Gridley which overstated his accomplishments and omitted critical information. Typical of these is Huntoon, "Major General Richard Gridley," *Magazine of History*, 7 (1908), 278-83, 336-42; 8 (1908), 29-38. That article referred to Gridley with the military rank that the Massachusetts legislature granted him but the Continental Congress never ratified and he therefore never used.

CHAPTER SIX: "SELLING WARLIKE STORES"

p 91. "their is two Iron guns": Peck finally told Gage about his cannon on April 24, 1775, the day Bostonians were to surrender their arms so they could leave the besieged town. One senses he did so ironically. Carl Seaburg and Stanley Paterson, *Merchant Prince of Boston: Colonel T. H. Perkins, 1764-1854* (Cambridge, Mass.: Harvard University Press, 1971), 25.

p 92. "seven or eight iron ordnance": John Andrews to William Barrell, August 21, 1774, "Letters of John Andrews, Esq., of Boston, 1772-1776," Winthrop Sargent, editor, *MHS Proceedings*, 8 (1866), 362-3. Welles's political activity in John W. Tyler, *Smugglers and Patriots: Boston Merchants and the Advent of the American Revolution* (Boston: Northeastern University Press, 1986), 276-7. For Welles's biography, see *Sibley's Harvard Graduates*, 11:606-8.

Royal Artillery guns: "Return of Light Brass Ordnance and Stores sent from New York to Boston, between 18th. May and 27th. July 1774," vol. 121, Gage Papers, Clements Library.

"22 pieces of cannon": Percy to Gen Harvey (?), August 21, 1774, *Letters of Hugh Earl Percy from Boston and New York, 1774-1776,* Charles K. Bolton, editor (Boston: Charles E. Goodspeed, 1902), 36.

p 93. "General Gage professes": William Tudor to John Adams, September 17, 1774, *The Papers of John Adams*, Robert J. Taylor, editor (Cambridge, Mass.: Harvard University Press, 1977), 2:167.

"[That] manoeuvre rais'd": Andrews, September 18, 1774, *MHS Proceedings*, 8:363.

p 94. "Last evening": Andrews, September 20, 1774, *MHS Proceedings*, 8:364.

"six good pieces of large cannon": Benjamin Kent to John Adams, September 23, 1774, *Papers of John Adams*, 2:170.

Timmins as Loyalist: *MHS Proceedings*, 11:392.

"the Admiral": Andrews, September 20, 1774, *MHS Proceedings*, 8:364. Thomas Newell also mentioned the loss of these guns; "Diary of Mr. Thomas Newell," September 20, 1774, *MHS Proceedings*, 15 (1877), 358.

"The people have lately": Vice Adm. Samuel Graves to Philip Stephens, Secretary of the Admiralty, September 23, 1774, Colonial Office, Great Britain, *Documents of the American Revolution, 1770-1783*, K. G. Davies, editor (Dublin: Irish University Press, 1975), 8:200.

p 95. "given his countrymen": Newell, "Diary," September 28, 1774, *MHS Proceedings*, 15:359.

"The Select Men and the Committee": *New-York Gazette*, October 10, 1774.

"ten cart-loads": Andrews, September 27, 1774, *MHS Proceedings*, 8:369.

"When about noon": Andrews, September 28, 1774, *MHS Proceedings*, 8:370.

p 96. "[N]ot content with disfiguring": Andrews, September 28, 1774, MHS Proceedings, 8:370.

"keeps incog.": Warren to Samuel Adams, September 29, 1774, Samuel Adams Papers, New York Public Library; printed in Richard Frothingham, *The Life and Times of Joseph Warren* (Boston: Little, Brown, 1865), 381-2.

"Scott had repeatedly": Andrews, September 28, 1774, *MHS Proceedings*, 8:370. *American Archives*, Peter Force, editor, 4th series (Washington, D.C.: U.S. Congress, 1837-53), 2:211.

"What is the meaning": *New-York Gazette*, October 10, 1774.

p 97. "It was difficult to still": Greenleaf to Paine, September 27, 1774, *Papers of Robert Treat Paine*, Stephen T. Riley and Edward W. Hanson, editors (Boston: MHS, 2005), 3:7. *American Archives*, 4th series, 1:806, 810.
"it is as much our grave": Warren to Samuel Adams, September 29, 1774, Samuel Adams Papers, NYPL.
"The countrymen that happen'd": Andrews, September 28, 1774, *MHS Proceedings*, 8:370.
"lying in the river": Joseph Warren to Samuel Adams, September 29, 1774, Samuel Adams Papers, NYPL. Samuel Phillips, identified as by surname only, could have been either father or son of that name.
"waited on Captain Bishop": Andrews, September 30, 1774, *MHS Proceedings*, 8:371.

p 98. "A Countryman": Frederick Mackenzie, *A British Fusilier in Revolutionary Boston*, Allen French, editor (Cambridge, Mass.: Harvard University Press, 1926), 42.
"pack'd in candle boxes": Andrews, March 18, 1775, *MHS Proceedings*, 8:401. Out in Charlestown, provincial commissary David Cheever sent "10 Boxes Bullets" and other material to James Barrett in Concord with a note saying: "this teem is sent away at 10 O'clock Satturday night in a Graite pannick Just having heard that the Kings Officers have seazed a cart load of Cartrages going thru Roxbury containing 19000 which must make you and I Extremely Cautious in our carrying on"; Cheever to Barrett, March 18, 1775, United States Revolution Collection, 1754-1928, AAS.
"two Custom house Officers": Deposition of Robert Pierpoint, March 20, 1775, Samuel Adams Papers, NYPL.
Gunpowder import ban: *The Correspondence of General Thomas Gage with the Secretaries of State, and with the War Office and the Treasury, 1763-1775*, Clarence Edwin Carter, editor (New Haven: Yale University Press, 1933), 2:176, 1:386.
"four double-fortified": *JHRM*, 52 (1776), 28. *JHRM*, 53 (1777), 83.

p 99. "2 Swivel Guns": Alice Hanson Jones, *American Colonial Wealth: Documents and Sources*, 2nd edition (New York: Arno Press, 1977), 2:959.
"passed a resolve": *JHRM*, 55 (1779), 57.
"to look out for": Gage to Graves, October 11, 1774, vol. 123, Gage Papers, Clements Library.
Massachusetts cannon purchase: *JHRM*, 49 (1772-73), 166, 193, 288, 292.
Guns sent to Pepperrell: Gage to Dartmouth, October 17, 1774, *Correspondence of General Thomas Gage*, 1:379. Great Britain Colonial Office, *Documents of the American Revolution*, 8:213, 243-4. Andrews, October 13, 1774, *MHS Proceedings*, 8:375.
"The Reputation of our Friend": Josiah Quincy, Sr., to Josiah Quincy, Jr., October 26, 1774, *MHS Proceedings*, 50 (1916-17), 482.

p 100. "that without Lord North's permission": Adm. Samuel Graves to Gage, November 1, 1774, vol. 124, Gage Papers, Clements Library.
"A dealer in cannon": *MHS Proceedings*, 32:139.

"Affairs here are worse": Gage to Barrington, September 25, 1774, *Correspondence of General Thomas Gage*, 2:654-5.

"many tumults": *Journals of Each Provincial Congress of Massachusetts in 1774 and 1775*, William Lincoln, editor (Boston: Dutton & Wentworth, 1838), 3-4.

p 101. Town participation in General Court: John J. Waters, Jr., *The Otis Family in Provincial and Revolutionary Massachusetts* (Chapel Hill: University of North Carolina Press, 1968), 84.

Men at first Provincial Congress: *JEPCM*, 7-15. Stephen E. Patterson, *Political Parties in Revolutionary Massachusetts* (Madison: University of Wisconsin Press, 1973), 110.

p 102. Stronger measures: *JEPCM*, 22.

Change in Parliament: Parliament was dissolved for new elections on September 30. Lord North hoped that new elections would strengthen his government, especially in regard to the American colonies, and that is what happened.

"consider what": *JEPCM*, 23.

CHAPTER SEVEN: "OUT OF BOSTON TO SOME PLACE IN THE COUNTRY"

p 103. "appear under arms": *Norwich Packet*, September 1, 1774.

"six half Barrels": *Boston News-Letter*, September 1, 1774.

"of the size and bigness": D. Hamilton Hurd, *History of Norfolk County* (Philadelphia: J. W. Lewis, 1884), 1:167.

p 104. "well stocked": *JEPCM*, 222.

"raise fifty pounds": John D. Washburn, *Address, Delivered July 4, 1876, at Lancaster, Massachusetts* (Lancaster, Mass.: n.p. 1876), 49-50. Walpole, Massachusetts, likewise dates its purchase of two cannon to September 26, 1774: "Historical Timeline of Walpole," www.walpole-ma.gov/library/pages/ historical-timeline-of-walpole. The town of Westborough bought a "four-pounder"; Herman Packard DeForest and Edward Craig Bates, *The History of Westborough, Massachusetts* (Westford: Westford, 1891), 161-2.

"Comittee To Provide Carriages": "Worcester Town Records from 1753 to 1783," Franklin P. Rice, editor, *Collections of the Worcester Society of Antiquity*, 4 (1882), 240, 247-50.

"bullets or lead": Samuel Adams Drake, *History of Middlesex County* (Boston: Estes & Lauriat, 1880), 1:443. See also William Barry, *History of Framingham* (Boston: James Munroe, 1847), 91.

p 105. "to procure a carriage": Lucas R. Paige, *History of Cambridge, Massachusetts, 1630-1877* (Boston: H. O. Houghton, 1877), 159.

"two pieces of Cannon": *Watertown Records* (Watertown, Mass.: Town of Watertown, 1928), 5:113.

"Great Guns": *Watertown Records*, 5:119-20.

"Several cannon were purchased": Lemuel Shattuck, *A History of the Town of Concord* (Boston: Russell, Odiorne, & Company, 1835), 92.

"that he may be paid": *JHRM*, 53, part 2 (1778), 161. Ingraham was paid £58.13s.4d. in March 1792, fourteen years after his initial request and after he had served a term in the legislature himself; *Massachusetts Acts and Resolves*, 1791-92, Chap. 122.

Duncan Ingraham: Robert A. Gross, *The Minutemen and Their World* (New York: Hill and Wang, 1976), 51, 54, 56. Elise Lemire, *Black Walden: Slavery and Its Aftermath in Concord, Massachusetts* (Philadelphia: University of Pennsylvania Press, 2011), 91-3.

"The mob unloaded": William Lee, *John Leigh of Agawam Massachusetts, 1634-1671: and His Descendants of the Name of Lee* (Albany: Joel Munsell's Sons, 1888), 158.

p 106. "most proper time": *JEPCM*, 28.

Ordnance budget: *JEPCM*, 30.

p 107. "his excellency General Gage": *JEPCM*, 31.

Commissaries and committee men: *JEPCM*, 35, 37-8.

"receiver general": *JEPCM*, 37-8.

Militia elections: *JEPCM*, 47-8.

p 108. "to take care of": *JEPCM*, 41.

"procure all the arms": *JEPCM*, 505.

"Voted, unanimously": *JEPCM*, 506.

"as the most proper person": *Massachusetts Mercury*, September 23, 1794. *Columbian Centinel*, September 24, 1794.

"upon furlough": *JEPCM*, 520.

p 109. "Entered the Service": "Notebook of Col. David Mason giving his Revolutionary service," Bryant-Mason-Smith Family Papers, held at MHS.

Letter of reference: Samuel H. Savage to Capt. Richard Derby, Sr., June 21, 1764, transcription, in Bryant-Mason-Smith Family Papers.

Richard Derby, Sr.: Robert E. Peabody, "The Derbys of Salem, Mass.," *EIHC*, 44 (1908), 195-7, 207-8. James Duncan Phillips, *The Life and Times of Richard Derby, Merchant of Salem* (Cambridge, Mass.: Riverside Press, 1929). Ronald N. Tagney, *The World Turned Upside Down: Essex County During America's Turbulent Years, 1763-1790* (West Newbury, Mass.: Essex County History, 1990), 46.

Richard Derby, Jr.: Ronald N. Tagney, *World Turned*, 90-1.

Wife and six surviving children: Mason genealogy (box 4, folder 9), Bryant-Mason-Smith Family Papers, held at MHS.

"all kinds of painting": Joseph B. Felt, *Annals of Salem* (Salem, Mass.: W. & S. B. Ives, 1849), 2:185, 38. *Essex Gazette*, July 31–August 7, 1770.

"2 large chests": Susan Smith, "Memoir of Col. David Mason—by his daughter Susan Smith, relict of Professor Smith of Hanover, N.H.—Novr, 1842, in her 80th year," Shaw Family Papers (reel 4, frames 272-80), Library of Congress.

"the newly discovered Electrical Fire": *Boston News-Letter*, February 21, 1765; *New-Hampshire Gazette*, November 21, 1766; and *Essex Gazette*, January 1, 1771. The Bryant-Mason-Smith Family Papers include a broadside promoting one of these lectures.

p 110. Gunpowder cartridges: Mason's accounts include charges for paper and flannel cartridges, the largest for "making 896 paper Cartridges"; "Notebook of Col. David Mason," Bryant-Mason-Smith Family Papers. To an eleven-year-old seamstress, that could easily feel like five thousand.

Mason's son's teacher: Invoice of "S. Holbrook," March 1, 1764, Bryant-Mason-Smith Family Papers.

p 111. "never dared venture": Susan Smith, "Biographical Sketch of Col. David Mason of Salem," *EIHC*, 48 (1912), 205.

"in the upper part": Smith, "David Mason," Shaw Family Papers, Library of Congress.

"went with Gen. Lincoln": "Memoirs of Col. David Mason," *New-York Review, and Atheneum Magazine*, 1 (1825), 305. Smith, "David Mason," *EIHC*, 48:204-5.

Salisbury ironworks: Robert B. Gordon, *A Landscape Transformed: The Ironmaking District of Salisbury, Connecticut* (New York: Oxford, 2001), 202.

"Marks & Number of Guns": Mason used the same stylized P to mean "pounder," "per," and "pair." "Notebook of Col. David Mason," Bryant-Mason-Smith Family Papers.

Rhode Island assembly: *Rhode Island Acts and Resolves, May 1774–April 1775*, 131-2.

p 112. "six twenty-four Pounders": Capt. James Wallace to Vice-Adm. Samuel Graves, December 12, 1774, *NDAR*, 1:15. I thank Bart Reynolds for calling this material to my attention.

"two eighteen-pounders": John Russell Bartlett, editor, *Records of the Colony of Rhode Island and Providence Plantation in New England, 1770 to 1776* (Providence: A. C. Greene & Brothers, 1862), 7:262-3.

"Train of Artillery": *Rhode Island Acts and Resolves, May 1774–April 1775*, 133-6, 141-4, 149. *Connecticut Courant*, December 19, 1774.

"into the Country": Nathaniel Shaw, Jr., to Eliphalet Dyer, December 14, 1774, *NDAR*, 1:20. *Connecticut Journal*, December 16, 1774.

"very frankly": Capt. James Wallace to Adm. Samuel Graves, December 12, 1774, *NDAR*, 1:15.

Raid on Fort William and Mary: *NDAR*, 1:18-9, 27, 31, 37-8, 40-1. Elwyn Page, "The King's Powder, 1774," *New England Quarterly*, 18 (1945), 83-92. David Hackett Fischer, *Paul Revere's Ride* (New York: Oxford University Press, 1994), 52-7.

"three four pounders": *NDAR*, 1:18.

p 113. "wait on Col. Robinson": *JEPCM*, 507.

Lemuel Robinson: Dorchester Antiquarian and Historical Society, *History of the Town of Dorchester, Massachusetts* (Boston: Ebenezer Clapp, Jr., 1859), 361, 364. John A. Schutz, *Legislators of the Massachusetts General Court, 1691-1780: A Biographical Dictionary* (Boston: Northeastern University Press, 1997), 327. *BTR*, 21:89, 264. *NEHGR*, 68:225-35.

"near the Lower Mills, in Dorchester": Francis S. Drake, *The Town of*

Roxbury: Its Memorable Persons and Places (Roxbury, Mass.: Drake, 1878), 73.

"under a compost heap": Drake, *Roxbury*, 73.

"Junr. Adjut. [with] Lieuts. Rank": John Boyle, "Boyle's Journal of Occurrences in Boston, 1759-1778," April 1, 1772, *NEHGR*, 84 (1930), 358.

William Dawes's role: Dawes's great-grandson Henry W. Holland set down the reminiscences of two family members in a book printed for other family members: *William Dawes and His Ride with Paul Revere* (Boston: John Wilson, 1878). Those descendants said Dawes had masterminded the theft from the gunhouse on the Common. However, Holland had Samuel Gore's story in two histories that he cited as sources: James Spear Loring's *Hundred Boston Orators* and Samuel A. Drake's *Old Landmarks and Historic Personages of Boston*. Gore had not mentioned Dawes, and Henry Burbeck gave credit for the second theft to members of the train, which Dawes was not.

p 114. "my father accidentally received": Holland, *William Dawes*, 34, 37.

"the person appointed": Audit Office 13/51, Massachusetts New Claims, S, 395-7, National Archives, UK.

"were put into a boat": William Tudor, *The Life of James Otis, of Massachusetts* (Boston: Wells and Lilly, 1823), 457.

p 115. "Mr. Williams, a respectable farmer": Tudor, *James Otis*, 457. Manure figures in almost every story of greater Boston's hidden artillery, perhaps a sign of how much of the stuff the culture produced. "Cannon, balls, and such like heavy stores, were put into carts and carried out over the neck, under the appearance of loads of dung"; Gordon, *History*, 1:473. "Have seen twenty load [of musket balls] cover'd with dung to go out of town myself"; John Andrews to William Barrell, March 18, 1775, "Letters of John Andrews, Esq., of Boston, 1772-1776," Winthrop Sargent, editor, *MHS Proceedings*, 8 (1866), 401.

Joseph Williams: Drake, *Roxbury*, 20-30, 34. The May 30, 1768, *Boston Evening-Post* referred to "Col. Joseph Williams's Seat in Roxbury," indicating his high standing.

Abigail Williams and Mehitable Dawes: Holland, *William Dawes*, 25.

"with an ox-team for offals": George R. T. Hewes, as told to "A Bostonian" [Benjamin Bussey Thatcher], *Traits of the Tea Party* (New York: Harper & Brothers, 1836), 257-8.

Jerusha Minot: *NEHGR*, 68:221.

"deposited them": Drake, *Roxbury*, 73.

African day-names: Gary B. Nash, *Race, Class, and Politics: Essays on American Colonial and Revolutionary Society* (Urbana: University of Illinois Press, 1986), 294-6.

James Brewer: *Columbian Centinel*, October 8, 1806.

Brewer at Massacre: *Legal Papers of John Adams*, L. Kinvin Wroth and Hiller B. Zobel, editors (Cambridge, Mass.: Harvard University Press, 1965), 3:112-4.

Brewer at Tea Party: "Minutes of the Tea Meetings," *MHS Proceedings*, 20 (1884), 13; Hewes and [Thatcher], *Traits of the Tea Party*, 261-2.
Brewer as captive: Timothy Newell journal, June 6, 1775, *MHS Collections*, 4th series, 1:262. Ezra Stiles, *The Literary Diary of Ezra Stiles, D.D., Ll.D.*, Franklin Bowditch Dexter, editor (New York: Scribner's, 1901), 1:570.
p 116. Brewer during war: *Massachusetts Soldiers and Sailors of the Revolutionary War* (Boston: Wright & Potter, 1896-1908), 2:466. "The United States to James Brewer," *MHS Proceedings*, 6 (1862-63), 261.
"6-inch brass mortars": "United States to James Brewer," *MHS Proceedings*, 6:261.
Richard Boynton: "An Alphabetical List of the Sons of Liberty who dined at Liberty Tree, Dorchester, August 14, 1769," *MHS Proceedings*, 11 (1871), 140.
Boston Committee of Correspondence members: Richard D. Brown, *Revolutionary Politics in Massachusetts: The Boston Committee of Correspondence and the Towns, 1772-1774* (Cambridge, Mass.: Harvard University Press, 1970), 59. Annotated list of Bostonians appointed to enforce the Association, *MHS Proceedings,* 32:140.
"He not being able": *MHS Proceedings*, 6:261.
p 118. "to secure for the country": Tudor, *James Otis*, 452.
"2 Brass 2¶": "Notebook of Col. David Mason giving his Revolutionary service," Bryant-Mason-Smith Family Papers, held at MHS.
"patrolled the street for several hours": Tudor, *James Otis*, 457, 465.

CHAPTER EIGHT: "TO ACT THE TRAITOR"

p 119. "getting magazines": Gage to Dartmouth, September 12, 1774, *The Correspondence of General Thomas Gage with the Secretaries of State, and with the War Office and the Treasury, 1763-1775*, Clarence Edwin Carter, editor (New Haven: Yale University Press, 1933), 1:374.
Gage's seconds-in-command: Percy, *Letters of Hugh Earl Percy*. Frederick Haldimand, *Sir Frederick Haldimand Papers: Unpublished Papers and Correspondence*, 115 reels (London: World Microfilm Publications, 1977).
p 120. Junior officers: John Barker, *The British in Boston: Being the Diary of Lieutenant John Barker of the King's Own Regiment from November 15, 1774 to May 31, 1776* (Cambridge, Mass.: Harvard University Press, 1924). W. Glanville Evelyn, *Memoir and Letters of Capt. W. Glanville Evelyn*. Martin Hunter, *The Journal of Gen. Sir Martin Hunter*, Anne Hunter and Elizabeth Bell, eds. (Edinburgh: Edinburgh Press, 1894). Stephen Kemble, *Journals of Lieut.-Col. Stephen Kemble, 1773-1789* (Boston: Gregg Press, 1972; reprint of *NYHSC*, vol. 16, 1883). Jeremy Lister, *Concord Fight* (Cambridge, Mass.: Harvard University Press, 1931). Mackenzie, *A British Fusilier in Revolutionary Boston*. Montresor, "The Montresor Journals," *NYHSC*, vol. 14. Archibald Robertson, *Archibald Robertson, Lieutenant-General Royal Engineers: His Diaries and Sketches in America, 1762-1780* (New York: New York Public Library, 1930). [Richard] Williams, *Discord and Civil Wars: Being a Portion of the Journal Kept by Lieutenant Williams*

of His Majesty's Twenty-third Regiment (Buffalo: East Hill Press, 1954). Marion Balderston and David Syrett, editors, *The Lost War: Letters from British Officers during the American Revolution* (New York: Horizon Press, 1975). I thank also Don Hagist for searching his database of general orders and courts-martial from the British army in Boston for mentions of brass cannon, without success.

"actually carried": Graves to Philip Stephens, Secretary of the Admiralty, September 23, 1774, Colonial Office, Great Britain, *Documents of the American Revolution, 1770-1783*, K. G. Davies, editor (Dublin: Irish University Press, 1975), 8:200.

"Commanded the Corps": AO 13/49, Massachusetts Claims P(I), 4-5, National Archives, UK.

"secretly removed": Henry Hulton, "Some Account of the Proceedings of the People in New England; from the Establishment of a Board of Customs in America, to the breaking out of the Rebellion in 1775," 262, André deCoppet Manuscript Collection, Manuscripts Division, Department of Rare Books and Special Collections, Princeton University Library. Published with the permission of the Princeton University Library.

"seized upon": James Wallace, December 12, 1774, *Parliamentary Register*, 1:60.

"imbecility of this government": John Wentworth, December 14, 1774, and December 16, 1774, *Parliamentary Register*, 1:100-2.

p 121. "The New England Provinces": Gage to Barrington, September 25, 1774, *Correspondence of Gage*, 2:654-6.

"Suspension of the Execution": Gage to Dartmouth, September 25, 1774, *Correspondence of Gage*, 1:375.

"an Army near twenty Thousand": Gage to Barrington, October 2, 1774, *Correspondence of Gage*, 2:656.

"This Province and the neighboring": Gage to Barrington, November 2, 1774, *Correspondence of Gage*, 659.

"the Province was in actual Rebellion": Thomas Hutchinson, *The Diary and Letters of His Excellency, Thomas Hutchinson, Esq.*, Peter Orlando Hutchinson, editor (Boston: Houghton-Mifflin, 1884), 1:297-8.

p 122. "What turned us all": William Knox, "Proceedings in Relation to the American Colonies," in Historical Manuscripts Commission, *Report on Manuscripts in Various Collections*, vol. 6 (Dublin: H.M. Stationery Office, 1909), 257.

"The account we have": *Parliamentary Register*, 1:29. Thanks to John K. Rowland for alerting me to this speech.

p 123. "any Gunpowder": Dartmouth to Gage and other colonial governors, October 19, 1774, *Correspondence of Gage*, 2:176. Gage acknowledged receiving this letter on December 15; Gage, *Correspondence of Gage*, 1:386.

"One Whiston": Warren to Adams, February 10, 1775, Samuel Adams Papers, New York Public Library. Richard Frothingham, *The Life and Times of Joseph Warren* (Boston: Little, Brown, 1865), 414-5, prints this letter but renders "Whiston" as "Wheston."

p 124. "Dr. Church and I": Warren to Adams, February 10, 1775, Samuel Adams Papers, NYPL. Frothingham, *Joseph Warren*, 414-5, posits that Warren meant the cannon should be moved "without [delay]," rather than "without" in the sense of "outside."

"wait on Col. Robinson": *JEPCM*, 508-9.

"became a tory": "Revolutionary Reminiscence," *Western Monthly Review*, 1:147.

Obadiah Whiston's depature: "List of the inhabitants of Boston, who . . . removed to Halifax with the army," *MHS Proceedings*, 18 (1880-81), 268. David E. Maas, *Divided Hearts: Massachusetts Loyalists, 1765-1790, A Biographical Directory* (Boston: Society of Colonial Wars and New England Historic Genealogical Society, 1980), 158. Maas's listing for Obadiah Wheaton probably refers to the same man.

Dr. Benjamin Church, Jr.: John A. Nagy, *Dr. Benjamin Church, Spy: A Case of Espionage on the Eve of the American Revolution* (Yardley, Penn.: Westholme, 2013). Allen French, *General Gage's Informers: New Material Upon Lexington and Concord, Benjamin Thompson as Loyalist and the Treachery of Benjamin Church, Jr.* (Ann Arbor: University of Michigan Press, 1932).

p 125. "Memorandums 21st. Feby.": Vol. 126, Gage Papers, Clements Library.

p 126. Ordnance costs: *JEPCM*, 30.

"Generall Constructions": "Notebook of Col. David Mason," Bryant-Mason-Smith Family Papers.

Newton's fieldpieces: Francis Jackson, *History of the Early Settlement of Newton* (Boston: Stacy & Richardson, 1854), 183-5.

"that the Committe appointed": *Watertown Records* (Watertown, Mass.: Town of Watertown, 1928), 5:113-4, 119-20.

p 126. "vote to have them fitted": Joseph B. Felt, *Annals of Salem* (Salem, Mass.: W. & S. B. Ives, 1849), 2:492.

p 127. "capable of taking sketches": Barker, *British in Boston*, 18.

"go through the counties": *General Gage's Instructions, of 22d February 1775* (Boston: J. Gill, 1779), 3-5.

"surveyors": *General Gage's Instructions*, 5-8.

p 128. "to assemble one fourth part": *JEPCM*, 510.

"have each two field pieces": *JEPCM*, 511-2.

"for the use of": *JEPCM*, 511.

"That eight field pieces": *JEPCM*, 512.

p 129. "to observe the motions": Notes dated February 24, 1775, vol. 126, Gage Papers. Gage enclosed a copy of this report, titled "Intelligence of Military Preparations in Massachusetts," in his letter to Dartmouth, March 4, 1775, Colonial Office, *Documents of the American Revolution*, 9:63-4.

Salem alarm: This description is based chiefly on Charles M. Endicott, "Leslie's Retreat, or the Resistance to British Arms, at the North Bridge in Salem," *PEI*, 1 (1856), 89-135, especially the newspaper accounts and reminiscences starting on page 122. Robert Rantoul's "The Affair at the North

Bridge, Salem, February 26, 1775," *EIHC*, 38 (1902), 321-52, rounds up British sources. Ronald N. Tagney, *The World Turned Upside Down: Essex County During America's Turbulent Years, 1763-1790* (West Newbury, Mass.: Essex County History, 1990), is a modern study of the event in well described context. See also David Hackett Fischer, *Paul Revere's Ride* (New York: Oxford University Press, 1994), 58-64. Peter Charles Hoffer, *Prelude to Revolution: The Salem Gunpowder Raid of 1775* (Baltimore: Johns Hopkins University Press, 2014), is the most recent study of the event, flawed by unreliable sources and the fact that no gunpowder was involved.

p 130. "two of the selectmen": *PEI*, 1:132.
"The regulars are coming": *PEI*, 1:127.
"a piece of thick oak trees": Susan Smith, "Biographical Sketch of Col. David Mason of Salem," *EIHC*, 48 (1912), 205.
"an oaken thicket": Felt, *Annals of Salem*, 2:516.
"was fond of exhibiting": *PEI*, 1:127.

p 131. "If he can find them": Felt, *Annals of Salem*, 2:516. By 1861 Derby's response became "Find them if you can! take them if you can! they will never be surrendered"; Perley Derby, "A Genealogy of the Derby Family," *EIHC*, 3 (1861), 162.
"expresses had gone out": Susan Smith, "Memoir of Col. David Mason—by his daughter Susan Smith, relict of Professor Smith of Hanover, N.H.—Novr, 1842, in her 80th year," Shaw Family Papers (reel 4, frames 272-80), Library of Congress.
"he would go over": *PEI*, 1:123.
"doing something": *PEI*, 1:130.
"pledged his honor": *PEI*, 1:123.
"went back of Colonel Sprague's": *PEI*, 1:128.

p 132. "an old country man": Smith, "Memoir of Col. David Mason," Shaw Family Papers, Library of Congress.
"on the top of his house": *PEI*, 1:129.
"Samuel Porter, a lawyer": Felt, *Annals of Salem*, 2:516.
"a crack in the breech": *PEI*, 1:130.
"The Circumstance": Gage to Dartmouth, 4 March 1775, *Correspondence of Gage*, 1:394.

p 133. "The Colonel landed": Pitcairn to the Earl of Sandwich, March 4, 1775, *The Private Papers of John, Earl of Sandwich, First Lord of the Admiralty, 1771-1782. Volume 1: August 1770-March 1778*, G. R. Barnes and J. H. Owens, eds. (London: Navy Records Society, 1932), 1:60-2.
"Twenty seven Pieces of Cannon": *Essex Gazette*, February 28–March 7, 1775.

CHAPTER NINE: "THIS TOWN IS FULL OF CANNON"

p 134. "officers of the army": *General Gage's Instructions, of 22d February 1775* (Boston: J. Gill, 1779), 9.
"the company of militia": *General Gage's Instructions*, 9-10.

p 135. "the people came out": *General Gage's Instructions*, 11-2.
Henry Barnes's horse: Dirk Hoerder, *Crowd Action in Revolutionary Massachusetts, 1765-1780* (New York: Academic Press, 1977), 237.
"swore to it": Pitcairn to the Earl of Sandwich, March 4, 1775, *The Private Papers of John, Earl of Sandwich, First Lord of the Admiralty, 1771-1782. Volume 1: August 1770-March 1778*, G. R. Barnes and J. H. Owens, eds. (London: Navy Records Society, 1932), 1:60-2.
"a great number": John Barker, *The British in Boston: Being the Diary of Lieutenant John Barker of the King's Own Regiment from November 15, 1774 to May 31, 1776* (Cambridge, Mass.: Harvard University Press, 1924), 25.

p 136. "the ignorance": "An Oration delivered March 15th 1775 from the Coffeehouse by Doctr. Thos. Bolton," Miscellaneous Bound Manuscripts, MHS.
"recover into The King's possession": Dartmouth to Gage, January 27, 1775, *The Correspondence of General Thomas Gage with the Secretaries of State, and with the War Office and the Treasury, 1763-1775*, Clarence Edwin Carter, editor (New Haven: Yale University Press, 1933), 2:182-3.
"An assumption": "Intelligence, March 3d. 1775," vol. 126, Gage Papers, Clements Library.
"upwards of 20": "Intelligence, March 4th. 1775," vol. 126, Gage Papers, Clements Library.

p 137. "the Books of the Committee": "Intelligence, March 8th, 1775." Gage's notes err in saying the committees met "at Charlestown."
Dividing food: *JEPCM*, 505.
"Four brass Cannon": Intelligence, March 8, 1775, vol. 126, Gage Papers, Clements Library.
Col. James Barrett: Robert A. Gross, *The Minutemen and Their World* (New York: Hill and Wang, 1976), 25, 57-8, 62-3, 69. The French version of the letter spelled out "Barret."
"Two pieces": Intelligence, March 8, 1775, vol. 126, Gage Papers, Clements Library.

p 138. Thomas Whiting: Gross, *Minutemen and Their World*, 54. William Whiting, *Memoir of Rev. Samuel Whiting, D.D.* (Boston: Rand, Avery, 1873), 218-20.
"pretre de Concord": "Il-ÿ-a des informations, (que L'on ne peut pas douter), d'un *Magazin Militaire*, ou Laboratoire, a Charlestown." Intelligence, March 9, 1775, vol. 126, Gage Papers, Clements Library. Allen French, *General Gage's Informers: New Material Upon Lexington and Concord, Benjamin Thompson as Loyalist and the Treachery of Benjamin Church, Jr.* (Ann Arbor: University of Michigan Press, 1932), 11-2, prints much of this letter.

p 139. "un certain *Salisbury*": Intelligence, March 11, 1775, vol. 126, Gage Papers, Clements Library.

p 140. "Les cannons de *Cuivre*": Intelligence, March 11, 1775, vol. 126, Gage Papers, Clements Library.

"account of all the Province Stores": United States Revolution collection, American Antiquarian Society. My thanks to Judy Cataldo for alerting me to this material. On February 24 the committee of safety and supplies appointed John Goddard of Brookline as "waggon master for the army"; *JEPCM*, 512. Goddard's record of what he carted to Concord is partially transcribed in "Extracts of the Account Book of John Goddard of Brookline," Brookline Historical Publication Society *Publications*, 15 (1898), 47-53. Goddard's records do not mention artillery. For more on him, see Henry G. Pickering, *Nathaniel Goddard: A Boston Merchant, 1767-1853* ([Cambridge]: Riverside Press, 1906), 17-27.

"Un certain nommé *Popkins*": Intelligence, March 11, 1775, vol, 126, Gage Papers, Clements Library.

John Popkin: Bradford Adams Whittemore, *Memorials of the Massachusetts Society of the Cincinnati* (Boston: Massachusetts Society of the Cincinnati, 1964), 489.

p 141. "There is a person": Charles Martyn, *The Life of Artemas Ward* (New York: Artemas Ward, 1921), 83.

"were mounted": *General Gage's Instructions*, 15-6.

"military stores": Gordon described the provincial artillery pieces this way: "There are four brass ones, of a small size, that may answer a good purpose. They have a few large iron cannon, two or three mortars and howitzers, cannon ball, and shells." William Gordon, *The History of the Rise, Progress, and Establishment, of the Independence of the United States of America* (London: the author, 1788), 1:492.

"Before our privateers": James Thacher, *A Military Journal During the American Revolutionary War, from 1775 to 1783* (Boston: Richardson & Lord, 1823), 43.

Dr. Preserved Clapp: Ebenezer Clapp, *The Clapp Memorial: Record of the Clapp Family in America* (Boston: David Clapp & Son, 1876), 43-4, 55-6.

p 142. "the real inventor": Statement by Richard Gridley, *Independent Chronicle*, November 28, 1776. See also *Massachusetts Acts and Resolves*, 1776-77, chap. 332; and *Journals of the Continental Congress*, 19:184. Clapp's rival for credit might have been Paul Revere; Elbridge Henry Goss, *The Life of Colonel Paul Revere* (Boston: J. G. Cupples, 1891), 1:278, states that he "invented a new carriage" for the cannon at Castle William.

"Dimensions of a Brass 3 ¶": David Mason notebook, page 88 (second page from the back), Bryant-Mason-Smith Family Papers, at MHS.

Royal Artillery standards: Adrian B. Caruana, *Grasshoppers and Butterflies: The Light 3 Pounders of Pattison and Townshend*, Historical Arms Series #39 (Bloomfield, Ont.: Museum Restoration Service, 1999), 3.

p 143. The "Hancock" bore: The mouth of the "Hancock" is now large enough to accommodate a four-pound cannonball. The diameter of the Royal Artillery's three-pound ball was 2.775 inches and the diameter of a four-pound ball 3.05 inches—a difference of slightly more than a quarter-inch, well within Mason's range of precision. Every artillerist who worked with that field-piece between its arrival in Boston in 1768 and its retirement sixty years later called it a three-pounder. But it was not a standard three-pounder, and that might have posed extra challenges.

"Had the enemy been": Thacher, *Military Journal*, 43.

"examine the road": *General Gage's Instructions*, 15-6.

p 144. "some British officers": Convers Francis, *An Historical Sketch of Watertown, in Massachusetts* (Cambridge, Mass.: E. W. Metcalf, 1830), 105.

"redcoats were at Jamaica Plain": Drake, *Roxbury*, 73.

"at Watertown": Barker, *British in Boston*, 27.

"The 38th & 52ed Regiments": Frederick Mackenzie, *A British Fusilier in Revolutionary Boston*, Allen French, editor (Cambridge, Mass.: Harvard University Press, 1926), 70.

Marches since December: Barker, *British in Boston*, 11.

p 145. "a number of letters": "Intelligence, March 26th. 1775," vol. 127, Gage Papers, Clements Library.

"the number of field pieces": *JEPCM*, 110.

"ordered the Committee": "Intelligence, March 26th. 1775," vol. 127, Gage Papers, Clements Library.

"the rules and regulations": *JEPCM*, 111.

"The marching": "Intelligence Received April 3d. 1775," vol. 127, Gage Papers, Clements Library.

"trois Grandes Caisses": Intelligence, April 6, 1775, vol. 127, Gage Papers, Clements Library.

p 146. "Le Coll. B——": Intelligence, April 6, 1775, Gage Papers, Clements Library. Mason's notebook likewise has an undated note about "James Barrett of Concord," confirming that they were linked. On the same page is "Worcester Timothy Bigilow." David Mason notebook, Bryant-Mason-Smith Papers, MHS.

"trois canons": Intelligence, April 6, 1775, vol. 127, Gage Papers, Clements Library.

"All things wear": James Warren to Mercy Warren, April 6, 1775, "Warren-Adams Papers," *MHS Collections*, 72 (1917), 46.

p 147. "all the Artillery": *NDAR*, 1:172-3, 186-7.

"Guns at fort Pownall": "Memorandum of Intelligence, April 11th. 1775," vol. 127, Gage Papers, Clements Library.

"Sixteen Peices of Cannon": Thomas Goldthwait to Thomas Cushing, April 16, 1775, vol. 127, Gage Papers, Clements Library.

"After a long debate": *JEPCM*, 137-8, 140.

"engaging six companies": *JEPCM*, 141-2.

"Six Companies of Matrosses": "Intelligence Received April 15th. 1775," vol. 127, Gage Papers, Clements Library.

p 148. "that Col. Barrett be desired": *JEPCM*, 515-6.

"the first & essential step": Dartmouth to Gage, February 27, 1775, *Correspondence of Gage*, 2:182-3. John R. Alden, "Why the March to Concord?", *American Historical Review*, 49 (1944), 446-54, discusses the importance of this dispatch in Gage's motivation.

"dans peu des Jours": Intelligence, April 14, 1775, vol. 127, Gage Papers, Clements Library.

CHAPTER TEN: "IF YOU MEET WITH ANY BRASS ARTILLERY"

p 149. Gage's focus on weaponry: After digesting more reports from New England, in April the secretary of state came around to the general's position, to an extent. He told Gage "That all Cannon, Small Arms, and other military Stores of every kind that may be either in any public Magazine, or secretly collected together for the purpose of aiding Rebellions, should also be seized and secured"—along with all traitors and rebels. Dartmouth to Gage, April 15, 1775, *The Correspondence of General Thomas Gage with the Secretaries of State, and with the War Office and the Treasury, 1763-1775*, Clarence Edwin Carter, editor (New Haven: Yale University Press, 1933), 2:191. By the time that dispatch reached Boston, the situation had changed drastically.

p 150. Committee members: *JEPCM*, 514-6. Though Joseph Palmer represented Braintree in the congress, he was staying with in-laws in Watertown; Frederick Tupper and Helen Tyler Brown, editors, *Grandmother Tyler's Book: The Recollections of Mary Palmer Tyler* (New York: G. P. Putnam's Sons, 1925), 37-8.

"most . . . are at Worcester": Notes dated February 24, 1775, vol. 126, Gage Papers, Clements Library.

p 151. Distance to Barrett's farm: David Hackett Fischer, *Paul Revere's Ride* (New York: Oxford University Press, 1994), 207, 317.

"Four Brass Cannon": Allen French, *General Gage's Informers: New Material Upon Lexington and Concord, Benjamin Thompson as Loyalist and the Treachery of Benjamin Church, Jr.* (Ann Arbor: University of Michigan Press, 1932), 29-30. French argues convincingly that Gage wrote a detailed first draft of instructions, then a more general final draft after learning about supplies being moved.

p 152. "The military Stores": "Intelligence, April 18th: 1775," vol. 127, Gage Papers, Clements Library. The word "four" was inserted over a crossed-out word, perhaps "two."

"With oxen and cart": Benson J. Lossing, *The Pictorial Field-book of the Revolution* (New York: Harper & Brothers, 1859), 1:551-2.

"Four cannon were carried": Lemuel Shattuck, *A History of the Town of Concord* (Boston: Russell, Odiorne, & Company, 1835), 34.

"where they were hidden": Olivia S. Crowell, *Stow, Massachusetts, 1683-1933* (Stow, Mass.: Rev. and Mrs. Preston R. Crowell, 1933), 71.

"Mrs. Barrett had concealed": Ezra Ripley, *A History of the Fight at Concord* (Concord, Mass.: Herman Atwill, 1832), 14.

p 153. "the men in the Barrett family": Margaret Sidney, *Old Concord: Her Highways and Byways* (Boston: D. Lothrop, 1888), 20. Frederic Hudson, "The Concord Fight," *Harper's Magazine*, 50 (December 1874–May 1875), 791, is the first mention in print of the Barretts plowing dirt over guns in their field—in that case, cannon.

"Having received Intelligence": French, *General Gage's Informers*, 31-2.

p 154. Troop strength and timing: Fischer, *Paul Revere's Ride*, 103-4, 146, 208, 313-6.

p 155. "a great number": Richard Frothingham, *History of the Siege of Boston*, 4th edition (Boston: Little, Brown, 1873), 57, suggests this is a quotation from Gerry's letter, but the source is not clear.

"it is said the officers": Transcription of the letter exhibited at the Concord Museum in April 2014. James T. Austin, *The Life of Elbridge Gerry* (Boston: Wells & Lilly, 1828), 1:68, provides a somewhat different transcription without the time of day included.

"by the occasional blowing": Elias Phinney, *History of the Battle at Lexington* (Boston: Phelps & Farnham, 1825), 33.

"a party of officers": Phinney, *Battle at Lexington,* 31.

Nathan Munroe mission: Phinney, *Battle at Lexington,* 38.

"two vessels": "Queries of George Chalmers, with the Answers of General Gage," *MHS Collections*, 4th series, 4:372.

Rev. Samuel Cooper: Charles W. Akers, *The Divine Politician: Samuel Cooper and the American Revolution in Boston* (Boston: Northeastern University Press, 1982), 195-7. The minister apparently made his final decision not to return to Boston on April 16; Samuel Kirkland Lothrop, *History of the Church in Brattle Street, Boston* (Boston: Crosby and Nichols, 1851), 102.

Cushing's departure: *Sibley's Harvard Graduates*, 11:388.

Isaiah Thomas's move: Thomas, *History of Printing in America*, 2nd edition (Worcester: American Antiquarian Society, 1874), 1:lxiii-lxv. Ray Raphael, *Founders: The People Who Brought You a Nation* (New York: New Press, 2013), 177-8.

p 156. "a cornfield": C.F.O., "Revolutionary Incident," *Cambridge Chronicle*, April 27, 1861. A similar account appeared in Samuel Abbot Smith, *West Cambridge 1775* (Arlington, Mass.: Arlington Historical Society, 1974), 16-7.

p 157. Soldiers searching tavern: Austin, *Elbridge Gerry*, 68-9.

"sudden arrest": Fischer, *Paul Revere's Ride*, 91. But see Gordon, *History of the Rise*, 1:476-7.

"The cannon at Concord": C. Stedman, *History of the Origin, Progress, and Termination of the American War* (London: J. Murray, 1794), 1:119.

p 160. "when they searched": *Pennsylvania Mercury*, April 29, 1775.

"proceeded to Concord": Gage to Dartmouth, April 22, 1775, *Correspondence of Gage*, 2:673-4.

"The detachment": Gordon, "An Account of the Commencement of Hostilities between Great-Britain and America, . . . in a letter to a gentleman in England," in Nathaniel Low, *An Astronomical Diary, or Almanack, for the Year of the Christian Æra, 1776* (Worcester: Isaiah Thomas, [1775]), 12. Gordon wrote much the same in *The History of the Rise, Progress, and Establishment, of the Independence of the United States of America* (London: the author, 1788), 1:479.

Two twenty-four-pounders: These big guns were repaired and sent to Marblehead in December; *JHRM*, 1775-76, 51:19-20.

p 161. "house where": *General Gage's Instructions, of 22d February 1775* (Boston: J. Gill, 1779), 18.

"Will you let them burn": Shattuck, *Concord*, 111.

"one of John Pigeon's guns": S. F. Smith, *History of Newton, Massachusetts* (Boston: American Logotype, 1880), 341.

"provide one field piece": *JEPCM*, 520.

p 162. Americans as underdogs: Fischer, *Paul Revere's Ride*, 327-8.

"a quantity of stores": *JEPCM*, 661, 665, 674.

"a Magazine": Gage, "A Circumstantial Account of an Attack that happened on the 19th of April 1775, on his Majesty's Troops" (Boston: John Howe, 1775).

"a large quantity": Gage to Barrington, April 22, 1775, *Correspondence of Gage*, 2:673.

"All the Cannon": "Intelligence Major Small," May 12, 1775, vol. 128, Gage Papers, Clements Library.

p 163. "wait on General Washington": *BTR*, 18:228.

Crafts's Continental army commission: George Washington to John Hancock, December 14, 1775, *The Papers of George Washington: Revolutionary War Series*, Philander D. Chase, editor (Charlottesville: University Press of Virginia, 1987), 2:546–549. Crafts to John Adams, December 16, 1775, *Papers of John Adams*, Robert J. Taylor, editor (Cambridge, Mass.: Harvard University Press, 1979), 3:366–367.

"Genl. Knox has two of the four": Stephen Higginson to John Lowell, March 4, 1783, in *Letters of Delegates to Congress, 1774-1789*, Paul H. Smith, editor (Washington, D.C.: Library of Congress, 1976-1998), 25:743. Higginson may have referred to the four guns having been lent to Massachusetts by Boston or Bostonians, or he may have meant to write "lent by Our State." Either way, it is clear he wanted the remaining two back from the national government.

p 164. "You will please to deliver": John Hancock to Henry Knox, May 9, 1788, *Papers of the Continental Congress,* microfilm edition, reel 165, 3:197.

"That there are, in the Arsenals": *Salem Mercury*, June 10, 1788. *Journals of the American Congress* (1823 edition), 4:816.

"two pieces of brass artillery": *American Herald*, June 5, 1788. *Massachusetts Gazette*, June 6, 1788. *Essex Journal*, June 11, 1788.

p 165. "Mr. Joseph Callender has just": *Salem Mercury*, May 26, 1789. *Independent Gazetteer*, May 30, 1789.

EPILOGUE: "THROUGH ALL OUR HISTORY, TO THE LAST"

p 167. Rhode Island brass cannon: *Pennsylvania Evening Post*, July 21, 1775.

p 168. "experimental gunnery": Oliver Ayer Roberts, *History of the Military Company of the Massachusetts, Now Called The Ancient and Honorable*

Artillery Company of Massachusetts, 1637-1888 (Boston: Alfred Mudge & Son, 1897), 2:146, 453.

The brass guns in storage: Around this time, it appears, the "Hancock" was etched with these small unexplained marks: "No. 2," "HBJ," and "IB / 1822."

"Virginian geese": Josiah Quincy, *Figures of the Past: From the Leaves of Old Journals*, 2nd edition (Boston: Little, Brown, 1926), 58. See also Adams to Benjamin Rush, November 11, 1807.

"I envy none": John Adams to William Wirt, January 5, 1818, *Works of John Adams*, Charles Francis Adams, editor (Boston: Little, Brown, 1856), 10:272.

p 169. "American independence was then": Adams to Tudor, March 29, 1817, *Works of John Adams*, 10:247.

Adams's letter published: *Novanglus and Massachusettensis* (Boston: Hews & Goss, 1819), 244-7.

Bunker Hill Monument: Carl Seaburg and Stanley Paterson, *Merchant Prince of Boston: Colonel T. H. Perkins, 1764-1854* (Cambridge, Mass.: Harvard University Press, 1971), 318-9.

One tradition, recorded as early as 1845: "The History and Journal of Jesse Wentworth Crosby," typescript at the Harold B. Lee Library, Brigham Young University. Transcribed at www.boap.org/LDS/Early-Saints/JWCrosby.html as of January 3, 2016.

Four-pounders: [Richard] Williams, *Discord and Civil Wars: Being a Portion of the Journal Kept by Lieutenant Williams of His Majesty's Twenty-third Regiment* (Buffalo: East Hill Press, 1954), 19.

"four small brass cannon": James Thacher, *A Military Journal During the American Revolutionary War, from 1775 to 1783* (Boston: Richardson & Lord, 1823), 43.

p 170. "bold, active, and defiant": David Hackett Fischer, *Paul Revere's Ride* (New York: Oxford University Press, 1994), 329.

Loring's description: James Spear Loring, *The Hundred Boston Orators*, 4th edition (Boston: John P. Jewett, 1852), 89-92. S. A. Drake cited "Loring's account" in *Old Landmarks and Historic Personages of Boston*, revised edition (Boston: Little, Brown, 1906), 314. Edward G. Porter, "The Beginning of the Revolution," in Justin Winsor, editor, *The Memorial History of Boston* (Boston: James R. Osgood, 1881), 3:62, cited Tudor but printed the names from Loring.

"stationed two brass field-pieces": William Wetmore Story, *The Life and Letters of Joseph Story* (Boston: Little & Brown, 1851), 1:9-12.

Elisha Story in Malden: Daybook for 1774, Elisha Story Papers, Massachusetts Historical Society.

Legend of John Pedrick: "Leslie's Retreat," *EIHC*, 17 (1880), 190-2. Joseph B. Felt received a version of this story from Elizabeth White by 1849; *Annals of Salem* (Salem, Mass.: W. & S. B. Ives, 1849), 2:514-5.

p 171. Pedrick as friend of royal government: *The Journals of Ashley Bowen (1728-1813) of Marblehead*, Philip Chadwick Foster Smith, editor (Boston:

CSM, 1973), 673. Colin Nicolson, "Governor Francis Bernard, the Massachusetts Friends of Government, and the Advent of the Revolution," *MHS Proceedings*, 101 (1991), 94-5. David E. Maas, *Divided Hearts: Massachusetts Loyalists, 1765-1790, A Biographical Directory* (Boston: Society of Colonial Wars and NEHGS), 1980), 118. *MHS Proceedings*, 12:187.

"she was a great talker": Story, *Joseph Story*, 1:15-6.

D'Berniere rewritten: *A Journal Kept by Mr. John Howe* (Concord, N.H.: Luther Roby, 1827). To complicate matters, there really was a young man named John Howe in Revolutionary Boston, helping to print the Loyalist *Boston News-Letter* before leaving with the British in 1776. The details of that man's life do not match up to those of the fictional "John Howe." See John N. Grant, "John Howe, Senior: Printer, Publisher, Postmaster, Spy," in *Eleven Exiles: Accounts of Loyalists of the American Revolution*, Phyllis R. Blakeley and John N. Grant, editors (Toronto and Charlottetown: Dundurn Press, 1982), 24-57.

p 172. Claim for Langdon: *MHS Proceedings*, 24 (1887-89), 193-4.

Claim for Hancock: Abram English Brown, *John Hancock, His Book* (Boston: Lee & Shepard, 1898), 189.

Claim for Knox: Noah Brooks, *Henry Knox: A Soldier of the Revolution* (New York: Putnam's, 1900), 20-1.

Usually an anecdote: There are noteworthy exceptions to this pattern. Neil R. Stout included the Patriots' seizures of cannon, including the Boston train's brass guns, in *The Perfect Crisis: The Beginning of the Revolutionary War* (New York: New York University Press, 1976), 182. Louis Birnbaum spotted those same cannon at Concord in *Red Dawn at Lexington* (Boston: Houghton Mifflin, 1986), 128.

p 173. "John Hall": John Bakeless, *Turncoats, Traitors and Heroes* (Philadelphia: J. P. Lippincott, 1959), 28, 30.

McKone's theorizing: Frank E. McKone to John Bakeless, April 11, 1958, and September 6, 1960, John Edward Bakeless Papers, New York Public Library. McKone's *General Sullivan: New Hampshire Patriot* (New York: Vantage Press, 1977) summarizes his research on Hall.

p 174. Gage's shaky hand: Gage to Percy, April 19, 1775, vol. 127, Gage Papers, Clements Library.

p 175. Gage family: *Burke's Peerage, Baronetage & Knightage*, 107th edition (Wilmington: Burke's Peerage, 2003), 2:1500.

Dr. Joseph Warren: Richard Frothingham, *The Life and Times of Joseph Warren* (Boston: Little, Brown, 1865). John Cary, *Joseph Warren: Physician, Politician, Patriot* (Urbana: University of Illinois Press, 1964). Samuel A. Forman, *Dr. Joseph Warren: The Boston Tea Party, Bunker Hill, and the Birth of American Liberty* (Gretna, La.: Pelican, 2012).

Oliver presiding over Council: Albert Matthews, editor, "Documents Relating to the Last Meetings of the Massachusetts Royal Council, 1774-1776," *CSM Publications*, 32 (1933-37), 499-501.

Vermont: The new state's name appeared first on Dr. Young's April 11, 1777, broadside "To the Inhabitants of Vermont, a Free and Independent State."

p 176. Bursting mortar: *The History of the Rise, Progress, and Establishment, of the Independence of the United States of America* (London: the author, 1788), 2:191. Gen. William Heath wrote the problem was that the mortars "were not properly bedded, as the ground was hard frozen"; *Memoirs of Major-General William Heath*, William Abbatt, editor (New York: William Abbatt, 1901), 32.

Adino Paddock: AO 13/49, Massachusetts Claims P(I), 4-13, National Archives, UK. Maas, *Divided Hearts*, 115. James H. Stark, *The Loyalists of Massachusetts and the Other Side of the American Revolution* (Boston: W. B. Clarke, 1910), 305-7.

Glass factory: Rhea Mansfield Knittle, *Early American Glass* (New York: Century, 1927), 183-5. Kenneth M. Wilson, *New England Glass and Glassmaking: An Old Sturbridge Village Book* (New York: Thomas Y. Crowell, 1972), 77, 84-6.

Obadiah Whiston: Maas, *Divided Hearts*, 158. *BRT*, 10:293, 22:118. Suffolk Deeds, 125:233; 201:46, 98-9; 206:179; 272:270-7. "Remarks by Brother F. C. Whiston on the Presentation of the Apron Worn by Lafayette," *Proceedings of the Grand Lodge of . . . Masons of the Commonwealth of Massachusetts*, June 9, 1875, 44-6.

William Dawes: Henry W. Holland, *William Dawes and His Ride with Paul Revere* (Boston: John Wilson, 1878). Roberts, *Ancient & Honorable Artillery*, 2:218-9, 2:194-5.

p 177. Duncan Ingraham: Eliza M. Gill, "Turell Tufts and His Family Connections," *Medford Historical Register*, 18 (1915), 57-9.

Dr. Benjamin Church: John A. Nagy, *Dr. Benjamin Church, Spy: A Case of Espionage on the Eve of the American Revolution* (Yardley, Penn.: Westholme, 2013).

John Derby's voyage: Robert S. Rantoul, "The Cruise of the 'Quero': How We Carried the News to the King," *EIHC*, 36 (1900), 1-30.

p 178. Lemuel Robinson's dispute: John R. Elting, *The Battle of Bunker's Hill* (Monmouth Beach, N.J.: Philip Freneau Press, 1975), 11.

ACKNOWLEDGMENTS

I have many institutions and people to thank for help with this book, starting with the Newton Free Library and the entire Minuteman Library Network. The Massachusetts Historical Society in Boston has been welcoming and invaluable, and the staff is second to none. I particularly want to thank Conrad E. Wright for hosting that seminar when I presented the first version of this study; Pat Leehey of the Paul Revere House, for his helpful comments on it; and Peter Drummey for assembling a temporary display of pertinent documents. My thanks also to Alan Rogers, Kate Viens, Ondine Leblanc, and many others there.

In addition, I am grateful for having been able to draw on resources at the William L. Clements Library at the University of Michigan, Ann Arbor; the Houghton, Widener, and Gutman Libraries at Harvard University; the American Antiquarian Society in Worcester; the Firestone and Mudd Libraries at Princeton University; the Mugar Memorial Library at Boston University; the Essex Institute in Salem; the Library of Congress and National Archives and Records Administration; the Massachusetts State Archives; the Boston Public Library; the New York Public Library; the National Archives of the United Kingdom and the British Library; the New England Historic Genealogical Society; the Bostonian Society; the Boston Athenæum; the Dartmouth College Library; the McGill University Library; the David Library of the American Revolution; and resources from Gore Place in Waltham, Massachusetts.

So many fellow researchers have offered me encouragement, sources, and feedback that I will undoubtedly forget some names. But I remember with gratitude Dave Ingram, Robert C. Mitchell,

Alfred F. Young, Ray Raphael, George C. Quintal, John K. Rowland, Don Hagist, Bart Reynolds, E. Jennifer Monaghan, Benjamin Carp, John C. Nagy, Kay Menand, Lisa Wilson, Cornelia Hughes Dayton, Steven Bullock, Laurel Thatcher Ulrich, William M. Fowler, Jr., Ben Irvin, Brent Simons, Bob Allison, Nathaniel Philbrick, Nick Bunker, Derek W. Beck, Judy Anderson, Sue Goganian, Charles Bahne, Rick Detwiller, Sam Forman, Gary Gregory, and Emmy Werner. Within the National Park Service I wish to thank Lou Sideris, Mark Nichipor, Nancy Nelson, Jim Hollister, Emily Murphy, Phil Hunt, Ethan Beeler, Matt Greif, Marty Blatt, Garrett Cloer, and all the folks at Longfellow House–Washington's Headquarters National Historic Site.

Jim Cunningham of Save Our Heritage and the Friends of Minute Man Park and Ross Tuttle of the *History Detectives* television show provided the impetus for some important research breakthroughs. Warren Little, the Massachusetts Society of the Cincinnati, and the Society of the Cincinnati's Anderson House Library in Washington, D.C., have been friendly and supportive.

A scholar outside the academy sometimes feels like a homeless waif. For providing forums where I could learn and share ideas, I thank the Massachusetts Historical Society, Peter Benes and the Dublin Seminar for New England Folklife, John Tyler and the Colonial Society of Massachusetts, the Omohundro Institute for Early American History and Culture, and the American Antiquarian Society.

After many years in development, this book became reality with a push from Todd Andrlik and his colleagues at the *Journal of the American Revolution* (allthingsliberty.com). I'm privileged to be part of that crew. Todd brought my manuscript to Bruce H. Franklin and the folks at Westholme, who have taken even more trouble with it than I have given to them.

I owe a great debt to all the brilliant people who created personal computers and the internet and thus allowed me to find connections that had eluded smarter and more learned historians without digital resources. I started this project before Google Books, HathiTrust, the Digitial Public Library of America, and similar digital sites had been launched. They have become stupendous scholarly resources. I'm delighted to use Readex's Archive of Americana and Early American Newspaper databases through the Boston Public Library and the New England Historic Genealogical Society, and the J-Stor archive of scholarly journals through the Newton Free Library. I have enjoyed several online discussion groups, including the H-Net lists, particularly H-OIEAHC and H-SHEAR, and the Revlist, 18cWoman, and NEREV groups. All offered valuable information and perspective. Another few years of progress like the last few, and I may never get up from my computer again.

I thank my writing friends, especially Greg Fishbone and Mitali Perkins for giving me the impetus to start the Boston 1775 blog, and everyone who took time away from the types of manuscripts we were supposed to be reading to critique my chapters.

Finally, I am grateful for the love of my family and friends. They would be loving, and I would be grateful, with or without this book.

INDEX

Abigail, 70
Adams, Abigail, 14, 40, 43
Adams, John, 6, 30, 37, 67, 92, 168, 219
Adams, Samuel, 5-6, 63, 74-79, 96-97, 123-124, 147, 149-150, 155, 157, 160, 165, 167-168
Allen, Ethan, 175
American Herald, brass artillery arrives in Boston and, 164
Ancient and Honorable Artillery Company, 168, 177, 190
Andrews, John, 14, 24, 26, 39-40, 42, 44, 54-56, 85, 89, 91-98, 171-172, 181, 193, 209
Austin, James T., 157
Avery, Jr., John, 63

Bakeless, John, 173
Balch, Joseph, 87, 170
Barker, John, 144
Barnard, Thomas, 131, 164
Barnes, Henry, 135
Barrett, James, 128, 137, 140, 146, 148, 151-153, 157, 204
Barrington, Viscount, 9, 100, 121
Batchelder, Josiah, 106
Beck, Derek W., 174
Bernard, Francis, 9, 14, 22, 48, 183
Bickham, George, 83
Bigelow, Timothy, 128, 139, 128, 173
Bishop, Thomas, 97
Black Horse Tavern, 155-156
Bliss, Daniel, 144
Bolton, Thomas, 136
Boston Chronicle
  founder's London creditors and, 75
  importing goods and, 68
  Theophilus Lillie letter and, 69
  tweaking Boston's prohibition against theater and, 71
Boston Evening-Post, attack on Richardson's home and, 72
Boston Gazette
  Isaiah Thomas and, 32
  marriage of William Dawes and, 67
  militia mobilization and, 24
  political spin on the Gores' spinning bee and, 70
  rumors of soldiers killing people and, 26
  Whig press and, 16
  wounding of Samuel Gore and, 73
Boston Massacre, 28, 74, 89, 115, 135, 182, 199
Boston News-Letter
  advertisement for "John Gore and Son" and, 76
  elaborate display at the militia training and, 50
  military conveying powder to Castle William and, 13
  missing artillery pieces and, 87
  Paddock promotion and, 53
Boston Patriots, 90, 93-94, 123, 155

Boston Port Bill, 1-2, 4, 19, 180, 184
Boston Post-Boy
"The Artillery Company divided into two Parties" and, 50
clearing the cannon and, 44
Governor's Island cannon batteries and, 45
Boston Tea Party, 21, 79, 115, 200
Bowdoin, James, 28, 181
Boyce, David, 130
Boyle, John, 75
Boynton, Richard, 88, 116
Bradford, John, 27-29, 185
Brattle, William, 9, 12, 14, 16-18, 25, 36, 63, 181-182
Brewer, James, 115-116
British East India Company, 2
Brooks, Noah, 172
Brown, Aaron, 61
Brown, Abram English, 172
Browne, William, 8
Brown, Solomon, 155
Brown, William, 127, 134-135, 138, 143-144, 150, 154
Bunker Hill, battle of, 85, 169, 171, 175
Bunker Hill Monument, 169, 176, 178
Bunker, Nick, 174
Burbeck, Henry, 49, 52, 54, 57, 192, 208
Burgoyne, John, 19
Burke, Edmund, 122

Calder, William, 42
Callender, Joseph, 164-165
Caner, Henry, 66, 76, 80
Carter, James, 86
Castle William, 4, 13, 38, 41, 49, 74, 78, 129, 142, 215
Charles River, 3, 25, 33, 40-41, 81, 94, 182, 196
Cheever, David, 107, 109, 113-114, 141, 150, 204
Chipman, Ward, 15-16
Church, Jr., Benjamin, 28, 68, 107-108, 124-125, 128, 132, 136, 145, 147, 150, 152, 177
Clapp, Preserved, 141-142
Clarke, Jonas, 157
Cleaveland, Samuel, 55, 95-96, 120
Clements Library, 173
Cochran, John, 112
Coercive Acts, 121, 180
Columbian Centinel
death of Samuel Gore and, 79
Gore obituary and, 57
Company of Cadets, 51, 53, 76-77
Condy, Foster, 77-78
Connecticut River, 36
Continental Congress, xiii, 6, 37, 54, 99, 112, 135, 149, 157, 163, 181, 203
Cooper, Samuel, 59, 155
Cooper, William, 27-30, 155
Copley, John Singleton, 58, 194
Crafts, Jr., Thomas, 48, 50, 53, 62-65, 68, 74, 80-81, 88, 95, 148, 163, 193
Crane, John, 112
Cudworth, Nathaniel, 29, 186
Cunningham, Andrew, 84, 177
Cushing, Thomas, 6, 76-77, 99-100, 149, 155
Cutler, Manasseh, 30

Danforth, Samuel, 24-26, 28-29
Dartmouth, 77-78
Dawes, Jr., William, 67, 88, 113-114, 156-157, 172, 177, 208
D'Berniere, Henry, 127, 134-135, 138, 143-144, 150, 161, 173
Derby, Elias Haskett, 177
Derby, Jr., Richard, 8, 109, 111, 126, 131, 177, 212
Derby, Sr., Richard, 109

Devens, Richard, 29, 32, 107, 150, 155-156
Dickinson, John, 68
Ditson, Thomas, 135
Drake, Francis S., 115, 192

East India Company, 2, 77, 112
Emerson, William, 138
Empire on the Edge (Bunker), 174
Essex County Convention, 7-8
Essex Gazette
  Richard Derby, Jr. and, 109
  stolen cannon and, 133
Eustis, William, 51, 118, 192

Faneuil Hall, 48, 69, 78, 94, 136
Felt, Joseph, 130
Fifty-ninth Regiment, 8
Fifty-second Regiment, 127, 144
Fischer, David Hackett, 162, 170
Folsom, Nathaniel, 112
Fort Edward, 45
Fort George, 112
Fort Louisburg, 90
Fort Pownall, 147
Fort William and Mary, 112, 120
Fort William Henry, 19, 45, 52
Forty-seventh Regiment, 135
Foster, Jedediah, 128
Foster, Robert, 130, 132
Fourth Regiment of Foot, 1-2, 33, 55, 82, 193
Franklin, Benjamin, 25, 76
Franklin, Bruce H., 224
French and Indian War, 7, 45, 90
Frothingham, Richard, 42

Gage, Margaret, 3
Gage, Thomas
  acting only on the defensive and, 93
  arrest of Warren and, 156
  Brattle letter and, 9
  Clements Library and, 173
  conversation with Benjamin Hallowell and, 31
  death of, 175
  doubling sentries in front of new gunhouse and, 82
  Essex County Convention and, 7-8
  fear of being attacked and, 33
  feeling pressure from London and, 136
  frustration with the populace and, 96
  guarding newer gunhouse and, 55
  idea that government was curtailing the people's rights and, 23
  instructions to Viscount Barrington and, 9
  last move in New England arms race and, 147
  letter from Oliver and, 35
  letter to Colonel Percy and, 174-175
  letter to Frederick Haldimand and, 36
  letter to Lord Dartmouth and, 160
  London authorizing military action and, 148
  Massachusetts General Court and, 5
  Massachusetts Government Act and, 6
  military conveying powder to Castle William and, 13
  political unrest in Boston and, 3-4, 7
  proposal of a "Suspension of the Execution of the late Acts" and, 121, 122
  protest from Suffolk County Convention and, 43
  report to Viscount Barrington and, 100
  revised instructions for Colonel Smith and, 153-154
  Richard Derby, Jr. and, 109

Robert Pierpoint's warning and, 98
seizing private property and, 98
South Writing School and, 85
spies and, 124-125, 129, 132, 137, 139, 143, 144, 145, 146, 148, 150-151, 173
stationing army regiments in Boston and, 80
summoning more regiments to Boston and, 40
suspected motives of, 122-123
tracking Boston train's guns and, 162-163
warning to Lord Dartmouth and, 38
William Brattle letter and, 14
Gamage, William, 29
Gardner, Henry, 107, 152
Gardner, Thomas, 32, 106, 128, 150
Garrick, Edward, 89
George III, 4
Gerry, Elbridge, 109, 150, 155-157
Gill, Moses, 107-108
Goldthwait, Joseph, 3, 12, 180
Gordon, William, 141, 160, 214
Gore, Christopher (Kit), 62, 176
Gore, Elizabeth, 58
Gore, Frances, 58, 60, 62, 70
Gore, John, 45, 58-61, 65-67, 69-70, 76, 80, 88, 110, 176
Gore, Samuel, 56-62, 64-65, 72-74, 76-77, 79, 81-85, 87, 118, 169-170, 172, 174, 176-177
Gore, Sarah, 66, 75
Governor's Guard, 52
Granary Burying Ground, 48
Grant, Moses, 77-79, 81-82, 87
Graves, Samuel, 31, 40, 94, 99, 120
Gray, Samuel, 131-132
Greenleaf, Joseph, 27, 29, 97
Greenleaf, Stephen, 84
Gridley, Jeremiah, 170
Gridley, Richard, 82, 87-90, 170, 203
Griffin's Wharf, 2, 78-79
Gross, Robert, 173

Haldimand, Frederick, 36-37, 120
Hall, Benjamin, 107-109
Hallowell, Jr., Benjamin, 31-33, 36, 77, 186-187
Hancock, Dorothy, 147
Hancock, John, 28, 53, 68, 75-77, 99, 107, 136, 142, 147, 150, 155, 157, 160, 164-165, 167-170, 172-173, 178, 191, 215, 219
Harvard University, 22, 61-63, 75
Hatch, Jabez, 50-51, 78, 148
Heath, William, 106, 108, 128, 150, 175, 178, 221
Henry, Patrick, 168-169
Henshaw, Joseph, 129
Hewes, George R. T., 79
Higginson, Stephen, 163, 219
Hill, Edward, 30
His Majesty's Commissioners of Customs for North America, 5
H.M.S. *Lively*, 40, 94, 97
Hoerder, Dirk, 173
Holbrook, Abiah, 83
Holbrook, Samuel, 55, 83-85, 110, 170
Hooper, Thomas, 61
Horrid Massacre, 4, 74
Hosmer, Joseph, 161
Hubbard, Ebenezer, 146, 151
Hudson River, 45
Hulton, Henry, 44, 120, 186, 210
The Hundred Boston Orators (Loring), 170
Hutchinson, Thomas, 51, 53, 63, 75-78, 80

Igniting the American Revolution (Beck), 174

Ingraham, Duncan, 105, 139, 177, 206
Isle of Jersey, 176

Jackson, Joseph, 49
Jackson, William, 71
John Hancock: His Book (Brown), 172
Johnston, John, 62, 65, 81
Johonnot, Francis, 54
Jones, Samuel, 146, 151
A Journal Kept by Mr. John Howe, 171

Keith, Zephaniah, 106
Kemble, Stephen, 127
Kent, Benjamin, 94
Knox, Henry, 52, 74, 163-165, 167-168, 172, 192
Knox, William, 122

Lake George, 19, 45
Lane, William, 42
Langdon, Nathaniel, 172
Lee, Jeremiah, 107, 109, 156-157
Lee, Joseph, 16, 24-26, 29, 36, 105, 139
Leonard, Daniel, 6-7, 23
Leslie, Alexander, 129-132, 134, 139, 170
Liberty-Tree, 14, 64, 66-67, 71, 113
The Life of James Otis (Tudor), 56, 169
Lillie, Theophilus, 69, 71, 74
Lincoln, Benjamin, 107, 111, 124, 150, 163
London Magazine, "No Taxation without Representation" and, 20
Long Wharf, 1
Lord Dartmouth, 4, 6, 9, 36, 38, 119, 132, 136, 148-149, 160
Lord North, 100
Loring, James Spear, 170, 172
Loring, Joshua, 7
Lovell, John, 61, 68, 86
Lowell, John, 163
Loyall Nine, 53, 63-64, 68, 78
Lyde, Byfield, 12

Mackenzie, Frederick, 98, 144
Maddison, George, 1, 3, 12-13, 55
Malcom, Daniel, 64
Marshall, Thomas, 163
Martin, Joseph Plumb, 37
Mason, David, 45-46, 48, 52, 59, 65, 108-111, 118, 125-126, 129-131, 139, 142-143, 146, 160-161, 169, 175-176
Mason, Susan, 45-46, 48
Mason, Thaddeus, 12-13, 30
Massachusetts Bay, 6, 87
Massachusetts General Court, 5
Massachusetts Government Act, 6-7, 17, 19, 21, 30, 34, 43, 101, 103
Massachusetts Historical Society, 116, 171-172, 223-224
Massachusetts militia, 9, 12, 49, 57, 64, 175, 183
Massachusetts Patriots, xii, 102, 134, 145, 156-157, 161
Massachusetts Provincial Congress, xi, 105, 111, 116, 161-162, 167, 170, 175, 177
Massachusetts Spy, Isaiah Thomas and, 31-32, 155
Massachusetts Supreme Court, 168
McKone, Frank E., 173
McNeil, Archibald, 17-19, 26, 34-35, 183
Mill Pond, 94
Minot, George, 115
Minot, Jerusha, 115
Minute Man National Historical Park, 178
Mitchell, Edward, 128
Molesworth, Ponsonby, 88

Molineux, William, 27, 29, 70, 98-99
Montagu, John, 78
Montresor, John, 41, 44
Muddy Pond Woods, 115
Munroe, Nathan, 155
Munroe, William, 155, 157
Mystic River, 3, 13

National Park Service, 178
Neponset River, 43
Ness, John, 88
The New England Primer, 60
Newell, Thomas, 40, 45, 88, 95, 193, 204
New-York Gazette, Gage's meeting with Warren and, 97
Nightingale, Joseph, 112
North American Review, biography of Otis and, 169
North End Caucus, 77
North Latin School, 75, 86
North River, 130-132
Nutting, John, 13

Old South Meeting-House, 78, 135
Oliver, Andrew, 63
Oliver, Elizabeth, 26
Oliver, Thomas, 25-28, 30-31, 33-36, 38, 175, 180, 184, 188
Orne, Azor, 106-107, 150, 156
Otis, Harrison Gray, 86
Otis, Jr., James, 168-169

Paddock, Adino, 45-46, 48-55, 65, 78, 80-81, 110, 120-121, 123, 128, 140, 142, 176, 192
Paine, Robert Treat, 6, 44, 54, 74, 97
Palmer, Joseph, 44, 54-55, 106-107, 150, 216
Parker, John, 155
Parker, Jonathan, 115
Parliament, 1-2, 4, 6, 20-21, 40, 66, 77, 102, 121-122, 174, 180, 184, 205
Patterson, Robert, 72, 74
Paxton, Charles, 77
Peck, Thomas Handasyd, 91, 203
Pedrick, John, 170
Pedrick, Mehitable, 171
Pepperrell, William, 99
Percy, Earl, 38, 44, 92, 119, 144-145, 157, 174, 190
Phillips, Samuel, 97
Phips, David, 3, 12-13, 29-30, 49, 180, 186
Pickering, Timothy, 177
Pierce, Mary (Polly), 81
Pierce, Samuel, 43
Pierpoint, Robert, 88, 98
Pigeon, John, 126, 150, 161
Pigot, Robert, 14
Pitcairn, John, 133, 135
Pitts, Lendell, 79
Pomeroy, Seth, 106
Pope Night, 63
Popkin, John, 140
Porter, Samuel, 132
Powell, William, 108
Prescott, William, 148
Preston, 94
Privy Council, 5
Provincial Congress, xi, 101-107, 110-111, 113, 116-118, 124, 135, 137, 143-150, 157, 161-162, 167, 170, 175, 177-178
Putnam, Israel, 37

Quakers, 130
Quarry Hill, 3, 12-13
Queen Street Writing School, 61, 86
Quincy, Dorothy, 157
Quincy, Edmund, 15
Quincy, Esther, 15
Quincy, Josiah, 99
Quincy, Jr., Josiah, 74
Quincy, Samuel, 74

Raphael, Marie, 174
Raphael, Ray, 174
Revere, Paul, 78, 112, 148, 156-157, 163, 215, 223
Rice, Jonathan, 104
Richardson, Ebenezer, 65, 71-76, 199
Ripley, Ezra, 152
Robinson, Lemuel, 53, 113, 118, 124, 128, 148, 178
Royal Artillery, 37, 45, 48, 52, 92, 95, 120, 142-143, 161
Royal Navy, 2, 5, 8, 20, 40, 44, 54, 78, 94, 97, 108, 112, 114-115, 120
Ruggles, Timothy, 6-7

Salem Mercury, inscription ordered by Congress and, 165
Salisbury, Stephen, 139
Sanderson, Elijah, 155
Sargent, John, 132
Scarborough, 8
Schoolhouse Hill, 42
Scott, Joseph, 94-96, 116
Searle, George, 62
Seider, Christopher, 72, 74, 198
Sewall, Esther, 15-16
Sewall, Jonathan, 14-16, 26-27, 36, 182
Shattuck, Lemuel, 152
Shays Rebellion, 177
Shirley, William, 22, 183
Sidney, Margaret, 153
Sixty-fourth Regiment, 129, 131
Small, John, 162
Smith, Francis, 151, 153, 156, 160-161
Smith, Susan, 110-111, 169-170
Solemn League and Covenant, 53, 80
Sons of Liberty, 64, 67, 80, 87, 113
South Latin School, 60-62, 79, 85-86, 200
South Writing School, 55, 82-85, 87, 90, 117
The Spirit of '74 (Raphael), 174
Stamp Act of 1765, 2-3, 9, 19-20, 22, 53, 62-64, 67, 100, 169
Stevens, Ebenezer, 78-79
Stiles, Ezra, 17, 34, 38, 183
Stone, Jonathan, 104
Story, Elisha, 170-171
Stow, Edward, 114
Suffolk County Convention, 43
Sullivan, John, 112

Temple, Robert, 3, 13, 180
Tenth Regiment, 127
Thacher, Benjamin Bussey, 79
Thacher, James, 141, 143
Thirty-eighth Regiment, 89, 93, 144
Thomas, 99
Thomas, Isaiah, 31-32, 155
Thompson, Timothy, 42
Townshend, Charles, 66, 69, 75
Trott, George, 50, 53
Tuckerman, Edward, 50
Tudor, William, 41, 56-57, 81, 84-85, 90, 93, 114, 118, 169-170, 172
Turncoats, Traitors and Heroes (Bakeless), 173
Twenty-third Regiment, 35

Universal Penman (Bickham), 83

Vassall, John, 36

Walden Pond, 151
Wallace, James, 112, 120
Wanton, Joseph, 112
Ward, Artemas, 128, 141
War of 1812, 171
Warren, James, 106
Warren, Joseph, 27-28, 36, 38, 72-73, 75, 96-97, 107-108, 113-114, 118, 123-124, 128, 135-136, 148-149, 156-157, 175, 211

Washington, George, 39, 163, 177
Watson, Abraham, 150, 155, 157
Webb, Joseph, 98-99
Welles, Arnold, 91-92
Welles, Susannah, 92
Whicher, Joseph, 130
Whigs, xii, 8, 20, 23, 27, 49, 63, 65-66, 69, 71, 73-74, 76-78, 80-81, 88, 116-117
Whiston, Francis C., 176
Whiston, Obadiah, 87-89, 118, 123-124, 169-170, 176, 202
Whiston, Priscilla, 176
White, Benjamin, 124, 150
White, Elizabeth, 170-171
Whiting, Thomas, 138
Williams, Abigail, 115
Williams, Job, 7
Williams, Joseph, 115
Wilmot, George, 72, 74
Wirt, William, 168
World War I, 172
Wyeth, Joshua, 124

Young, Alfred F., 173
Young, Thomas, 27-28, 30, 32, 36, 38, 72, 75, 79, 175